FOUNDATIONS OF SOFTWARE DEVELOPMENT ENGINEERING

Essential Concepts, Design Strategies, Coding Standards, Testing Techniques, and Project Leadership

Santiago Guido

Copyright © 2024 Santiago Guido

All rights reserved

The characters and events portrayed in this book are fictitious. Any similarity to real persons, living or dead, is coincidental and not intended by the author.

No part of this book may be reproduced, or stored in a retrieval system, or transmitted in any form or by any means, electronic, mechanical, photocopying, recording, or otherwise, without express written permission of the publisher.

ISBN-13: 9798301717161
ISBN-10: 1477123456

Cover design by: Art Painter
Library of Congress Control Number: 2018675309
Printed in the United States of America

I would like to express my deepest gratitude to the love of my life, Nancy, for being my constant source of inspiration, my greatest support at every step of this journey, and for giving me two wonderful children, who are my driving force and my daily joy.

To my mother, who taught me the values of generosity and hard work, which have been essential in both my life and my work.

To my siblings and my dear uncles Araceli, César, Pepe, and Lulú, who have always supported me with love; their affection and presence are with me wherever I go.

CONTENTS

Title Page
Copyright
Dedication

CHAPTER 1	3
1.1. What is Software Development Engineering?	6
1.2. Importance of Software Principles	9
1.3. Book Structure and Objectives	12
CHAPTER 2	16
2.1. History and Evolution of Software Engineering	17
2.2. TYPES OF Software	21
2.3. Software Development Life Cycle (SDLC)	25
2.4. Development Methodologies: Agile, Traditional, and Hybrid	29
2.5. Legacy Software and Its Management	34
2.6. Relationship Between Software Engineering and Other Engineering Disciplines	38
2.7. Documentation Practices and International Standards	43
2.8 Chapter conclusions	48
Chapter 3	50
3.1. Fundamentals of Requirements Engineering	51
3.2. Basic Techniques for Requirements Gathering	55
3.3. Analysis and Prioritization of Requirements	56
3.4. Specification of Requirements According to the IEEE 830 Standard	60

3.5. Software Requirements Specification (SRS)	64
3.6. Implementation of the Requirements Specified in the SRS in the Software Development Process	68
3.7. Requirements Validation and Verification	72
3.8. Requirements Management Tools	76
3.9. Benefits of Using Requirements Management Tools	80
3.10. Challenges in Using Requirements Management Tools	81
3.11. chapter conclusions	82
Chapter 4	84
4.1. Basic Principles of Software Design	85
4.2. Design Patterns: Usage and Examples	89
4.3. User Interface design	100
4.4. Object-Oriented Design and Component-Based Design	103
4.5. Software Design Documentation	106
4.6. Jacob Nielsen's Principles for Developing Attractive Websites and Interfaces	109
4.7. Design of Relational and NoSQL Databases	112
4.8. API and Microservices Design (SOA)	115
4.9. chapter conclusions	118
Chapter 5	120
5.1. Fundamental Concepts of Software Architecture	121
5.2. Common Architectural Patterns	124
5.3. Software Architecture Modeling	127
5.4. Evaluation and Selection of Architectures	130
5.5. Microservices-Based Architecture	134
5.6. Serverless Architecture	137
5.7. Event-Driven Architectures (EDA)	141
5.8. Scalability and Performance in Software Architectures	145
5.9. Security in Software Architecture	149
5.10. Software Architecture Documentation	152
5.11. Service-Oriented Architecture	155

5.12. Software Architecture Practices for High Availability Systems	158
5.13. Chapter Conclusions	161
CHAPTER 6	163
6.1. Coding Fundamentals	164
6.2. Most Used Programming Languages	168
6.3. Algorithms	173
6.4. Programming Logic	177
6.5. Basic Design Patterns	182
6.6. Code Optimization	187
6.7. Secure Programming Practices	192
6.8. Technical Debt (code debt)	197
6.9. Code Refactoring	201
6.10. Unit Testing in Coding	205
6.11. Programming Styles	209
6.12. Error and Exception Handling	213
6.13. Code Documentation	217
6.14. Industry Coding Standards	220
6.15. Continuous Integration and Its Relationship with Coding	223
CHAPTER 7	227
7.1. Fundamentals of Clean Code	228
7.2. Naming and Conventions	231
7.3. Eliminating Redundancy	234
7.4. code organization	237
7.5. Code Maintenance	240
7.6. Practical Examples	243
7.7. Code Simplification Techniques	246
7.8. Continuous Refactoring	250
7.9. Chapter Conclusions	253
Chapter 8	255
8.1. Introduction to Version Control in Software	256

8.2. Git	259
8.3. GitHub and Remote Repositories	262
8.4. GIT WORKFLOW	265
8.5. Git Branching Strategies	268
8.6. Git Integration with CI/CD Tools	271
8.7. chapter conclusions	274
Chapter 9	276
9.1. Types of Software Testing: Unit, Integration, Functional	277
9.2. Test Automation: Tools and Strategies	280
9.3. Black-Box and White-Box Testing	283
9.4. Test Case Management & Software Quality	286
9.5. Security and Performance Testing	290
9.6. A/B Testing and Usability	293
9.7. Load Testing and Stress Testing	297
9.8. Chapter conclusions	301
Chapter 10	303
10.1. SOLID Principles	304
10.2. Test-Driven Development (TDD)	307
10.3. Code Reviews and Pair Programming	310
10.4. Effective Documentation	313
10.5. Six Sigma and Software Quality	319
10.6. Software Quality Models and Standards	322
10.7. Knowledge Management in Development Teams	326
10.8. DevSecOps Implementation	330
10.9. Chapter Conclusions	333
CHAPTER 11	335
11.1. Talent Development and Training	336
11.2. Project Management Tools: Jira, Trello, etc	339
11.3. Project Measurement and Tracking: KPIs and Metrics	342
11.4. Risk Management and Planning	345

11.5. Agile Methodologies in Project Management — 348
11.6. Project Scope and Requirements Management — 352
11.7. Time and Resource Estimation — 356
11.8. Quality Management in Software Projects — 359
11.9. Project Closure and Post-Mortem Evaluation — 362
11.10. Chapter Conclusions — 366
CHAPTER 12 — 368
12.1 Introduction to Ethics in Software Development — 369
12.2. Basic Principles of Intellectual Property — 371
12.3. Regulations and Compliance in Simple Terms — 373
12.4. Ethics in Artificial Intelligence and Machine Learning — 376
12.5. Cybersecurity Practices and Legal Aspects — 379
12.6. Legal Implications of Software Use in Different Sectors — 382
12.7. CHAPTER CONCLUSIONS — 385
Capítulo 13 — 387
13.1. Artificial Intelligence in Software Development — 388
13.2. DevOps and CI/CD — 391
13.3. Cloud Computing and Cloud-Native Application Development — 393
13.4. Future of Software Engineering: Low-Code and No-Code — 396
13.5. Edge Computing and Its Impact on Development — 399
13.6. Applications in Augmented and Virtual Reality — 402
13.7. chapter conclusions — 405
Capítulo 14 — 407
14.1. Recap of Key Concepts — 408
14.2. Key Skills for Software Developers — 410
14.3. Recommended Resources for Further Learning — 412
14.4. Farewell and Acknowledgments — 415
Chapter 15 — 417
15.1. Glossary of Terms — 418
15.2. Documentation Templates — 421

15.3. Useful Resources and Tools 432
15.4. References 435
About The Author 437

FOUNDATIONS OF SOFTWARE DEVELOPMENT ENGINEERING

CHAPTER 1
INTRODUCTION

Today, technology and software are essential for the functioning of nearly every aspect of our lives, from the mobile applications we use daily to the complex systems that manage business, financial, educational, and entertainment operations. From the moment we wake up and check our smartphones to how we interact with the world through social media, online shopping, or transportation services, software is present at every stage of our day. This has created a profound dependency, where the stability of many of our daily activities relies on the quality and proper functioning of software.

Modern organizations, regardless of their size or industry, rely on software to optimize processes, enhance communication with customers, manage inventories, control supply chains, and perform other critical functions. As a result, the demand for robust, scalable, and secure systems has grown exponentially in recent years. Companies in all sectors, from tech startups to large corporations, invest significant resources in developing software that enables them not only to remain competitive but also to innovate and adapt quickly to market changes and user expectations.

In this context, Software Development Engineering has emerged as a vital discipline for creating technological solutions that are not only functional but also meet high standards of efficiency, security, and adaptability. Unlike traditional programming, which focuses on writing code to achieve specific objectives, software engineering takes a systematic and disciplined approach to solving complex problems. It considers not only initial development but also the software's ability to evolve, be maintained, and meet long-term expectations.

Software Development Engineering addresses the challenges of building applications that meet immediate needs while adapting to a constantly evolving environment. This includes tackling issues such as ensuring security against cyber threats, optimizing performance to handle large volumes of data, and scaling applications to support an increasing number of users. In a world where technological obsolescence can occur rapidly, software engineering provides the tools and methodologies needed to create solutions that endure over time and adapt to changing market realities.

The purpose of this book is to offer a comprehensive guide to understanding and applying the key principles and practices in this field. With both theoretical and practical approaches, it aims to equip readers not only with knowledge on how to design and develop software efficiently but also with a deep understanding of what makes software high-quality, scalable, and aligned with industry best practices. Furthermore, it explores critical aspects such as collaboration within development teams, managing software projects, and using modern tools that facilitate work in agile and collaborative development environments.

By exploring these topics, this book is intended to serve as a valuable resource for students, developers, and professionals who want to strengthen their understanding of software engineering. You will learn to tackle the challenges of modern software development and apply practical solutions that contribute to the success of technology projects of any scale. From creating a minimum viable product for a startup to the continuous improvement of a complex system for a large corporation, this book aims to provide the knowledge needed to become a software engineer capable of developing robust applications with a significant impact in the digital world.

1.1. WHAT IS SOFTWARE DEVELOPMENT ENGINEERING?

Software Development Engineering is a branch of engineering focused on the systematic, controlled, and efficient design, development, implementation, and maintenance of software systems. Unlike basic programming, which concentrates on writing code to solve specific tasks, software engineering encompasses a broader, methodical approach. It applies engineering principles and practices to treat software creation as a comprehensive process. This includes not only addressing a system's basic functionality but also ensuring its scalability, maintainability, security, and quality, so the software not only works but adapts and evolves over time.

Modern software development involves solving complex problems that extend beyond writing lines of code. Software engineers must analyze real-world problems and translate them into viable technological solutions. This process includes breaking down large problems into manageable components, understanding the interactions between those components, and integrating them to form a coherent, functional system. The principles of software engineering provide a framework for tackling these tasks, ensuring that software is built in an organized manner with a long-term perspective.

Software engineering is not limited to programming. It also involves applying software design and architecture principles to ensure the system is modular and its parts can be updated, improved, or replaced without affecting the overall functionality. This is crucial in a rapidly evolving technological environment where systems must be flexible enough to adapt to new demands and requirements. Software engineers face the challenge of anticipating future changes and designing systems that can evolve without being completely rebuilt.

It is an integral process that spans from defining system requirements to design and coding, followed by rigorous testing and maintenance throughout the software's lifecycle. This lifecycle, known as the Software Development Life Cycle (SDLC), includes several carefully managed phases to ensure the project is developed efficiently and meets established quality standards. The first phase, requirements gathering and analysis, is critical as it involves thoroughly understanding client or end-user needs and translating them into technical specifications that guide system development.

Once the requirements are defined, the system design phase begins. This phase establishes the architecture and plans how the software components will interact. This step is vital to ensure the system's scalability and to allow future updates without significant changes. The coding phase then turns the design into reality through the writing of source code, while the testing phase ensures the software meets functional requirements and is free of performance-affecting errors.

Maintenance is another critical aspect of software engineering. Often, a system's lifecycle doesn't end with its initial deployment; in fact, the real work often begins once the software is in use. Updates, bug fixes, performance improvements, and adaptations to new requirements are all part of maintenance, ensuring the software continues to perform optimally over time.

Software Development Engineering focuses not only on creating code but also on fostering collaboration within teams, meticulous planning, and product optimization to meet end-user needs. In a professional setting, software projects are often developed by multidisciplinary teams, including software engineers, user experience (UX) designers, quality assurance specialists, and project managers. Collaborative teamwork is essential for project success as it aligns technical objectives with business expectations and user needs.

Meticulous planning is also key to avoiding cost overruns, delays, and quality issues. This involves using development methodologies such as Scrum or Kanban, which facilitate task organization and progress tracking, allowing teams to adapt quickly to changing requirements. Through an agile and collaborative approach, software engineering aims to minimize risks and ensure that delivered software not only meets initial requirements but can also be swiftly adapted to the changing needs of the market and users.

Finally, product optimization extends beyond code efficiency to include usability, security, and user experience. Efficient software is not only fast and resource-friendly but also easy to use and delivers a positive experience to its users. Software engineers must balance technical efficiency with user satisfaction, ensuring the final product is functional while adding value and fulfilling user expectations.

In conclusion, Software Development Engineering is far more than writing code; it is a disciplined and collaborative process aimed at building high-quality technological solutions to solve complex problems and deliver products that evolve alongside user needs and technological advancements. By applying engineering principles, professionals in this field ensure that software not only fulfills its initial purpose but is also prepared to adapt and grow in an increasingly dynamic and competitive environment.

1.2. IMPORTANCE OF SOFTWARE PRINCIPLES

Software principles form the foundation for developing applications and systems that not only function correctly but are also sustainable and capable of evolving alongside user and industry demands over time. These principles serve as a set of guidelines that enable developers to make informed decisions, align their efforts with industry best practices, and create software that is not only functional but also robust, adaptable, and durable. Embracing solid principles from the beginning of software development equips teams to better handle industry challenges such as rapidly evolving technology, shifting client demands, the need for secure and high-quality products, and the pressure to deliver solutions within increasingly tight timeframes.

Adopting well-established development principles ensures a systematic approach, reducing complexity and enhancing team collaboration. This is especially crucial in large-scale software projects, where multiple developers and teams must work together, ensuring consistent system development and seamless integration of different software components. By adhering to software principles, teams can minimize technical debt, referring to quality compromises made to speed up development but which may lead to long-term maintenance challenges. This disciplined focus on principles helps prevent future issues, making the software easier to maintain and scale.

Benefits of Applying These Principles

- Quality and Reliability: Well-designed software minimizes errors and ensures that systems operate correctly under various conditions. Principles like Separation of Concerns and modular design enable developers to create software that is easier to understand, test, and debug. This results in more reliable software capable of handling errors gracefully and maintaining performance, even in unforeseen scenarios. Software quality is not only about functionality but also about delivering a seamless and consistent user experience, which is critical in areas like finance, healthcare, and public infrastructure.

- Scalability: An engineering-driven approach allows software to grow systematically, adapting to new features and higher user loads. Design principles like the Open/Closed Principle help developers build software that can be extended without altering its core, enabling new features to be added without introducing system errors. This is essential in a rapidly changing environment where user demands and market expectations evolve quickly. Scalability also involves adapting to incorporate new integrations and services that complement the original solution, ensuring the software evolves rather than becomes obsolete.

- Maintainability: Proper design and coding practices make it easier to improve and fix software without compromising its core functionality. Principles like DRY (Don't Repeat Yourself) and the Single Responsibility Principle contribute to clean and organized code, where each part of the system has a clear and defined purpose. This not only helps new developers quickly understand the code but also allows safe modifications, reducing the risk of one change affecting other system areas. Maintainability is particularly valuable in long-term projects, where software must adapt to new needs and technologies without requiring complete redesigns.

- Resource Optimization: Adhering to good development practices enables efficient use of system resources like processing time and memory. This is particularly important for applications that handle large data volumes or need to run on resource-constrained devices like smartphones or IoT devices. Applying principles like early optimization and efficient consideration of data structures and algorithms ensures the software runs efficiently while lowering operational costs in terms of energy consumption and server capacity. This can make a significant difference in the long-term profitability of software projects, especially those that need to scale to thousands or millions of users.

These principles help engineers and developers make informed decisions that positively impact the software lifecycle, ensuring that products meet their initial goals and adapt to technological changes and business needs. By establishing a solid foundation early in the development process, teams create software that can be extended and improved without significant restructuring, enabling companies and development teams to respond more agilely to market opportunities. Moreover, adopting software principles promotes sustainable development, where every line of code and design decision is made with the software's future and its impact on the end-user experience in mind. In a fast-paced environment where technology and user expectations advance rapidly, a solid foundation of principles is crucial for the long-term success of any software project.

1.3. BOOK STRUCTURE AND OBJECTIVES

This book is structured to guide both beginners and those seeking to deepen their knowledge of Software Development Engineering. Across its chapters, the book covers topics ranging from basic concepts to advanced practices, always with a practical and industry-oriented approach. Each chapter builds upon the previous one, providing a comprehensive view of software engineering to establish a strong foundation and deep understanding of all aspects of software development, from conceptualization to delivery and maintenance.

The book's approach is gradual and sequential, allowing readers to progress naturally from fundamental concepts to more complex practices. By the end of the book, readers should be able to actively participate in software development projects, applying both technical knowledge and management skills. Additionally, the book addresses best practices and current industry trends to help readers stay updated in a rapidly evolving field.

Book Objectives

• Understand the Fundamentals: Through a detailed explanation of the history and principles that underpin software engineering, readers will understand how this discipline has evolved and the pillars supporting it. This knowledge is essential for situating any practice or methodology within a broader context and understanding why certain strategies are more effective than others for specific project types.

• Develop Design Skills: Exploring design patterns and architectures to create robust and scalable software. Readers will learn how to design solutions that work today and remain relevant and functional in the future, adapting to changing user needs and technological evolution.

- Improve Coding Practices: Introducing techniques for clean coding and code maintenance to ensure project sustainability. This includes principles like Clean Code, refactoring, and the importance of automated testing to ensure code remains functional and understandable over time.

- Apply Testing Strategies: Understanding the importance of software testing and how it improves the quality and security of the final product. The book covers unit tests, integration tests, and test automation, demonstrating how each type of test contributes to more robust and secure software.

- Adopt Best Practices: Including agile methodologies, programming principles, and modern approaches to collaborative development. The book emphasizes Scrum, Kanban, and effective communication within development teams.

- Manage Software Projects: Providing tools and techniques for effective project management, from planning to delivery, aligning team efforts with client objectives and product vision.

Book Structure

1. Foundations of Software Engineering: An overview of the theoretical and practical base underpinning software development, including its history, lifecycle, and methodologies.

2. Software Design: Approaches to creating architectures and designs that meet client needs.

3. Coding and Best Practices: Principles for clean and maintainable code.

4. Software Testing: Strategies for implementing automated and manual tests.

5. Best Practices in Software Development: Advanced principles and agile methodologies.

6. Software Project Management: Leading teams and managing projects effectively.

7. Current and Future Trends: Emerging technologies like AI,

cloud-native applications, DevOps, and Machine Learning.

Each chapter includes exercises and case studies to enable readers to apply their knowledge practically, providing an immersive learning experience.

CHAPTER 2
FUNDAMENTALS OF SOFTWARE ENGINEERING

Software engineering is a vital discipline for the creation, development, and maintenance of applications and computer systems. Throughout history, this field has evolved, adopting new methodologies, principles, and practices aimed at improving the efficiency, quality, and sustainability of software products. This chapter delves into the fundamentals of software engineering, exploring its history, types, development lifecycle, methodologies, ethical considerations, legacy software management, its relationship with other engineering disciplines, and the importance of documentation and international standards.

2.1. HISTORY AND EVOLUTION OF SOFTWARE ENGINEERING

The history of software engineering dates back to the 1960s, a pivotal era when the term "software crisis" emerged. This crisis reflected the challenges faced by the industry as software systems became increasingly complex and difficult to manage. Software projects often exceeded budgets and deadlines, and final products failed to meet quality expectations, resulting in inefficient and unstable systems. These issues highlighted the need for more systematic and rigorous approaches to software development, giving rise to software engineering as a formal discipline.

2.1.1 The Early Years: 1960–1970

The 1960s witnessed the emergence of formal concepts in software engineering, primarily driven by the complex computing projects of the space race and military developments. The "software crisis" became evident when ad hoc methods and a lack of structure proved insufficient to handle the growing complexity of systems. The NATO Software Engineering Conference in 1968 was a significant milestone, addressing the need for an engineering approach to software development and laying the groundwork for defining the discipline.

During this era, methodologies oriented towards structured programming were adopted, aiming to improve code clarity and management through control structures like loops and well-defined conditionals. Structured programming allowed developers to build systems with more readable and maintainable code, marking an essential step toward the professionalization of software development.

2.1.2 The 1970s and Structured Programming

The 1970s marked a transition to more disciplined methods in software development. Structured programming, popularized by pioneers like Dijkstra, emphasized clear control structures (e.g., loops and conditionals) and modular design, facilitating code comprehension and maintenance. Languages like Pascal and C reflected these principles, and software development began to resemble a controlled and methodical process rather than intuitive craftsmanship.

This period also saw the introduction of formal project management models, such as the Waterfall Model, which became a reference point for subsequent years. This model defined a sequence of phases for software development, from requirements specification to maintenance, promoting a linear and predictable project structure.

2.1.3 The 1980s and 1990s: Object-Oriented Programming and Computing Expansion

The 1980s introduced a significant shift with the advent of object-oriented programming (OOP), a paradigm that revolutionized software design. Languages like Smalltalk initially proposed this approach, which was later popularized by C++ and Java. OOP enabled developers to organize code into objects representing real-world entities, enhancing the ability to model complex systems and reuse software components—a key factor in scalable and maintainable development.

Object-oriented principles, such as encapsulation, inheritance, and polymorphism, became foundational in software design. This paradigm helped development teams create more robust and flexible systems while addressing software challenges from a reality-based perspective.

Simultaneously, software development became increasingly integrated into the business environment, and project management tools and version control systems emerged to facilitate collaborative team work. Organizations began adopting more formal development methodologies to improve predictability and project quality.

2.1.4 The 2000s: Agility and Adaptability

The turn of the millennium brought new challenges, including the rise of the internet and the need to deliver products faster and with greater adaptability. Agile methodologies emerged, focusing on flexibility, rapid software delivery, and client collaboration. The Agile Manifesto, published in 2001, marked a paradigm shift by emphasizing communication, iterative work, and adaptability to changing requirements.

Scrum, Kanban, and Extreme Programming (XP) became popular agile methodologies, equipping teams with tools to manage projects efficiently and adapt continuously to client needs. Agility reduced the time to deliver functional software, improved client satisfaction, and fostered a culture of continuous improvement within development teams.

2.1.5 Recent Years: DevOps, Cloud Computing, and Software Modernization

In the last decade, software engineering has evolved through the integration of development and operations (DevOps), which promotes collaboration between these teams to accelerate the software delivery cycle. DevOps practices, such as continuous integration (CI) and continuous delivery (CD), have transformed the deployment and maintenance of applications, enabling faster and more secure delivery.

Cloud computing has also been a major catalyst in software engineering evolution, allowing companies to scale applications flexibly and manage vast amounts of data. Technologies like containers (Docker) and orchestrators (Kubernetes) have simplified the development and deployment of distributed applications.

Simultaneously, artificial intelligence and machine learning have started influencing software development, from optimizing processes to creating more intelligent and adaptive software.

2.1.6 Current Challenges and the Future of Software Engineering

Today, software engineering faces new challenges, such as the growing importance of cybersecurity, the need to create sustainable and ethical software, and the integration of emerging technologies like artificial intelligence and augmented reality. As the industry continues to evolve, robust approaches, suitable methodologies, and a steadfast commitment to quality remain essential.

The history of software engineering demonstrates how the discipline has evolved from an urgent need to manage complexity to a cornerstone of the digital age. With a clear understanding of its origins and evolution, software engineers are better equipped to tackle present and future challenges, building systems that not only meet current standards but also adapt to technological and market changes.

2.2. TYPES OF SOFTWARE

Software, due to its diversity and versatility, is classified into different types based on its purpose, functionality, and the environment in which it operates. This classification enables software engineers to choose the best approach for development, tailoring software to user needs and the technical specifications of the hardware and environment where it will be implemented. The main software categories are:

2.2.1 System Software

System software is essential for the operation of computers and electronic devices, enabling interaction between hardware and application software. This type of software acts as a mediating layer that controls and coordinates hardware usage.

- Operating Systems: The most well-known component of system software, examples include Windows, macOS, Linux, and Android. An operating system manages hardware resources, such as memory, the processor, and input/output devices, providing an environment where user applications can run. It also handles system security and file management.

- Device Drivers: Drivers are specific programs that allow the operating system to communicate with hardware devices, such as printers, graphics cards, or storage devices. Without them, many peripherals would not be compatible with the system.

System software is crucial for the stability and efficiency of devices, ensuring applications run smoothly and system resources are managed optimally.

2.2.2 Application Software

Application software is designed to assist users in performing specific tasks and is the most visible and familiar software category to end users.

- Productivity Applications: These include office suites (Microsoft Office, Google Workspace), project management software, and collaboration tools. These applications are essential in office environments for tasks such as document editing, spreadsheet management, and email handling.

- Web Browsers: Fundamental applications for accessing the internet, such as Google Chrome, Mozilla Firefox, and Safari. Their importance has grown exponentially with digitalization, as many applications are now accessible via browsers.

- Creative and Multimedia Software: Tools for graphic design (Adobe Photoshop, Illustrator), video editing (Premiere Pro, Final Cut Pro), and 3D modeling (Blender). These are vital in creative industries such as advertising, film, and animation.

Application software is designed to enhance productivity and facilitate specific tasks, providing an intuitive experience tailored to the needs of end users.

2.2.3. Embedded Software

Embedded software is integrated into electronic devices to perform specific functions, often focusing on efficiency and stability. Unlike application software, embedded software is deeply tied to the hardware it operates on and is generally invisible to the end user.

- Home Appliances and Consumer Devices: From microwaves to smart TVs, many everyday devices contain embedded software that manages their internal functions.

- Cars: Modern cars feature numerous embedded software systems controlling everything from engines and brakes to entertainment and navigation systems. This software must be robust and secure, as it often affects occupant safety.

- Medical Devices: In healthcare, embedded software is used in devices like pacemakers, ultrasound machines, and patient monitoring systems. Reliability and precision are critical for this type of software.

Embedded software is essential for devices requiring quick and efficient responses, and its design must consider the memory and processing constraints of the devices it is implemented on.

2.2.4. Development Software

Development software includes tools that enable programmers to create other programs, simplifying the software development process. This type of software is essential for software engineers as it provides resources for writing, testing, and debugging code.

- Integrated Development Environments (IDEs): Tools like Visual Studio, Eclipse, and IntelliJ IDEA combine a code editor, debugger, and compiler, facilitating programming by offering a unified experience. IDEs accelerate development by providing auto-completion, syntax highlighting, and project management.

- Compilers and Interpreters: These transform source code written in a programming language into machine-executable code, such as C++ compilers or Python interpreters.

- Version Control Systems: Tools like Git enable developers to collaborate and manage changes in source code, streamlining teamwork and tracking project evolution.

Development software is fundamental for creating high-quality software, providing a structured environment and tools that enhance developer efficiency.

2.2.5. Enterprise Software

Enterprise software is designed to meet the needs of large organizations, helping them manage their business processes more efficiently. This type of software is often complex and integrates with multiple systems and databases.

- ERP (Enterprise Resource Planning): Solutions like SAP and Oracle ERP integrate different business areas, such as accounting, human resources, supply chain, and inventory management. This provides a comprehensive view of operations and facilitates decision-making.

- CRM (Customer Relationship Management): Tools like Salesforce and HubSpot manage customer relationships, track interactions, handle sales, and analyze customer behavior data. These are essential for optimizing marketing, sales, and customer service.

- BI (Business Intelligence): Business intelligence

applications like Tableau and Power BI help organizations analyze large volumes of data, generating reports and visualizations that facilitate strategic decision-making.

Enterprise software optimizes resource management, improves internal process efficiency, and enables organizations to adapt quickly to market changes.

2.2.6 Importance of Software Classification

Understanding these categories is essential for software engineers, as each type of software requires a different approach during development. For example, an embedded system has resource constraints not present in enterprise software, while development software must be intuitive for programmers who will use it.

By recognizing the differences between these types of software, engineers can design more efficient and appropriate solutions aligned with user expectations and market needs. This classification also helps to understand the role of software in modern society, from the technology we use daily to the complex systems operating in the background of large organizations and critical devices.

2.3. SOFTWARE DEVELOPMENT LIFE CYCLE (SDLC)

The Software Development Life Cycle (SDLC) is a framework that describes the systematic stages that must be followed to develop software, from its initial conception to its final retirement. This structured approach helps ensure that the software is developed efficiently, meets quality expectations, and satisfies user needs. The SDLC phases provide a clear plan for project management and allow development teams to maintain control throughout the process. Below is a detailed explanation of each of the most common phases:

2.3.1. Requirements Gathering

The requirements gathering phase is the starting point of the SDLC, where the needs and expectations of the client or end-users are identified. In this phase, the functionalities that the software must have, its constraints, and any other technical or business requirements are defined.

• Requirements Gathering Techniques: Interviews, surveys, focus groups, and document analysis are some of the techniques used to understand what the user needs. These techniques help gather a list of functional requirements (what the system must do) and non-functional requirements (performance, security, usability).

• Requirements Documentation: The result of this phase is often a Software Requirements Specification (SRS) document that acts as a guide for the following stages of development. The quality of this documentation is crucial, as errors or ambiguities in the requirements can lead to problems during development.

2.3.2. Analysis

Once the requirements are defined, the analysis phase focuses on evaluating the project's feasibility and understanding in-depth what is required to develop the solution.

- **Feasibility Study**: This study analyzes whether it is possible to develop the software with the available resources (time, budget, technical skills). It also evaluates the technical, economic, and operational feasibility of the project.

- **Use Case Modeling**: Use cases are tools that describe how users will interact with the software. Diagrams are created to show interactions between the user and the system, facilitating a more detailed understanding of the requirements.

- **Risk Analysis**: Identifying and assessing potential risks, such as changes in project scope or technical problems, helps develop contingency plans and mitigate issues before they affect development.

2.3.3. Design

In the design phase, a technical roadmap is created that will guide the construction of the software. This phase turns the requirements and analysis into an architecture and detailed design that developers can follow.

- **System Architecture Design**: The system architecture defines the high-level structure of the software, including its division into modules and how they interact with each other. Design patterns and technologies to be used are selected.

- **User Interface (UI) Design**: The user experience (UX) and graphical user interface (UI) are designed, ensuring that interaction with the software is intuitive and satisfying for the end-user.

- **Detailed Design**: This defines how each software module will be implemented, including class diagrams, sequence diagrams, and data flow diagrams. It provides a clear plan for coding.

2.3.4. Implementation

The implementation phase, also known as development or coding, involves programming the functionalities and features described in the design.

- **Coding**: Developers write the code using programming languages appropriate for the defined architecture (such as Java, Python, C++). It is important to follow best coding practices to ensure code maintainability.

- **Code Review**: Code reviews help detect errors early and ensure the code meets quality standards. These reviews can be formal, using static analysis tools, or informal, through peer reviews.

- **Continuous Integration**: In large projects, continuous integration (CI) systems are used to integrate the code into a common repository and run automated tests, ensuring that new changes do not introduce errors.

2.3.5. Testing

The testing phase is crucial to verify that the software works correctly and meets the defined requirements. Different types of tests are conducted to ensure the product's quality.

- **Unit Testing**: Verifies the functionality of individual units of code, such as functions and methods, ensuring that each component works correctly on its own.

- **Integration Testing**: Focuses on verifying the interaction between different modules or components of the software, ensuring they work well together.

- **System and Acceptance Testing**: System testing evaluates the software as a whole, ensuring it meets the client's requirements. Acceptance testing, often performed by the client or end-user, ensures the software is suitable for its purpose.

Testing helps identify and correct defects before the software reaches the users, ensuring greater customer satisfaction and reducing the cost of fixing errors in later stages.

2.3.6. Deployment

The deployment phase involves moving the software from the development environment to the production environment, where it will be available to users.

- **Production Environment Setup**: Servers are configured, and network and database connections are secured for the software to function. In some cases, a pilot deployment is done for a small group of users before the general release.

- **Deployment and Data Migration**: This includes transferring user data from previous systems to the new software, ensuring the information remains intact and secure during the process.

- **Deployment Strategies**: Strategies such as gradual deployment, blue-green deployment, or continuous deployment may be used, depending on the project's type and tolerance for service interruptions.

2.3.7. Maintenance

Once the software is in operation, the maintenance phase ensures it continues functioning correctly, adapts to new requirements, and remains secure.

- **Bug Fixing**: Even though pre-deployment tests are thorough, bugs may be identified during real-world use of the software. These bugs are fixed through patches and updates.

- **Updates and Enhancements**: Over time, client needs may change or new improvement opportunities may arise. Software updates allow for adding new features and improving existing ones.

- **Preventive and Adaptive Maintenance**: Preventive maintenance focuses on avoiding future problems by optimizing code and improving performance. Adaptive maintenance adjusts the software to remain compatible with new environments, such as new versions of operating systems or hardware.

Maintenance is an ongoing phase that ensures the software's longevity and its ability to adapt to technological and market changes.

2.3.8. Importance of SDLC in Software Development

Each phase of the SDLC plays a fundamental role in developing high-quality software and ensuring user satisfaction. A structured approach allows for anticipating problems and mitigating risks, ensuring projects are delivered on time, within budget, and with a quality level that meets expectations. Additionally, the SDLC is adaptable and can be adjusted to different development methodologies, such as agile, traditional, or hybrid methodologies, allowing development teams to choose the best approach based on the needs of each project.

2.4. DEVELOPMENT METHODOLOGIES: AGILE, TRADITIONAL, AND HYBRID

Development methodologies are frameworks that provide a set of practices and processes to organize, plan, and execute software development efficiently. Choosing the right methodology can be a determining factor in the success of a project, as each approach offers advantages and limitations that fit different types of projects and teams. Below are the three main development approaches: traditional, agile, and hybrid methodologies.

2.4.1 Traditional Methodologies
Traditional methodologies, also known as predictive approaches, follow a linear and structured sequence in software development. Each phase of the project must be completed before moving on to the next, allowing for detailed planning from the start of the project. Some of the most well-known traditional methodologies include:

- **Waterfall Model**: This model was one of the first systematic approaches for software development and is characterized by a series of sequential phases: requirements, design, implementation, testing, deployment, and maintenance. It is particularly useful in projects where the requirements are clear, complete, and unlikely to change throughout development.

-**Advantages**: Its structured approach facilitates planning and tracking progress. It is suitable for projects with well-defined and stable requirements, such as critical systems that require strong documentation.

-**Disadvantages**: It has limited flexibility to adapt to changes in requirements once the development phase has started. Additionally, the client does not see a functional product until the later stages of the project, which can lead to unmet expectations if the initial requirements were not precise.

- **V-Model**: Similar to the Waterfall model, the V-Model emphasizes verification and validation at each stage of development. For each development phase, there is a corresponding testing phase, forming a "V" shape. This helps identify errors before moving on to the next stage.

-**Advantages**: Provides high-quality development and testing due to its detailed approach to verification and validation. It is ideal for software projects where quality is a critical aspect.

-**Disadvantages**: It is rigid, and like the Waterfall model, it is unsuitable for projects where requirements may change during development.

2.4.2 Agile Methodologies

Agile methodologies are iterative and incremental approaches that prioritize flexibility, rapid delivery of value, and constant collaboration with the client. These methodologies emerged as a response to the limitations of traditional approaches and aim to adapt to a changing requirements environment. Some of the most popular agile methodologies include:

- **Scrum**: Scrum is based on performing short iterations called sprints, typically lasting between 2 and 4 weeks. During each sprint, the development team works on a specific set of features that are reviewed at the end of the cycle to receive feedback from the client and adjust the course of development.

-**Advantages**: It facilitates adaptation to changes in requirements and allows the client to continuously see and evaluate progress. This reduces the risk of developing a product that does not meet the client's expectations.

-**Disadvantages**: It requires constant communication and active commitment from the client, which can be difficult to maintain in some environments. Additionally, without proper discipline, the project scope can easily become uncontrolled (known as scope creep).

- **Kanban**: Kanban focuses on visualizing the workflow and managing work in progress. It uses a board that shows pending, in-progress, and completed tasks, which helps identify bottlenecks and optimize the workflow.

-**Advantages**: Kanban is highly flexible and allows development teams to quickly adapt to changes. It is ideal for teams that need to improve efficiency without adopting a full agile process.

-**Disadvantages**: Being less structured than Scrum, it can be difficult for some teams to manage priorities without a clear framework of iterations.

- **Extreme Programming (XP)**: XP focuses on continuous improvement of the code and close collaboration with the client. Some of its practices include pair programming, continuous testing, and frequent integration.

-**Advantages**: It promotes a high level of code quality and a rapid response to changes in requirements.

-**Disadvantages**: It requires a highly disciplined and experienced development team to effectively implement all its practices.

2.4.3 Hybrid Methodologies

Hybrid methodologies combine elements of both traditional and agile approaches, adapting to the specific needs of each project. These approaches aim to leverage the structure and predictability of traditional methodologies along with the flexibility and adaptability of agile methodologies. Examples of hybrid methodologies include:

- **V-Agile Model**: This approach combines the verification and validation principles of the V-Model with the flexibility of agile iterations. Requirements and design are performed in detail, as in the V-Model, but implementation and testing are carried out in iterative cycles.

-**Advantages**: Allows for detailed planning and high-quality testing while still enabling adaptation to changes through iterations. It is ideal for projects with complex requirements that, nevertheless, require greater flexibility during implementation.

-**Disadvantages**: Combining both approaches can be difficult to manage, especially if the team is not familiar with the practices of both methodologies.

- **Agile-Waterfall**: In this approach, the Waterfall model is used for the early stages of the project, such as requirements gathering and design, while implementation and testing are carried out iteratively using agile practices.

-**Advantages**: Allows for better definition of requirements at the beginning of the project, which facilitates planning, while agile implementation allows for adjustments and improvements as the product is developed.

-**Disadvantages**: It can be challenging to maintain a balance between linear and iterative phases, potentially causing conflicts between initial planning and adaptations during implementation.

- **Scrumban**: A mix of Scrum and Kanban, Scrumban uses the sprint structure of Scrum to organize work but with the flexibility and focus on continuous improvement of Kanban.

-**Advantages**: Provides a balance between Scrum's organization and Kanban's adaptability, making it ideal for teams that need some structure but also want to improve workflow efficiency.

-**Disadvantages**: It can be difficult to implement if the team does not fully understand the principles of both methodologies, and the lack of a rigid framework can be a challenge for projects requiring more formal planning.

2.4.4 Choosing the Right Methodology

Choosing the right development methodology depends on several factors, such as the size and experience of the team, the nature of the project, the complexity of requirements, and the level of client involvement. In projects where the requirements are stable and well-defined, traditional methodologies may be the best option. However, when requirements are changing and the client needs to see results quickly, agile methodologies may offer more flexibility and adaptability. Hybrid methodologies are useful in situations where a balance between structure and adaptability is desired.

Ultimately, the success of a software development project does not depend solely on the selected methodology but on the team's ability to adapt, communicate, and collaborate effectively to meet the project's objectives.

2.5. LEGACY SOFTWARE AND ITS MANAGEMENT

Legacy software refers to old computer systems that, despite their age, are essential to the operations of many organizations. These systems are often critical to the functioning of businesses as they handle essential processes such as financial data management, production operations, and other business processes. However, as technology advances, legacy software presents several challenges that make its maintenance and evolution difficult. Companies face a dilemma between maintaining and modernizing these systems, as their complete replacement is a complex, costly task that carries significant risks.

Therefore, it is important to delve into the main strategies and considerations for efficiently managing legacy software:

2.5.1. Challenges of Legacy Software

Legacy software presents a number of problems that make it difficult to manage and update, including:

- **Technological Obsolescence:** These systems are often built with technologies that are no longer used or supported, making it difficult to find skilled personnel to maintain them. Old programming languages and discontinued platforms can create incompatibilities with new technologies and complicate integration with modern systems.

- **High Maintenance Costs:** Correcting errors, making adaptations, and maintaining the functionality of legacy software involves significant costs. These costs can exceed the budget for developing a new system, as they require in-depth knowledge of the system and time spent on maintenance tasks.

- **Security Issues:** Since legacy systems were not designed with modern cybersecurity threats in mind, they are often vulnerable to attacks. The lack of security updates and official support from vendors increases the risk of exposure to vulnerabilities.

- **Organizational Dependency:** Organizations often rely heavily on these systems for their daily operations, making the transition to new systems risky. The lack of detailed documentation on how these systems work adds complexity to any attempt at modernization or migration.

2.5.2. Strategies for Managing Legacy Software

Since completely replacing legacy systems is a risky and costly process, organizations often adopt intermediate strategies to maintain their functionality while minimizing the issues associated with their obsolescence. Below are the main strategies for managing legacy software:

•**Refactoring**: Refactoring involves improving the code of a legacy system without changing its behavior or functionality. This includes making the code more understandable, modular, and efficient, which facilitates long-term maintenance. Refactoring may involve:

- Improving the structure of the code: Breaking complex code into simpler modules, renaming variables for clarity, and improving code organization.

- Performance optimization: Identifying and eliminating bottlenecks in the code that affect system performance.

- Updated documentation: Providing accurate documentation of the refactored code, which facilitates future maintenance.

Refactoring is an effective option when the legacy system still meets most of the organization's requirements but requires improvements in maintainability and performance.

•**Migration to New Platforms**: This strategy involves adapting legacy software to run on newer hardware or software environments. Unlike complete replacement, migration preserves the core functionality of the system while updating the environment in which it runs. Migration approaches include:

-**Rehosting**: Moving legacy software to a more modern environment (such as a cloud server) without modifying its underlying code. This can improve scalability and accessibility but does not address code obsolescence issues.

-**Replatforming**: Adapting legacy software to work on a new operating system or database platform, with minimal changes to the code. This allows leveraging performance and security features of modern platforms.

-**Containerization**: In some cases, legacy software can be encapsulated in containers (e.g., Docker) to facilitate deployment in new environments without significant modifications.

·**Encapsulation**: Encapsulation involves using APIs or interfaces so that legacy software can interact with newer systems without needing to modify its core code. This allows the legacy system to continue functioning as a "core" while new functionalities are built independently around it. Examples of encapsulation include:

-**Creating REST APIs**: Enabling legacy software to offer services through REST APIs, making it easier to integrate with mobile applications, modern web systems, and other services.

-**Integration with Middleware**: Using middleware software to interconnect the legacy system with new applications and databases, facilitating communication and data transfer between different systems.

Encapsulation is particularly useful when there is a desire to preserve the functionality of the legacy system but also integrate it with new technologies to extend its capabilities.

· **Gradual Replacement (Partial Modernization):** Rather than replacing the entire legacy system at once, this strategy focuses on gradually modernizing specific parts of the system. This could involve redesigning specific modules or creating new services that gradually replace legacy software functions. As each module is developed, it is integrated with the rest of the system, minimizing the risk of significant operational disruption.

-**Advantages**: Allows for a smoother transition and reduces the risk of catastrophic failures by having parts of the system functioning while others are being modernized.

-**Disadvantages**: It can be a lengthy and complex process, requiring meticulous planning to ensure that new components work properly with existing systems.

2.5.3. Benefits of Proper Legacy Software Management

Proper management of legacy software not only extends the life of critical systems but also offers several key benefits for organizations:

- **Reduction of Operational Risks:** By maintaining and gradually modernizing legacy software, organizations can minimize the risk of unexpected disruptions and ensure their critical systems remain reliable.

- **Cost Optimization:** While maintaining and modernizing legacy software requires investment, it is generally less costly than a complete replacement. This is especially important when legacy systems are deeply integrated into the organization's operations.

- **Adaptation to New Needs:** Through strategies such as encapsulation and migration to new platforms, organizations can adapt their legacy systems to current demands, such as integration with mobile technologies, cloud connectivity, and improved user experience.

- **Preservation of Organizational Knowledge:** Legacy systems often contain valuable knowledge about an organization's business processes and logic. By keeping these systems updated, that knowledge is preserved and makes the transition to new solutions easier.

2.5.4. Conclusions on Legacy Software

Managing legacy software is a common challenge in the field of software engineering. While these systems present significant difficulties due to their obsolescence and complexity, various strategies exist to optimize their use and extend their lifespan. Whether through refactoring, migration to new platforms, encapsulation, or gradual replacement, the key lies in finding a balance between maintaining the critical functionality of the system and adopting necessary technological improvements to face future challenges. In this way, organizations can continue to benefit from their prior investments while preparing for the demands of the current digital environment.

2.6. RELATIONSHIP BETWEEN SOFTWARE ENGINEERING AND OTHER ENGINEERING DISCIPLINES

Software engineering shares principles, approaches, and techniques with other engineering disciplines, facilitating collaboration in multidisciplinary projects and enabling the creation of comprehensive solutions that combine software, hardware, and processes. This synergy is essential in a technological environment where systems require the integration of multiple components to function efficiently.

It is important to recognize some of the key relationships between software engineering and other branches of engineering:

2.6.1. Systems Engineering

- Systems engineering and software engineering share a common focus on managing complex systems that include both software and hardware components. While software engineering focuses on the development and maintenance of software, systems engineering addresses the design and integration of the entire system, ensuring that each part works together to achieve project goals. This collaboration is crucial in projects such as:

- Hardware and Software Integration: In systems involving coordination of physical devices and software, such as industrial control systems, autonomous cars, and telecommunications networks. In these cases, systems engineering ensures proper integration of hardware and software, while software engineering develops the applications and drivers necessary for that integration.

- Requirements Management and Systems Modeling: Systems engineering helps define the overall system requirements and model its behavior, which is essential for software engineers to design architecture that meets those requirements. This is common in aerospace system development, where safety and performance requirements are critical.

- Development of Critical Systems: In critical applications like defense systems, military simulations, or air traffic control systems, systems engineering and software engineering work hand in hand to ensure that each component operates under strict safety and reliability conditions.

2.6.2. Electronic Engineering

- The relationship between software engineering and electronic engineering is particularly relevant in the development of embedded systems and IoT (Internet of Things) devices. Embedded systems are those where the software is designed to perform specific functions within a device that combines hardware and software. Some key areas of collaboration include:

- Firmware Development: Software engineering is responsible for developing the firmware that controls the behavior of microcontrollers and processors in electronic devices. This includes everything from household appliances and medical equipment to industrial automation systems.

- IoT Devices: The integration of sensors, actuators, and wireless communication in internet-connected devices requires the collaboration of electronic engineers who design the hardware and software engineers who develop the control applications and platforms. This enables the creation of solutions for smart cities, connected homes, and environmental monitoring.

- Resource Optimization: In systems with limited resources, such as low-power microcontrollers, software engineers must closely collaborate with electronic engineers to optimize memory, processing, and energy usage. This is essential in the design of portable devices and wearables, where battery life and efficiency are crucial.

2.6.3. Industrial Engineering

Industrial engineering and software engineering share the goal of optimizing processes, albeit in different contexts. While industrial engineering seeks efficiency in production and logistics processes, software engineering focuses on optimizing software development processes. Collaboration between these disciplines is beneficial in areas such as:

- Process Optimization in Development: Principles of continuous improvement and lean manufacturing from industrial engineering are applicable in software development, especially in agile methodologies. For example, concepts such as waste reduction, productivity improvement, and quality management can be implemented to improve efficiency in software creation.

- Software Project Management: Industrial engineering contributes project planning and control methods, such as earned value analysis and risk management, which are applicable in software project management. This helps development teams better manage deadlines, resources, and budgets.

- Business Process Automation: In business process automation projects (Business Process Automation), software engineering develops the necessary tools to digitize and optimize workflows, while industrial engineering analyzes and defines the processes to be automated. This collaboration is essential for implementing ERP (Enterprise Resource Planning) systems and robotic process automation (RPA).

2.6.4. Mechanical Engineering and Robotics

The collaboration between software engineering and mechanical engineering is crucial in the development of automated and robotic systems. These systems combine precision mechanics with advanced control algorithms and programming software, enabling the creation of innovative solutions such as:

- Control Systems Development: Software engineers develop control systems that allow robots and industrial machines to perform complex tasks. This includes everything from trajectory programming to integrating sensors that enable automated decision-making.

- Mechanical Systems Simulation: Software engineering enables the simulation of mechanical systems to predict their behavior under various conditions, which is essential for mechanical engineering in validating and optimizing designs before manufacturing.

- **Industrial Automation**: Programming programmable logic controllers (PLCs) and integrating SCADA (Supervisory Control and Data Acquisition) systems requires collaboration between software engineers and mechanical engineers to automate manufacturing processes, improve production line accuracy, and ensure safety in industrial environments.

2.6.5. Data Engineering and Data Science

Software engineering and data engineering are increasingly interdependent, especially in contexts where data value is key for decision-making. Software engineering provides the necessary infrastructure for data collection, storage, and processing, while data engineering focuses on managing and analyzing large volumes of information. Some areas of collaboration include:

- **Big Data Infrastructure Development**: Software engineers are responsible for creating scalable architectures for data ingestion and processing, using technologies such as Hadoop, Spark, and NoSQL databases. Data engineers design the data structure and create pipelines that allow the extraction of valuable insights.

- **Artificial Intelligence and Machine Learning**: Implementing AI and machine learning models depends on collaboration between software engineers who develop the necessary platforms and APIs and data scientists who train and tune the models. This is crucial in applications like demand prediction, image analysis, and natural language processing.

- **Enterprise Data Integration**: Software engineering facilitates the integration of various enterprise data sources through APIs and ETL (Extract, Transform, Load) systems, while data engineering organizes and cleans that data to make it useful for analysis and reporting.

The relationship between software engineering and other engineering disciplines is essential for addressing the complex challenges of today's technological environment. These collaborations allow for the creation of robust solutions that integrate software and hardware components, optimize processes, and deliver value to organizations. The interdisciplinary approach not only fosters innovation but also ensures that systems are efficient, scalable, and adaptable to the changing needs of industries. Understanding and leveraging these synergies is key for software engineers seeking to develop solutions that are not only technically solid but also aligned with the strategic goals of organizations.

2.7. DOCUMENTATION PRACTICES AND INTERNATIONAL STANDARDS

Documentation is a fundamental pillar in software development, as it facilitates understanding, maintenance, and evolution of the system for both the development team and other stakeholders, such as users, project managers, and support personnel. Properly documenting each stage of the development process is crucial to ensure quality, efficiency, and the transfer of knowledge throughout the software's lifecycle. Below are some of the most common documentation practices and the international standards that guide these processes:

2.7.1. Common Documentation Practices

2.7.1.1. Technical Documentation:

- **Design and Architecture Details**: Describes how the software is structured, including architecture diagrams, class diagrams, flowcharts, and other representations that help understand the system's structure and behavior. This documentation is essential for developers to understand the system's overall structure and how different components interact.

- **Code Documentation**: Includes comments within the source code that explain the purpose of functions, classes, and modules, as well as external documentation on the structure and functionality of the code. Tools like Javadoc (for Java) and Doxygen (for C++) help generate technical documentation automatically from commented code.

- **Interface Specifications**: Documents how different software modules interact with each other and with external systems through APIs (Application Programming Interfaces). This documentation facilitates integration and collaboration between development teams and allows third parties to understand how to use the API.

2.7.1.2. User Documentation::

- **End-User Guides:** Describes how to use the software from the user's perspective. These guides include detailed instructions on the application's features, usage examples, and solutions to common problems. They are essential for reducing the software's learning curve and ensuring that users can take full advantage of its features.

- **Operation Manuals:** Targeted at system administrators and IT personnel who need to install, configure, and maintain the software. This includes instructions for installation, environment setup, maintenance, and updates.

- **FAQs and Online Documentation**: Frequently asked questions and online documentation are important supplements to user documentation. They allow users to quickly find answers to common problems and stay updated on new software features as updates are released.

2.7.1.3. Requirements Documentation::

- **Functional Requirements**: Describes the specific functionalities that the software must fulfill, such as the operations it must perform and the use cases it must cover. These requirements help understand what the software is expected to do from the user's perspective.

- **Non-Functional Requirements:** Includes aspects like performance, security, scalability, and usability. They are essential for defining quality standards and ensuring that the software functions optimally under various conditions.

- **User Stories and Use Cases**: In agile methodologies, user stories document what the user expects from the system in a simple manner, while use cases detail the interactions between the user and the software. Both are fundamental for guiding the development of features that align with the user's real needs.

2.7.2. International Standards

International standards play a crucial role in standardizing software development processes, ensuring that best practices are followed and that a consistent level of quality is maintained in the developed products. Some of the most notable standards include:

2.7.2.1. ISO/IEC 12207: Software Lifecycle Process:

This international standard establishes a framework for the software lifecycle, defining processes, activities, and tasks to be performed during development, maintenance, and retirement of software. It provides a standardized approach to documentation and practices, ensuring that all stakeholders involved in the project have clarity on responsibilities and expected quality.

ISO/IEC 12207 covers both internal software development and third-party software acquisition, making it applicable to projects with different development approaches. It also promotes continuous improvement of the development process, contributing to the optimization of productivity and software quality.

2.7.2.2. ISO/IEC 90003: Software Quality Management:

This standard is an extension of ISO 9001 and focuses on quality management in the development and maintenance of software. It provides guidelines for applying the principles of ISO 9001 in a software development context, helping organizations ensure that their development processes meet international quality standards.

By applying this standard, companies can improve customer satisfaction, reduce software errors, and optimize development processes. Additionally, ISO/IEC 90003 is useful for projects that must meet specific regulatory requirements, such as those in the medical or aerospace industries.

2.7.2.3. CMMI (Capability Maturity Model Integration):

CMMI is a process improvement model used to assess the maturity of an organization's software development processes. It provides a framework for identifying best practices and guiding companies in improving the quality of their products and development processes.

This model defines maturity levels ranging from an initial process, characterized by ad-hoc management, to an optimized process, where practices are standardized and continuous improvement is an essential component. Implementing CMMI helps organizations manage risk, improve project planning, and achieve a high level of quality in software development.

2.7.2.4. IEEE 830: Software Requirements Documentation:

This standard provides guidelines for creating software requirements specification (SRS) documents. A well-written SRS is crucial to ensure that customer requirements and project objectives are clear from the beginning, reducing the risk of misunderstandings and errors during development.

IEEE 830 specifies the content, structure, and format that requirements documents should have, promoting the creation of a clear and detailed specification that serves as a foundation for design, implementation, and validation of the software.

2.7.3. Importance of Documentation and Standards
Proper documentation and compliance with international standards not only improve software quality but also facilitate collaboration and communication among different project stakeholders. Moreover, they make the software more maintainable, easing future updates and modifications, and help minimize risks associated with a lack of knowledge when new developers join the team.

The use of standards like ISO/IEC 12207 or CMMI also offers companies a competitive advantage in the market, as they demonstrate their commitment to quality and continuous improvement, which can be a decisive factor for customers when choosing a software provider. In an increasingly regulated and demanding software development environment, mastering these practices and standards is essential for project success and customer satisfaction.

In conclusion, a combination of solid documentation practices and adherence to international standards is key to ensuring success in software development. It guarantees that delivered products meet user expectations and remain reliable throughout their lifecycle.

2.8 CHAPTER CONCLUSIONS

Software engineering is a discipline that has evolved significantly since its early days, adapting to changing technology challenges and market demands. Throughout this chapter, an overview of its history, different types of software, and structured approaches to managing systems development through the Software Development Lifecycle (SDLC) has been presented. The importance of adopting appropriate methodologies for each project, whether agile, traditional, or hybrid, has also been emphasized, as well as the relevance of ethical principles in creating responsible and sustainable technological solutions.

The management of legacy software and the relationship of software engineering with other disciplines reinforce the idea that software development does not occur in isolation but requires a broad understanding of its environment and the operational needs of organizations. Finally, documentation and compliance with international standards ensure the consistency and quality of software products, facilitating their maintenance and evolution over time.

This chapter sets the foundation for understanding the context, principles, and best practices that guide the creation of quality software. The topics covered not only offer an overview of the essential knowledge for every software engineer but also pave the way for exploring, in the next chapters, the specific details of each phase and technique that comprise software engineering.

CHAPTER 3
REQUIREMENTS ENGINEERING

Requirements engineering is a fundamental discipline within software engineering that focuses on identifying, analyzing, documenting, verifying, and managing the requirements that a software system must fulfill. Requirements define what the software must do and under what conditions it should operate, serving as a vital guide for design and development. Proper requirements engineering ensures that the final product meets the expectations of customers and users while minimizing misunderstandings and costly changes in later stages of the project.

3.1. FUNDAMENTALS OF REQUIREMENTS ENGINEERING

Requirements engineering is one of the most critical phases in the software development life cycle. It is responsible for thoroughly understanding the problem the software aims to solve and translating user needs and stakeholder expectations into clear, precise, and manageable specifications. Accurate identification and documentation of requirements establish a solid foundation for the entire system, reducing risks of misunderstandings and costly changes in later stages.

The requirements engineering process encompasses more than the initial collection of needs; it also includes the management and tracking of these requirements throughout the project lifecycle. This ensures that the developed software aligns with the client's goals and that any changes in requirements are efficiently managed.

3.1.1.Functional Requirements

Functional requirements describe the specific functions, behaviors, and services that the system must provide. They focus on what the software must do and how it should interact with users and other systems. Common examples include:

- **Operations:** Functions the system must perform, such as transaction processing, report generation, or user management.

- **System Reactions:** Expected behaviors in response to user actions, such as displaying an error message when invalid data is entered.

- **Interactions with Other Systems:** Specifications on how the software should integrate with external systems like databases, APIs, or web services.

Clarity in functional requirements is essential to ensure the system meets customer expectations and delivers the desired functionality.

3.1.2. Non-Functional Requirements

Non-functional requirements, also known as quality attributes, focus on how the system should operate beyond its functionalities. They refer to the quality expectations stakeholders have regarding the system's performance, efficiency, and user experience. Key types of non-functional requirements include:

• **Performance:** The speed at which the system processes requests or handles a certain number of simultaneous users.

• **Security:** Mechanisms to protect information, such as user authentication, authorization, and data encryption.

• **Usability:** The system's ease of use, including aspects like user experience (UX) and user interface (UI).

• **Scalability:** The ability of the system to grow and adapt to increased workload without losing efficiency.

• **Maintainability:** How easily the system can be modified to fix errors, implement improvements, or adapt to new environments.

While non-functional requirements do not directly address system functionalities, they are critical to a project's success as they significantly impact user satisfaction and system longevity.

3.1.3. Stakeholders

Stakeholders are all individuals or groups with an interest in the software development process. Including all relevant stakeholders in the requirements engineering process is essential to consider diverse perspectives and avoid overlooking key requirements. Main stakeholder types include:

• **End Users**: Those who will interact directly with the software. Their feedback is crucial for ensuring the system is intuitive and meets their expectations.

- **Clients**: Represent the business or organization funding the project and have expectations about the software's return on investment (ROI).
- **Developers and Technical Teams**: Responsible for building the system. Their technical expertise can influence the feasibility and implementation of requirements.
- **Project Managers**: Oversee alignment between requirements and project goals, as well as plan and execute activities.
- **Regulators**: In cases where the software must comply with specific legal or regulatory requirements, such as data protection laws, regulators are critical stakeholders influencing requirements.

Effective stakeholder identification and communication from the early stages help avoid misunderstandings and ensure the software meets the expectations of all parties involved.

3.1.4. Importance of Requirements Engineering

Requirements engineering bridges the gap between the client's vision and system development. When done correctly, it provides a clear understanding of what is expected from the software and establishes a solid foundation for design and implementation. Key benefits include:

- **Risk Reduction:** Clear requirements help identify and mitigate risks before they impact development.
- **Improved Communication:** Enhances communication between the development team and stakeholders, minimizing misunderstandings and misaligned expectations.
- **Time and Cost Optimization:** Precisely defining the software's scope reduces the need for changes and corrections in later stages, saving time and costs.
- **Quality of the Final Product:** Ensuring requirements reflect actual user needs increases the likelihood of delivering valuable and useful software.

Thus, requirements engineering is not just about defining what the software should do but creating a shared understanding among all involved parties to ensure project success.

3.2. BASIC TECHNIQUES FOR REQUIREMENTS GATHERING

Requirements gathering is the process of obtaining information about what stakeholders expect from the system. Common techniques include:

- **Interviews**: Direct interactions with stakeholders to explore their needs and expectations.

- **Questionnaires and Surveys:** Used to collect information from a large number of users, helping identify patterns and trends.

- **Requirements Workshops**: Collaborative sessions where different stakeholders discuss and agree on system requirements.

- **Direct Observation**: Analyzing how users interact with the current system to better understand their needs.

- **Analysis of Existing Documentation:** Reviewing previous documents, manuals, and reports to gather valuable insights on past requirements and existing issues.

3.3. ANALYSIS AND PRIORITIZATION OF REQUIREMENTS

Once requirements are gathered, the next crucial step in requirements engineering is their analysis and prioritization. This phase ensures that the requirements are complete, consistent, and feasible, and that there are no ambiguities that could impact the software's implementation. The goal of the analysis is to understand the relationships between different requirements, identify potential conflicts, and ensure alignment with the project's objectives. Additionally, prioritizing requirements allows the development team to focus their efforts on aspects that are most valuable to stakeholders, maximizing the project's impact based on available resources.

3.3.1. Requirements Analysis

Requirements analysis involves several activities that delve deeper into each requirement's details. The key activities include:

- **Requirements Validation**: Verifying that requirements are clear, precise, and understandable for all stakeholders. It also involves assessing whether the requirements are feasible within the project's constraints, such as budget, timelines, and technical capabilities.

- **Conflict Detection:** Identifying potential conflicts between requirements. For instance, a high-performance requirement might contradict a security requirement that involves encrypting data, which could slow down the system. Detecting these conflicts early enables informed and balanced decisions before they affect development.

- **Requirements Modeling:** Using diagrams such as use

cases, flowcharts, or entity-relationship diagrams to visualize how different requirements relate to each other and the system. This helps clarify the scope of each requirement and identify possible omissions.

Detailed analysis of requirements provides a clearer view of the project's scope and the challenges that may arise during development, allowing the development team to plan effectively.

3.3.2. Requirements Prioritization

Prioritizing requirements is essential for efficient resource management, ensuring that the development team focuses first on the most important and critical functionalities. This is particularly useful when time or resources are limited. Common techniques for prioritizing requirements include:

- MoSCoW Method (Must Have, Should Have, Could Have, Won't Have):

-Must Have (Critical): Requirements that are indispensable for the system to function minimally.

-Should Have (Desirable): Important but non-critical requirements whose absence wouldn't compromise the software's core functionality.

-Could Have (Optional): Requirements that enhance user experience but are not essential for basic functionality.

-Won't Have (Excluded): Requirements that are not considered for the current project version but may be relevant for future updates.

This method is particularly useful for managing expectations and helping stakeholders understand project limitations and priorities.

- Weighted Analysis:

Assigning a score to each requirement based on its importance to users and the complexity of implementation. For example, a requirement that holds high value for stakeholders but is technically challenging may have a different priority than one that is simple to implement but less critical.

This approach balances what is valuable to the client with what is feasible for the development team, aiding decision-making during planning.

- Cost-Benefit Analysis:

This technique evaluates the positive impact of implementing each requirement against the costs and resources needed to do so. It involves analyzing how much value a requirement adds to the system and whether that value justifies the implementation effort.

This is especially useful for business decisions, allowing stakeholders to identify high return-on-investment (ROI) requirements and prioritize the most profitable ones.

- Kano Model:

This classifies requirements into three categories: Basic, Performance, and Delight. Basic requirements are those users take for granted, performance requirements increase satisfaction as they are better fulfilled, and delight requirements are unexpected but highly satisfying features.

This approach helps identify which requirements truly surprise and satisfy users, enabling the creation of a product that exceeds expectations.

3.3.3. Importance of Effective Analysis and Prioritization

Analyzing and prioritizing requirements helps development teams better align stakeholder expectations with the project's technical realities and capabilities. Some key advantages of these activities include:

- **Resource Optimization**: By focusing on the most valuable requirements first, resources like time and budget are utilized most efficiently.
- **Reduction in Rework**: Identifying and resolving conflicts early prevents costly modifications during development.
- **Alignment of Expectations**: Prioritization helps stakeholders understand which features will be available in each development phase, avoiding misunderstandings and frustrations.
- **Adaptability to Change**: A flexible prioritization approach allows the development team to better respond to changes in requirements during the process, which is particularly relevant in Agile

projects.

Requirements analysis and prioritization are, therefore, fundamental steps for the success of any software development project. They establish a solid foundation for planning, ensure the team focuses on what matters most, and facilitate delivering a product that meets client and user expectations.

3.4. SPECIFICATION OF REQUIREMENTS ACCORDING TO THE IEEE 830 STANDARD

The IEEE 830 standard provides a detailed framework for creating Software Requirements Specification (SRS) documents. This framework aims to standardize how project requirements are described and communicated. Following this standard ensures that the SRS is clear, concise, complete, and comprehensible to both technical teams and stakeholders, fostering a shared vision of the system to be developed.

3.4.1. Key Elements of the IEEE 830 Standard

The IEEE 830 standard outlines that an SRS document should be structured into three main sections: Introduction, General Description, and Specific Requirements. Each section plays a crucial role in effectively communicating and understanding the software's needs.

    1) Introduction:

       ·   **Purpose**: Describes the purpose of the requirements document, specifying who its intended users are and how they should use it. This helps define the scope of the SRS and clarify stakeholder expectations.

       ·   **Scope**: Defines what will and will not be included in the system. It specifies the system's boundaries and its relationship with other systems, providing a global vision of the software to be developed.

       ·   **Definitions, Acronyms, and Abbreviations**: Includes a glossary of technical terms and abbreviations used in the document. This facilitates understanding and ensures a shared vocabulary among stakeholders.

- **References**: Lists relevant documents or standards used as references during the preparation of the SRS, such as design documents, feasibility analyses, or other applicable standards.

- **Document Overview**: Explains the document structure and what can be found in each section, enabling readers to navigate it efficiently.

2) General Description:

- **Product Perspective:** Describes how the system interacts with other systems, defining its context and interfaces with external modules or systems. This helps understand how the software will integrate into its operational environment.

- **Product Features**: Summarizes the functionalities the system will offer. This section provides a general overview, without detailing each function, to help stakeholders understand the product's value.

- **User Characteristics**: Identifies system users, describing their skills and needs, which is crucial for designing appropriate user interfaces and experiences.

- **Constraints**: Defines technical, regulatory, or design limitations the team must consider, such as hardware restrictions, compatibility issues, or compliance with specific regulations.

- **Assumptions and Dependencies**: Specifies assumptions made during the SRS creation and the software's dependencies on other systems, tools, or processes. This helps identify risks and plan mitigation strategies.

3) Specific Requirements:

- **Functional Requirements**: Provides detailed descriptions of the functionalities the system must fulfill, specifying actions it should perform under certain conditions. These are often documented using use cases, flowcharts, or user stories to illustrate expected behaviors.

- **Non-Functional Requirements**: Details software quality

attributes such as security, performance, scalability, and usability. These requirements define success factors beyond system functionality.

- **External Interfaces**: Specifies how the software will connect to other systems, detailing user interfaces, APIs, communication protocols, and other external interactions. This ensures seamless integration with other applications or systems.

- **Design Constraints**: Includes limitations affecting design decisions, such as architectural constraints, mandatory technologies, or security policies.

- **Interoperability and Compatibility Requirements**: Describes how the system should interact with other environments and platforms, ensuring proper functionality in different configurations.

3.4.2. Advantages of Using the IEEE 830 Standard

Adopting the IEEE 830 standard for requirements specification provides several benefits that directly impact the quality of a software project:

- **Clarity and Consistency**: By following a defined structure, all critical aspects of the system are covered, facilitating understanding and avoiding ambiguous interpretations. This ensures the development team, testers, and stakeholders share a common vision of the project.

- **Enhanced Communication**: A well-structured SRS acts as a contract between developers and stakeholders, specifying what needs to be built and how the system should function. This minimizes misunderstandings and aligns expectations.

- **Foundation for Design and Testing**: The SRS serves as the primary reference for system design and test plan creation. Every specified requirement should be traceable throughout design and testing, ensuring the software meets described needs.

- **Change Management**: A detailed requirements document simplifies change management by enabling tracking and evaluating the impact of modifications before implementation. This is especially useful in long-term projects where requirements may evolve.

3.4.3. Best Practices for Writing an SRS According to IEEE 830

To create an effective SRS, it's important to follow certain best practices during its preparation:

- **Be Clear and Precise**: Each requirement should be written unambiguously to leave no room for misinterpretation. This includes using clear language and specifying technical terms precisely.

- **Avoid Ambiguity**: Ensure requirements do not contain vague terms that could be misinterpreted. For instance, instead of saying a functionality should be "fast," specify that it should respond in "less than 2 seconds."

- **Maintain Traceability**: Each requirement should be identifiable and traceable throughout the project lifecycle, allowing for tracking how and where each need is addressed in design and development.

- **Include Examples and Diagrams**: Using examples, flowcharts, use cases, and other graphical elements helps clarify requirements and facilitates understanding among all involved parties.

The IEEE 830 standard is a fundamental tool for software requirements specification, ensuring detailed, clear, and coherent documentation. Using this standard enables all project participants to share a common understanding of system expectations and functionalities, which is critical for successful software development. Furthermore, it establishes a solid foundation for subsequent development stages, such as design, coding, and testing, ensuring the final product meets customer and user needs.

3.5. SOFTWARE REQUIREMENTS SPECIFICATION (SRS)

The Software Requirements Specification (SRS) document is essential for developing a software system as it establishes the system's requirements in a structured and precise manner and serves as a comprehensive reference throughout the development cycle. A well-crafted SRS helps align expectations between stakeholders and the development team, ensuring that the final product meets stated needs and facilitates decision-making during the design, development, and testing process. The key elements of an SRS are as follows:

3.5.1. Main Elements of an SRS

1) Detailed Functional Requirements:

- **Specific Functionality Description**: Functional requirements detail each function or behavior the system must perform. This includes how the software processes data, interacts with other systems, and responds to specific user inputs. Each functional requirement must be well-defined and broken down to avoid ambiguities in interpretation.

- **Use Cases and Diagrams:** To clarify these requirements, use cases and interaction diagrams, such as sequence diagrams, are commonly used. Use cases provide practical examples of how users will interact with the system, helping developers and testers understand the context of each functionality.

2) User Interfaces:

- **Interface Description**: This section details how users will interact with the system, including graphical user interface (GUI) elements, navigation flows, and screen designs. This is crucial for ensuring the system is intuitive and user-friendly for the end-users.

- **Interface Prototypes and Wireframes**: To represent the user experience, the SRS may include low-fidelity prototypes, wireframes, or even mockups of the software screens. These visual elements help stakeholders envision the final product and identify potential improvements before development begins.

- **User Flow Diagrams**: User flow diagrams are useful for illustrating how users will navigate the system and the actions available at each step. This helps design an efficient workflow and identify critical points in the user experience.

3) Constraints and Assumptions:

- **Technical Constraints:** These are limitations imposed by the technological environment, such as hardware or software restrictions, compatibility with specific operating systems, and other technical requirements. For instance, if the software must operate on a particular platform or be compatible with legacy systems.

- **Regulatory and Legal Constraints**: If the software must comply with specific regulations, such as data protection laws (e.g., GDPR or HIPAA), these must be documented in the SRS. This ensures development is carried out in compliance with current regulations and avoids future legal issues.

- **Environmental Assumptions:** The SRS should also describe the assumptions under which the system is designed, such as the operational environment, resource availability, and user profiles. These assumptions are important since any changes to them could impact the development or operation of the software.

4) Quality Requirements:

- **Performance Expectations:** Performance requirements specify how the software should behave under certain conditions, such as response time, load time, and the ability to handle a specified number of concurrent users. These requirements ensure a satisfactory user experience even under high demand.
- **Security and Privacy:** This section details the security measures the system must implement, such as user authentication, encryption of sensitive data, and protection against security vulnerabilities. Data privacy is also critical, especially for applications handling personal information.
- **Scalability and Maintainability:** The system's ability to scale as user needs grow is a key aspect, especially for systems expected to expand over time. Additionally, the software must be easy to maintain and update, describing aspects like modular code structure and ease of implementing future changes.
- **Usability and Accessibility:** Usability refers to how easy it is for users to learn and operate the system. Accessibility requirements ensure the software can be used by people with disabilities, complying with guidelines like the WCAG (Web Content Accessibility Guidelines).

3.5.2. Importance of the SRS in the Development Cycle

A properly crafted SRS provides significant benefits throughout the software lifecycle:

- Clear Communication: The SRS serves as a reference document for all project members, ensuring everyone—developers, testers, and project managers—has a uniform understanding of the system requirements. This minimizes misunderstandings and avoids developing features that deviate from expectations.
- Foundation for Design and Testing: Each SRS requirement should be traceable through the design and testing phases. During design, each aspect of the system can be verified against a defined requirement, and during testing, each functionality can be ensured to meet the specified requirements.
- Change Management: As development progresses, new needs may arise, or original requirements may change. A well-documented SRS facilitates the evaluation of these changes, allowing

analysis of their impact on the system and informed decisions about implementation.

In conclusion, a clear and comprehensive SRS document is essential for the success of any software development project. It precisely defines what the system must do and the conditions it must meet, providing a solid foundation for design, implementation, and testing. Following standards like IEEE 830 ensures the SRS is a structured, high-quality document that facilitates collaboration among all stakeholders and guarantees the final software meets users 'and clients 'expectations and needs.

3.6. IMPLEMENTATION OF THE REQUIREMENTS SPECIFIED IN THE SRS IN THE SOFTWARE DEVELOPMENT PROCESS

The implementation of the requirements specified in the Software Requirements Specification (SRS) document is a crucial phase within the development cycle, as it defines how user needs and expectations are transformed into concrete code and functionalities. This phase requires detailed planning and a methodical approach to ensure that the final product meets the initial specifications. Below are the main activities involved in this phase:

3.6.1. Sprint Planning (in Agile Methodologies)

• **Decomposition of Requirements into User Stories**: In Agile approaches, the requirements defined in the SRS are broken down into user stories. Each user story represents a functionality from the end user's perspective and allows for incremental implementation. This helps the development team focus on delivering value quickly.

• **Effort Estimation and Task Planning**: User stories are prioritized and estimated in terms of effort (e.g., story points). They are then grouped into sprints, which are short development iterations (typically 2 to 4 weeks). During sprint planning, specific tasks for each user story are defined, ensuring structured progress in development.

- **Adapting to Changes**: Sprint planning also allows for adjusting requirements based on feedback from stakeholders. This is particularly useful when new needs arise or when initial requirements are misinterpreted.

3.6.2. Software Design

- **System Architecture**: Once the requirements are defined, the system's architecture is designed, establishing how different components interact and integrate with the chosen technologies (databases, APIs, services, etc.). This ensures that the technical design meets the functional and non-functional requirements specified in the SRS.

- **Detailed Module Design**: Building on the overall architecture, a detailed design for each system module is created, including class diagrams, sequence diagrams, and data flows. These diagrams help translate requirements into a technical structure developers can follow during coding.

- **Design Considerations for Non-Functional Requirements:** Aspects such as security, performance, and scalability must be addressed during the design phase. For instance, if a non-functional requirement specifies high concurrency support, the architecture should include techniques like load balancing or caching.

3.6.3. Coding and Development

- **Module Functionality Implementation:** Developers write the code needed for each module, following the specifications and detailed design. It is essential that the code is clear, maintainable, and adheres to established coding principles (e.g., the DRY principle - Don't Repeat Yourself).

- **Continuous Integration (CI):** CI allows developers to frequently integrate their changes into a shared repository, where automated tests ensure that the code meets functional requirements. This helps identify issues early and ensures that system components work well together.

- **Code Review:** Code reviews are essential to ensure that the software meets the requirements specified in the SRS. Through code reviews, developers can confirm that each implemented function follows best practices and aligns with the described needs.

- **Unit Testing:** Unit tests verify that the individual functions of each module meet the expected requirements. This ensures that the system's basic components align with the SRS specifications before being integrated into a broader testing environment.

3.6.4. Requirement Tracking and Change Management

- **Requirement Traceability:** As implementation progresses, maintaining traceability of requirements is essential. This means that every module or system component should be linked to the original requirements in the SRS. This facilitates verifying that all requirements are correctly implemented and helps identify any unaddressed requirements.

- **Change Management**: During development, requirements may change due to new needs or adjustments in project scope. A good change management system allows for evaluating how a requirement change will impact development and coordinating its implementation without compromising product consistency.

3.6.5. Testing and Validation

- **Acceptance Testing:** To verify that the requirements specified in the SRS have been correctly implemented, acceptance testing is performed with stakeholders. These tests validate that the software meets user expectations and that the developed functionalities address the scenarios defined in the SRS.

- **Integration and System Testing:** In addition to acceptance testing, integration testing ensures that the system's different modules work together. System testing evaluates the software's overall behavior, ensuring it meets non-functional requirements such as performance and usability.

3.6.6. Documentation and Feedback

- **Technical Documentation Update**: As different modules are developed and requirements implemented, the technical documentation should be updated to reflect the current state of the system. This includes any adjustments made during implementation.

- **Stakeholder Feedback Collection**: Feedback from

stakeholders during the implementation phase is valuable for ensuring the product meets their expectations. This allows for timely adjustments before the system is completed.

3.6.7. Importance of Proper Implementation of SRS Requirements

Accurately implementing the requirements specified in the SRS is key to the project's success. If developers understand and adequately translate each requirement into functionalities, the final software will meet user needs, avoiding costly rework and last-minute adjustments. Furthermore, an implementation aligned with the SRS facilitates effective testing and reduces the likelihood of critical errors, contributing to delivering a quality product within the established timelines and budget.

3.7. REQUIREMENTS VALIDATION AND VERIFICATION

Requirements validation and verification are critical processes in software engineering that ensure the developed software not only meets the established technical specifications but also satisfies the needs and expectations of end users. These complementary processes help maintain alignment with initial project objectives and minimize the risks of errors and misunderstandings during development. Below are the key aspects of each process:

3.7.1. Verification

Verification evaluates whether the requirements have been correctly defined and whether each one has been implemented as specified in the Software Requirements Specification (SRS). It focuses on the consistency and integrity of the requirements document and its alignment with the developed product, ensuring all technical aspects are duly addressed. Common verification activities include:

- **Documentation Review**: Requirements specification documents are meticulously reviewed to ensure completeness, consistency, and clarity. This includes reviewing functional and non-functional requirements, as well as diagrams or models describing the system.

- **Traceability Analysis**: A traceability matrix links each SRS requirement to corresponding design elements, tests, and code. This ensures no critical requirements are overlooked during development.

- **Static Testing**: Performed without executing the software, these activities include peer reviews, technical audits, and code analysis.

They help identify early issues, such as inconsistencies in developers' interpretation of requirements.

- **Prototypes and Models**: Prototyping verifies requirement interpretations before coding. Prototypes may include user interfaces or diagrams illustrating the system's intended operation.

3.7.2. Validation

Validation ensures the software meets end-user needs and performs as expected in real-world scenarios. It evaluates the product from the client or end-user perspective to confirm its usefulness and relevance to the problem it aims to solve. Key validation activities include:

- **User Testing**: Involving end users to interact with the software and verify that it meets their expectations. Feedback from users often highlights usability and functionality issues missed during development.

- **Acceptance Testing**: A critical step before deployment, ensuring the software meets all requirements specified in the SRS. Scenarios simulating daily user tasks are used to verify its readiness for production.

- **Real-World Environment Simulation**: Testing in environments closely replicating real-world conditions ensures the system operates as intended under actual workload and environmental factors.

- **Functional Prototypes**: High-fidelity prototypes or beta versions are validated by users to ensure core functionalities are properly implemented before the final release.

3.7.3. Differences Between Verification and Validation

While verification and validation share the goal of ensuring software quality, they differ significantly:

- **Focus**: Verification ensures the product is developed correctly based on specifications ("Did we build it right?"), while validation ensures the product meets user needs ("Did we build the right thing?").

- **Method**: Verification involves technical processes such as documentation and code reviews, whereas validation engages users and stakeholders through testing and evaluation.

- **Timing**: Verification is ongoing throughout development, while validation primarily occurs towards the end, when the software is near its final state.

3.7.4. Benefits of Requirements Validation and Verification

Properly implementing validation and verification activities provides several advantages:

- **Reduced Rework**: Early identification of issues or misunderstandings prevents costly changes in advanced development or production stages.

- **Improved Customer Satisfaction**: Ensuring the software meets user needs enhances customer loyalty and market positioning.

- **Enhanced Software Quality**: Rigorous validation and verification result in robust, secure, and efficient systems that meet all requirements.

- **Project Acceptance Facilitation**: Stakeholders gain confidence in the product when a clear validation and verification process is followed, easing project approval.

3.7.5. Challenges in Requirements Validation and Verification

Despite their benefits, validation and verification also present challenges:

- **Requirement Ambiguity**: Poorly defined requirements can lead to misinterpretations and unmet needs. Continuous reviews and clarity in requirement drafting are essential to avoid this.

- **Stakeholder Involvement**: Validation relies heavily on end-user and stakeholder participation. Lack of availability or engagement can result in software that fails to meet expectations.

- **Adapting to Changes**: Frequent requirement changes in projects can complicate traceability and testing, requiring a flexible and agile approach.

In conclusion, requirements validation and verification are

complementary processes that ensure the developed software meets SRS specifications and fulfills end-user expectations. Their proper execution contributes to high-quality products and reduced risks and costs throughout the software development lifecycle.

3.8. REQUIREMENTS MANAGEMENT TOOLS

Requirements management tools are essential to facilitate the organization, tracking, and maintenance of requirements throughout the software development lifecycle. These tools help ensure that requirements are accessible, up-to-date, and maintain traceability from definition to implementation and validation. Below are some of the most popular tools and their features:

3.8.1. Jira

- Widely used by Agile teams, Jira is ideal for managing user stories, tasks, and defects, providing a clear view of project requirements.

- Integrates with tools like Confluence for documentation and Git for version control, enabling traceability from requirement specification to code.

- Supports creating Kanban and Scrum boards to visualize the progress of requirements through development stages, ensuring efficient backlog management and task prioritization.

- Its flexibility in configuring custom workflows makes it adaptable to various types of projects, from simple to complex.

3.8.2. IBM Rational DOORS

- A robust tool designed for large-scale projects, especially useful in regulated industries such as aerospace, automotive, and defense.

- Provides a collaborative environment where teams can define, analyze, and manage requirements while handling large data volumes.

- Enables bidirectional traceability, linking each requirement with its tests, designs, and use cases to ensure alignment with initial specifications.

- Includes advanced reporting capabilities, allowing detailed reports on requirements status and compliance.

3.8.3. Confluence

- A documentation tool that complements Jira, ideal for collaborating on writing and discussing requirements.

- Allows teams to create workspaces to document requirement specifications, discuss changes, and maintain historical revision records.

- With templates and macros, teams can structure documentation clearly, supporting technical specifications, flow diagrams, and meeting notes.

- Integration with other Atlassian tools, like Jira, enhances visibility and control by linking documented requirements to development tasks.

3.8.4. Azure DevOps

- Provides a comprehensive suite of tools for managing software projects, from planning to deployment.

- In requirements management, Azure DevOps allows the creation of work items, definition of user stories and tasks, and linking them directly to code commits and CI pipelines.

- Ensures complete traceability from requirement definition to production delivery, helping identify requirement changes and their impact on development.

- Integration with tools like GitHub and automation features for testing and deployment make it a powerful option for projects aligning with DevOps principles.

3.8.5. Jama Connect

- Focused on requirements, testing, and risk management, this tool is ideal for complex projects requiring rigorous traceability control.

- Facilitates collaboration in defining and validating requirements, offering a visual environment to link requirements with tests and use cases.

- Its notification and review system ensures teams stay informed of requirement changes, streamlining stakeholder approval for modifications.

- Particularly valuable in compliance-critical environments, it provides detailed audits for each requirement change and its documentation.

3.8.6. ReqSuite RM

- Known for its ease of use and focus on automating requirement collection and analysis processes.

- Supports collaborative requirement definition and management, offering predefined workflows for tracking changes and validating requirements.

- Integrates with popular development tools like Jira and Azure DevOps, making it suitable for diverse development environments.

- Features export and import capabilities in formats like Excel and Word, simplifying communication with stakeholders who prefer traditional formats.

3.8.7. Helix RM (Perforce)

- Designed for effective requirements management in software and complex system projects, Helix RM is popular for requirements and change traceability.

- Facilitates the creation of traceability matrices, allowing teams to visualize how requirements link to development artifacts, such as test cases and design elements.

- Offers an intuitive interface to visualize requirement statuses and dependencies, identifying and resolving potential conflicts before impacting development.

- Especially valuable in projects requiring high collaboration and rigorous requirements configuration management.

3.9. BENEFITS OF USING REQUIREMENTS MANAGEMENT TOOLS

The use of these tools in requirements management provides numerous benefits, including:

- **Improved Collaboration:** They facilitate collaboration among teams, allowing developers, analysts, and stakeholders to access and update information in a centralized manner.

- **Complete Traceability:** Ensure that each requirement is linked to its implementation, testing, and validation, enabling clear project progress tracking and quick issue identification.

- **Error Reduction:** By automating change tracking and maintaining a detailed history of requirements, these tools minimize errors and misunderstandings that may arise from changes in specifications.

- **Ease of Auditing and Compliance:** Many of these tools enable the generation of detailed reports that facilitate auditing and compliance with regulations, which is critical in regulated industries.

3.10. CHALLENGES IN USING REQUIREMENTS MANAGEMENT TOOLS

While requirements management tools offer many advantages, they also present certain challenges:

- Learning Curve: Some tools, especially more robust ones like IBM Rational DOORS, can be complex to configure and use, requiring additional training for the team.

- Cost: Advanced tool licenses can be expensive, which may be a constraint for small teams or startups with limited budgets.

- Integration with Other Systems: Ensuring that requirements management tools integrate well with other development and testing tools is critical to avoid duplication of effort and data.

In conclusion, selecting the right requirements management tool depends on the specific needs of the project, team size, and system complexity. Effectively using these tools can make a significant difference in the final product's quality and stakeholder satisfaction, ensuring software development aligns with client expectations and business goals.

3.11. CHAPTER CONCLUSIONS

Requirements engineering is a crucial component of software development as it defines the roadmap that guides the development team. Proper requirements specification and management reduce the risk of deviations during the project and ensure the final software meets customer expectations.

By employing suitable techniques for gathering, prioritizing, and specifying requirements, and leveraging management tools, teams can stay focused on actual user needs and achieve a high-quality end product. Constant collaboration with stakeholders and the adoption of standards such as IEEE 830 ensure an orderly and consistent process, facilitating the delivery of software that not only meets but exceeds market expectations.

CHAPTER 4
SOFTWARE DESIGN

Software design is a fundamental phase in system development, as it establishes the structure and architecture of the solution before implementation begins. A good design ensures the software is efficient, maintainable, and scalable, facilitating its evolution over time. Below are the most relevant aspects of software design:

4.1. BASIC PRINCIPLES OF SOFTWARE DESIGN

The basic principles of software design are essential for creating robust, scalable, and maintainable systems. These principles help developers organize code so it is understandable and adaptable to future changes, ensuring software quality. Here are some of the most important principles:

4.1.1. Modularity

Modularity involves dividing the system into independent modules or components that perform specific functionalities. This makes the system easier to understand since each module can be analyzed in isolation. Additionally, it enables changes and updates without affecting the rest of the system. Modularity improves:

- **Code Reusability**: By creating independent modules, they can be reused in other projects or parts of the system.

- **Maintainability**: Errors can be identified and corrected more easily when they are localized within a specific module.

- **Testing**: Modules can be tested individually (unit testing), simplifying the functionality verification process.

4.1.2. Abstraction

Abstraction focuses on the essential aspects of a system while hiding implementation details. This allows developers to work at a high level without worrying about how internal details are implemented. Benefits of abstraction:

- **Simplicity:** Hiding complexity results in cleaner and more understandable designs.

- **Flexibility**: It allows internal implementation changes without affecting those using the abstraction.

- **Clear Interfaces**: Well-designed abstractions define interfaces that facilitate interaction between different system components.

4.1.3. Coupling and Cohesion

These two concepts are key to evaluating design quality:

- **Cohesion:** Refers to how closely the responsibilities of a module are related. A highly cohesive module performs a specific task and focuses on a single purpose, making it easier to maintain and understand.
- **Coupling**: Refers to the degree of dependency between modules. Low coupling is desired to minimize the impact of changes in one module on others, resulting in more flexible and easily modifiable systems.

An ideal design aims for high cohesion and low coupling, contributing to a more robust and adaptable system.

4.1.4. Single Responsibility Principle (SRP)

The SRP states that each module, class, or function should have only one reason to change, meaning it should have a single responsibility. This leads to cleaner and more organized code because:

- **Clarity:** Each module is responsible for a specific task, making the code easier to read and understand.
- **Ease of Testing:** Clear responsibilities make it easier to create unit tests to verify each module's behavior.
- **Reduced Risk of Errors:** Changes affect only the part of the code corresponding to that responsibility, minimizing the risk of errors elsewhere in the system.

4.1.5. Open/Closed Principle (OCP)

The OCP suggests that software entities (classes, modules, functions) should be open for extension but closed for modification. This means new functionality can be added without modifying existing code, achieved through inheritance and the use of interfaces. This principle is essential for:

- **Extensibility:** Allows adapting the system to new requirements without altering the base code.

- **Safe Maintenance:** Avoiding modifications to existing classes reduces the risk of introducing errors into previously tested functionalities.

- **Use of Polymorphism:** In object-oriented programming, interfaces and abstract classes facilitate creating new behaviors without altering base classes.

4.1.6. Liskov Substitution Principle (LSP)

This principle states that derived classes must be interchangeable with their base classes without altering system behavior. If a class B inherits from class A, it should be usable wherever an instance of A is expected. Benefits of LSP:

- **Interchangeability**: Facilitates polymorphism and enhances system flexibility.

- **Correctness Assurance**: Ensuring subclasses maintain expected behavior reduces errors in object interactions.

4.1.7. Interface Segregation Principle (ISP)

The ISP suggests that clients should not be forced to depend on interfaces they do not use. In other words, it is better to have several purpose-specific interfaces than a single general interface. This allows classes to implement only the methods they truly need:

- **Improved Modularity:** Facilitates creating classes with only the functionalities they require, reducing unnecessary code.

- **Flexibility:** Enables greater customization in interface implementation.

- **Reduced Dependencies**: Minimizes dependency overhead, improving code maintainability.

4.1.8. Dependency Inversion Principle (DIP)

This principle states that high-level modules should not depend on low-level modules; both should depend on abstractions. Additionally, abstractions should not depend on concrete details; rather, details should depend on abstractions. This is achieved using interfaces and abstract classes:

- **Decoupling:** Depending on abstractions instead of concrete implementations reduces dependency between components.

- **Ease of Testing:** Using interfaces simplifies creating unit tests, as class behaviors can be simulated through mocks.

- **Maintainability**: Changing the implementation of a module without affecting others improves system flexibility.

Applying these basic principles in software design helps create systems that are robust, adaptable to changes, and easier to maintain over time. By adopting approaches such as modularity, abstraction, and managing coupling and cohesion, developers build systems that not only meet current requirements but also evolve efficiently to meet new needs.

4.2. DESIGN PATTERNS: USAGE AND EXAMPLES

Design patterns are proven and reusable solutions to common problems encountered in software development. They act as templates that can be applied in various situations, facilitating the creation of more efficient and maintainable systems. Design patterns are categorized into three main groups: creational, structural, and behavioral patterns.

4.2.1. Creational Patterns

Creational patterns focus on object creation and help decouple the instantiation logic from the classes. This allows developers to change the type of objects created without affecting the code that uses them. Some notable examples are:

-Singleton

The Singleton pattern ensures that a class has only one instance and provides a global point of access to it. This is useful when controlling access to shared resources, such as database connections or application settings.

Usage:

- Storing global application configuration.
- Managing connections to external resources like databases.

Example: (All example codes are written in python)

class Singleton:

 _instance = None

 def __new__(cls):

> if cls._instance is None:
>
> cls._instance = super(Singleton, cls).__new__(cls)
>
> return cls._instance

singleton1 = Singleton()

singleton2 = Singleton()

assert singleton1 is singleton2

Both variables point to the same instance

This code implements the Singleton design pattern, ensuring that a class has only one instance and provides a global point of access to it.

1. Singleton Class Definition: A class named Singleton is defined.
2. Class Variable _instance: A class variable _instance is initialized to store the only instance of the class.
3. _new_ Method: This special method controls instance creation:

- if cls._instance is None: Checks if an instance already exists. If _instance is None, no instance has been created yet.
- cls._instance = super(Singleton, cls).**new**(cls): If no instance exists, a new one is created using the class base's new method.
- return cls._instance: Returns the instance, either newly created or pre-existing.

4. Instance Creation:

- singleton1 = Singleton(): Creates the first instance of Singleton.
- singleton2 = Singleton(): Attempts to create a second instance but returns the existing instance due to the Singleton pattern.

5. **Instance verification**: The line assert singleton1 is singleton2 verifies that both variables (singleton1 and singleton2) point to the same instance.

This code example ensures that any attempt to create a new instance of the Singleton class always returns the same instance, ensuring that there is only a single object of that class in the entire application.

-Factory Method

The Factory Method pattern defines an interface for creating objects but allows subclasses to decide which class to instantiate. This promotes flexibility and code reuse by enabling the creation of different types of objects without specifying the exact class.

Usage:

- Creating objects of different types implementing the same interface.
- Providing instantiation logic that can be changed without affecting other components.

Example: (All example codes are written in python)

class Product:

def operation(self):

pass

class ConcreteProductA(Product):

def operation(self):

return "Resultado de Producto A"

class ConcreteProductB(Product):

def operation(self):

return "Resultado de Producto B"

class Creator:

def factory_method(self):

pass

class ConcreteCreatorA(Creator):

def factory_method(self):

return ConcreteProductA()

class ConcreteCreatorB(Creator):

def factory_method(self):

return ConcreteProductB()

This code implements the Factory Method design pattern, which provides a way to create objects without specifying the exact class of the object to be created.

1. **Base class product**: A class named Product is defined with a method called operation. This method is empty (with a pass statement) because it will serve as an interface for the concrete products derived from this class.

2. **Concrete Product Classes**:

- ConcreteProductA: Inherits from Product and implements the operation method, returning a specific string ("Result of Product A").

- ConcreteProductB: Also inherits from Product and implements the operation method, returning another specific string ("Result of Product B").

3. **Base class creator**: A class named Creator is defined with a method called factory_method. This method is also empty and will be implemented in concrete subclasses.

4. **Concrete creator classes**:

- ConcreteCreatorA: Inherits from Creator and implements the factory_method, creating and returning an instance of ConcreteProductA.

- ConcreteCreatorB: Inherits from Creator and implements the factory_method, creating and returning an instance of ConcreteProductB.

The Factory Method pattern allows ConcreteCreatorA and ConcreteCreatorB to create objects of types ConcreteProductA and ConcreteProductB, respectively, without requiring the client to know the exact class of the object being created. This makes the code more flexible and easier to extend, as new products and creators can be added without modifying existing code.

4.2.2. Structural Patterns

Structural patterns facilitate the composition of objects and classes to form more complex structures. They enable developers to build flexible and scalable systems. Examples include:

-Adapter

The Adapter pattern allows two incompatible classes to work together through a common interface. This is achieved by creating an adapter that translates calls between the two classes.

Usage:

- Integrating existing systems with new implementations.
- Enabling different interfaces to work together.

Example (All example codes are written in Python):

class Target:

def request(self):

return "Solicitud del Target"

class Adaptee:

def specific_request(self):

return "Solicitud específica del Adaptee"

class Adapter(Target):

def **init**(self, adaptee):

self.adaptee = adaptee

def request(self):

return self.adaptee.specific_request()

This code implements the Adapter pattern, enabling two incompatible interfaces to work together.

1. **Target class**: Represents the interface expected by the client, with a request method returning "Request from Target".
2. **Adaptee class**: Represents the incompatible class, with a specific_request method returning "Specific request from Adaptee".
3. **Adapter class**:

• Inherits from Target, allowing it to be used where a Target is expected.

• Receives an instance of Adaptee and translates calls from request to specific_request.

The Adapter pattern allows the client to use an Adaptee object through the Target interface. When the client calls the Adapter's request method, the Adapter translates that request into a specific_request that the Adaptee can handle. This allows two incompatible classes to work together without modifying their original code.

-Decorator

The Decorator pattern dynamically adds functionality to an object without modifying its original structure. It is useful for extending object capabilities flexibly and conditionally.

Usage:

- Adding extra features to objects without altering existing code.
- Implementing functionalities conditionally.

Example: (All example codes are written in python)

class Component:

    def operation(self):

        pass

```
class ConcreteComponent(Component):
    def operation(self):
        return "Basic behavior"

class Decorator(Component):
    def __init__(self, component):
        self._component = component

    def operation(self):
        return f"Decorated: {self._component.operation()}"
```

This code implements the Decorator design pattern, which allows you to add additional functionality to an object dynamically.

1. **Component class**: A base class defining the operation method, representing a component to be decorated.
2. **ConcreteComponent class**: Inherits from Component and implements the operation method, returning "Basic behavior".
3. **Decorator class**:

• Inherits from Component and wraps a ConcreteComponent.

• In its init method, it receives an object of type Component (the component to be decorated) and saves it as an attribute (self._component).

• Its operation method calls the operation method of the original component and adds a prefix to the result, thus returning a decorated string: "Decorated: [result of the component]".

The Decorator pattern allows you to extend the behavior of an object without modifying its structure. In this case, you can create a ConcreteComponent and then wrap it in a Decorator to add new functionality. When you call the decorator's operation method, you get the original behavior, but with the extra functionality provided by the decorator.

4.2.3. Behavioral Patterns

Behavioral patterns focus on communication between objects and the delegation of responsibilities. They help define object interactions and improve code organization.

-Observer

The Observer pattern establishes a dependency relationship between objects so that when one changes, others are automatically notified. This is particularly useful when multiple components need to react to events.

Usage:

- Implementing events in graphical interfaces.
- Synchronizing states in distributed systems.

Example: (All example codes are written in python)

```python
class Observer:
    def update(self, message):
        pass


class Subject:
    def __init__(self):
        self._observers = []

    def attach(self, observer):
        self._observers.append(observer)

    def notify(self, message):
        for observer in self._observers:
            observer.update(message)
```

This code implements the Observer design pattern, which allows one object (the subject) to notify other objects (the observers) about changes in its state.

1. Observer class: This class defines the update method, which is called when the subject notifies the observers. In this case, it has no implementation (it is defined as an empty method), since each specific observer will implement its own update logic.

2. Subject class:

• _observers attribute: This is a list that stores the observers that are interested in receiving updates from the subject.

• attach method: Allows you to add a new observer to the observer list. When this method is called, the observer is added to the _observers list.

• notify method: This is responsible for notifying all observers about a change, passing a message as an argument. This method goes through the observer list and calls their update method, sending them the message.

The Observer pattern allows a subject to maintain a set of observers and automatically notify them when there is a change in their state. This is useful in situations where multiple objects need to react to events on a central object without needing to be directly coupled.

-Strategy

The Strategy pattern enables a family of algorithms to be interchangeable, allowing behavior to vary without modifying the client code. This promotes separation of concerns and flexibility.

Usage:

• Implementing algorithms interchangeably, such as different search or sorting strategies.

• Facilitating behavior selection at runtime.

Example: (All example codes are written in python)

class Strategy:

```python
    def execute(self):
        pass

class ConcreteStrategyA(Strategy):
    def execute(self):
        return "Execution of Strategy A"

class ConcreteStrategyB(Strategy):
    def execute(self):
        return "Execution of Strategy B"

class Context:
    def __init__(self, strategy):
        self._strategy = strategy

    def execute_strategy(self):
        return self._strategy.execute()
```

This code implements the Strategy design pattern, which allows selecting a strategy or algorithm at runtime.

1. **Strategy Class:** This is an abstract base class that defines the execute method. This method will be implemented in the concrete strategy classes.
2. **ConcreteStrategyA and ConcreteStrategyB Classes:** These are concrete implementations of the Strategy class. Both implement the execute method:

- ConcreteStrategyA returns the string "Execution of Strategy A".
- ConcreteStrategyB returns the string "Execution of Strategy B".

3. **Context class**:

- **Constructor init**: Constructor (__init__): Receives a Strategy object (one of the concrete strategies) and stores it in the _strategy attribute..

- **Execute_strategy method**: Calls the execute method of the stored strategy and returns the result.

The Strategy pattern allows defining a family of algorithms (in this case, ConcreteStrategyA and ConcreteStrategyB), encapsulating each of them and making them interchangeable in the context of use. This enables the behavior of an object (in this case, the Context) to adapt based on the selected strategy, facilitating code extensibility and maintainability.

In summary, design patterns are powerful tools for addressing recurring software development problems in a structured and efficient way. Adopting these patterns leads to cleaner, more modular, and maintainable code, enhancing software quality and sustainability over time. The choice of pattern depends on the problem's nature and project requirements, but knowing these patterns provides a solid framework for software design decision-making.

4.3. USER INTERFACE DESIGN

User interface (UI) design is fundamental to the user experience (UX), as a good interface must be not only aesthetically pleasing but also intuitive and accessible. The quality of UI design directly impacts user satisfaction and software effectiveness. To achieve successful UI design, several key aspects must be considered:

- **Low-Fidelity and High-Fidelity Prototypes:** Prototypes are essential tools in the design process as they allow designers and developers to visualize the interface before full implementation. They are divided into two categories:

- **Low-Fidelity Prototypes:** Simple, schematic representations of the interface used to explore design ideas and navigation flows. These can be created with paper and pencil or basic digital tools. Their purpose is to facilitate discussion and gather initial feedback without delving into specific details.

- **High-Fidelity Prototypes:** Closer to the final design, including graphic details, colors, typography, and the actual layout of elements. These prototypes simulate user interaction with the interface and are useful for more advanced usability testing. They can be created using specialized tools such as Adobe XD, Figma, or Sketch.

4.3.1. User-Centered Design Principles

User-centered design (UCD) prioritizes the needs, behaviors, and expectations of the end user throughout the design process. Key UCD principles include:

- **User Research**: Understanding who the users are and their needs through interviews, surveys, and behavioral studies.

- **Usability**: Ensuring the interface is easy to use, intuitive, and efficient. This involves minimizing cognitive load and ensuring users can navigate and complete tasks without frustration.

- **Accessibility**: Considering all users, including people with disabilities, by following guidelines like WCAG (Web Content Accessibility Guidelines) to make the interface usable for as many people as possible.

- **Iteration and Testing**: Testing the interface with real users and making adjustments based on their feedback. Design should be an iterative process, with continuous improvements driven by user experience.

4.3.2. Wireframes and Mockups

Wireframes and mockups are key tools that help define the structure and layout of elements in the interface, facilitating communication between designers and developers.

- **Wireframes**: Low-detail representations showing the basic structure of the interface, including the placement of elements like buttons, menus, and text fields. Wireframes focus on functionality and visual hierarchy without emphasizing visual design or colors.

- **Mockups**: More detailed and realistic representations of the interface, including colors, typography, and visual elements. Mockups allow stakeholders to visualize the final product and are useful for obtaining approval before development begins.

4.3.3. Style Guides and Design

Creating style guides is another recommended practice to ensure the visual and functional consistency of the interface. These guides establish:

- **Colors and Typography**: Defining the color palette and fonts to maintain a consistent visual identity.

- **UI Components**: Establishing design patterns for buttons, forms, menus, and other interface elements, ensuring all components behave consistently.

- **Spacing and Alignment**: Standards for the spacing and alignment of elements to create a clean and organized design.

4.3.4. Responsive Design

Responsive design ensures the interface works well across various devices and screen sizes, automatically adapting to the user's environment. This involves:

•**Using Flexible CSS**: Techniques such as grid layout and relative units to adjust the interface for different screen sizes.

•**Device Testing**: Testing on multiple devices and resolutions to ensure optimal user experience regardless of how the software is accessed.

UI design is an essential component of creating successful software. By focusing on usability, accessibility, and aesthetics, designers can create experiences that not only meet user needs but also foster loyalty and long-term satisfaction. Implementing prototypes, user-centered design principles, wireframes, and mockups are fundamental steps in this process, ensuring the final product not only works well but is also attractive and easy to use.

4.4. OBJECT-ORIENTED DESIGN AND COMPONENT-BASED DESIGN

Object-oriented design (OOD) and component-based design (CBD) are widely used approaches for creating modular, scalable, and reusable systems. Below are the definitions and characteristics of each:

4.4.1. Object-Oriented Design (OOD)

OOD is a programming paradigm that focuses on using classes and objects to represent and manipulate real-world entities. This approach has several key characteristics:

• **Classes and Objects:** A class is a template defining the properties and behaviors of a type of object. An object is an instance of a class, containing data and methods. This enables logically organizing code related to the problem domain.

- Principles of OOD:

•**Encapsulation**: Grouping related data and methods in a single component (the class) and controlling access to them through access modifiers. This protects the object's internal state and hides implementation details.

•**Inheritance**: Creating new classes based on existing ones, facilitating code reuse. Derived classes inherit features from base classes and can add new functionality or modify inherited behavior.

•**Polymorphism**: Allowing different classes to implement methods with the same name differently. This enables treating objects of different classes uniformly, simplifying program logic.

-Advantages of OOD:

·Code Reuse: Classes can be reused in different projects.

·Simplified Maintenance: Encapsulation and modularity make maintaining and evolving software easier.

·Better Understanding: Modeling real-world objects enhances system comprehension.

4.4.2. Component-Based Design (CBD)

CBD organizes the system into independent, reusable components. This approach is commonly used in modern software applications, particularly in microservices architectures and web interface development. Its main characteristics include:

·Components: Independent units encapsulating specific functionality and exposing well-defined interfaces for interaction with other components. This enables separate development, testing, and maintenance of each component.

·Interoperability: Designing components to communicate through interfaces, facilitating integration across platforms and environments.

·Reusability: Like OOD, components can be reused in different contexts and applications, reducing development time and effort by leveraging already implemented functionalities.

·Scalability and Flexibility: Component-based architecture allows easy scaling of systems by adding or removing components as needed, particularly useful in cloud applications and microservices architectures.

·Agile Development: CBD aligns well with agile methodologies, prioritizing rapid delivery of functionalities through parallel work on different components.

4.4.3. Comparison between OOD and CBD

·Focus: OOD focuses on creating classes and objects, while CBD emphasizes reusable, autonomous components.

- **Reusability**: Both promote reusability; OOD achieves this through inheritance and polymorphism, while CBD does so by encapsulating functionality in components.

- **Maintenance**: OOD may be harder to maintain in large systems due to class dependencies, whereas CBD simplifies maintenance and scalability through component independence.

4.4.4. Conclusion

Object-oriented design and component-based design are complementary approaches that help developers create modular and reusable systems. The choice between them depends on project requirements, the desired architecture, and the development team's preferences.

4.5. SOFTWARE DESIGN DOCUMENTATION

Software design documentation is a crucial element in the development process as it provides clear guidance on the system's structure and logic, facilitating team collaboration and ensuring that requirements are effectively translated into functional solutions. Below are the main components of this documentation:

4.5.1. UML Diagrams

Unified Modeling Language (UML) diagrams are visual tools that help represent various aspects of software design. Some of the most commonly used diagrams include:

- **Class Diagrams**: Show the system's classes, their attributes, methods, and relationships (such as inheritance and associations). These diagrams are essential for understanding the system's structure and how different objects interact.

- **Sequence Diagrams**: Illustrate the interaction between objects over time, showing how messages are sent and in what order. These are useful for visualizing control flow and how operations are performed within the system.

- **Use Case Diagrams**: Represent interactions between users (or actors) and the system, describing the functionalities it offers. This helps understand user requirements and how the system is expected to respond to different actions.

4.5.2. Architecture Specification

The **architecture specification** describes the system's overall structure, providing a high-level view of the main components and their interactions. It includes:

- **Key Components**: Identification of the system's modules, services, or core components, along with a brief description of their functions.

- **Component Relationships**: Details on how different components interact, including communication protocols and dependencies.

- **Integration**: Explanation of how the components are integrated into a broader system, including underlying infrastructure, databases, and other external interfaces.

- **Technologies Used**: A list of the technologies, frameworks, and programming languages to be employed in system development.

4.5.3. Style Guides and Code Conventions

Style guides and code conventions are documents that establish standards for writing and organizing code. These guides are essential for ensuring the team's work is:

- **Readable**: Naming conventions, file organization, and indentation make the code easier to read and understand.

- **Maintainable**: Following a consistent style facilitates error detection and correction, as well as the addition of new features without introducing bugs.

- **Collaborative**: When all team members adhere to the same conventions, collaboration and code review are streamlined, resulting in a smoother development process.

4.5.4. Importance of Design Documentation

Software design documentation serves as a reference during development and is also useful in subsequent stages:

- **Onboarding New Members:** Eases the integration of new developers by providing a clear understanding of the system's architecture and functioning.

- **Long-Term Maintenance**: Reduces learning curves and maintenance costs by enabling developers to quickly understand the existing system.

- **Software Evolution**: Helps identify areas for improvement or expansion by providing a clear view of the system's design.

4.5.5. Conclusion

Software design documentation is an essential component that ensures all team members have a clear and consistent understanding of the system's structure and functioning. Investing time in creating and maintaining this documentation early in the development process can lead to a more efficient workflow, fewer errors, and greater user satisfaction.

4.6. JACOB NIELSEN'S PRINCIPLES FOR DEVELOPING ATTRACTIVE WEBSITES AND INTERFACES

Jacob Nielsen, an expert in usability and interaction design, has established fundamental principles for creating effective and attractive user interfaces. These principles enhance user experience while contributing to the overall efficiency of applications and websites. Below are the most relevant principles:

1. Visibility of System Status

Maintaining visibility of system status is crucial for keeping users informed about what is happening in the application. This can be achieved through:

•**Feedback Messages:** Providing clear notifications when the system performs an action, such as saving a file or loading information (e.g., "Loading data…").

•**Progress Indicators:** Using loading bars or wait icons to show operation progress, helping users understand the system is working and they should wait.

•**Active/Inactive States**: Clearly indicating which options are available at any given moment, such as buttons that change state based on the user's actions.

2. Consistency and Standards

Consistency and standards ensure users feel comfortable and confident when interacting with the system. This involves:

•**Uniform Design**: Using similar colors, fonts, and visual styles across all pages or sections of the application to help users familiarize themselves with the environment and navigate without confusion.

•**Common Terminology**: Employing consistent language and terms throughout the system, avoiding mixing different words or phrases for the same action or element.

•**Compliance with Standards**: Adhering to design conventions of popular platforms (such as Android or iOS) so users can apply their previous experiences to the new system.

3. Flexibility and Efficiency of Use

Flexibility and efficiency of use enable users to personalize their experience and access functions more quickly. To achieve this, implement:

•**Shortcuts:** Provide hotkeys or gestures for experienced users, allowing them to perform common actions more efficiently.

•**Customization Options:** Allow users to adjust interface settings according to their preferences, such as font size, colors, and element layout.

•**Guides and Suggestions**: Offer options tailored to the user's experience level, with guides for beginners and advanced features for more experienced users.

4. Error Prevention

Error prevention is a key principle for improving usability, achieved by:

•**Preventive Design**: Creating interfaces that minimize the possibility of user errors, such as disabling buttons under certain conditions or validating data entry in real-time.

•**Clear Error Messages**: Providing clear and understandable error messages that explain what went wrong and how to fix it. Messages should be specific and not vague.

•**Confirmations for Critical Actions**: Implementing

confirmations when users perform actions with significant consequences, such as deleting a file or making a purchase. This provides an opportunity to review and cancel the action if needed.

Conclusion

Jacob Nielsen's principles are fundamental for developing attractive and effective websites and interfaces. Applying these principles helps developers create user experiences that are not only visually appealing but also intuitive and functional. This increases user satisfaction and contributes to system effectiveness, fostering smoother and more efficient application usage. Implementing these guidelines from the early stages of design can result in a more successful final product aligned with user expectations.

4.7. DESIGN OF RELATIONAL AND NOSQL DATABASES

Database design is a fundamental aspect of a software system's performance and scalability. The choice between relational and NoSQL databases depends on the nature of the data being handled and the project's specific requirements.

1. Relational Databases

Relational databases (RDBMS) are a traditional approach to storing and managing data. These databases use a tabular model, organizing data into tables composed of rows and columns. Key features and concepts include:

- **Table Structure:** Each table represents an entity (e.g., customers, products), and each row contains a unique record, while columns represent attributes of those records. This structure is ideal for well-defined data and complex relationships.

- **Referential Integrity:** Relational databases enable the establishment of relationships between tables using primary and foreign keys, ensuring data integrity and supporting complex queries across multiple tables.

- **Examples**: Popular relational database systems include MySQL, PostgreSQL, and Microsoft SQL Server. These platforms are widely used in applications requiring complex transactions and rigorous data management.

-Normalization

- **Normalization**: A fundamental process in relational database design that organizes data to minimize redundancy and improve integrity. It involves splitting data into tables and establishing appropriate relationships among them. There are several normal forms (1NF, 2NF, 3NF, etc.), each with its own rules and objectives for achieving optimal design.

-ER (Entity-Relationship) Modeling

• **ER Modeling:** This technique graphically represents the logical structure of the database. Entity-relationship diagrams help designers identify entities, their attributes, and relationships among them. This visualization ensures that all system requirements are addressed before implementation.

2. NoSQL Databases

NoSQL databases provide solutions for handling unstructured data and scenarios requiring high horizontal scalability. These databases are more flexible than relational ones and are categorized into several types:

·**Flexible Data Structure**: Unlike relational databases, NoSQL allows a more dynamic data structure, eliminating the need for a rigid schema before storing data. This adaptability accommodates changing system requirements.

·**Examples**: Popular NoSQL databases include MongoDB, Cassandra, and Couchbase. These are ideal for applications needing high-speed read and write operations and handling large volumes of unstructured data.

-Document Modeling

• **Document Modeling:** A hallmark of document-oriented databases like MongoDB. Instead of storing data in tables, each record is stored as a JSON or BSON document, enabling nested data and complex structures. This flexibility is valuable for applications requiring adaptable data structures and access patterns.

-Graph Databases

• **Graph Databases:** Designed for applications modeling complex relationships such as social networks, recommendation systems, or fraud management. They use nodes and edges to represent entities and relationships, enabling efficient queries on data connections. Examples include Neo4j and Amazon Neptune.

Proper database design is crucial for a software system's performance, scalability, and maintainability. By understanding the differences between relational and NoSQL databases and the key concepts of each, developers can make informed decisions aligning with project goals. This ensures that the chosen database not only handles current data efficiently but can also scale and adapt to future needs.

4.8. API AND MICROSERVICES DESIGN (SOA)

Designing APIs (Application Programming Interfaces) and microservices is essential for building modern systems that are scalable, maintainable, and capable of agile evolution. These approaches allow developers to construct distributed applications that facilitate communication between components and services.

1. RESTful APIs

RESTful APIs are a widely used standard for creating web services that enable application communication over HTTP. Key characteristics include:

•**Resource Orientation:** In REST, each resource (e.g., a user, product) is identified by a unique URL. Operations on these resources use standard HTTP methods: GET (retrieve), POST (create), PUT (update), and DELETE (remove).

•**Statelessness**: Each client-server request is independent, meaning the server does not retain client state between requests. This enhances scalability and simplifies infrastructure management.

•**Response Format:** RESTful APIs typically use data exchange formats like JSON or XML, making integration with different platforms and programming languages easier.

2. GraphQL

GraphQL is an alternative to RESTful APIs, offering greater flexibility and efficiency in data retrieval:

•**Specific Queries:** With GraphQL, clients request exactly the data they need, avoiding information overload common in REST API responses. This optimizes queries and reduces data transfer.

·**Single Endpoint:** Unlike REST, where each resource may have its own endpoint, GraphQL operates through a single endpoint that handles all requests, simplifying API structure and code organization.

·**Strict Typing:** GraphQL uses a type system that allows developers to define the structure of available data, aiding validation and autocompletion in development tools.

3. Microservices Architecture

The **microservices architecture** divides an application into small, independent services, each responsible for specific functionality:

·**Independence**: Each microservice can be developed, deployed, and scaled independently, supporting agile development and efficient software lifecycle management.

·**Diverse Technologies**: Microservices can use different technologies, programming languages, and databases based on each service's specific needs, providing flexibility in tool selection.

·**Scalability**: Microservices architecture enables independent scaling of services based on demand, especially beneficial for functions requiring more resources during specific periods.

4. Service-Oriented Architecture (SOA)

Service-Oriented Architecture (SOA) is a broader approach that also focuses on creating distributed applications through services:

·**Service Integration:** SOA integrates different services via an Enterprise Service Bus (ESB), enabling communication between heterogeneous applications. This is particularly useful in enterprise environments where multiple systems must interact.

·**Interoperability**: SOA services are designed to work together regardless of the platforms they run on, achieved through open standards and communication protocols.

·**Maintenance Ease**: Like microservices, SOA promotes separation of concerns, simplifying system evolution and maintenance. Changes to a service do not directly impact others, provided service contracts are respected.

Conclusion

API and microservices design, along with approaches like SOA, are fundamental in modern application development. They enable the creation of scalable, efficient, and maintainable systems, adapting to changing business needs and improving user experience. As technology evolves, implementing these architectures becomes a standard for building robust and flexible software.

4.9. CHAPTER CONCLUSIONS

Software design is an iterative process that translates requirements into a viable technical solution, balancing usability, efficiency, and maintainability. Good design not only facilitates development but also ensures that the system can adapt to future changes and respond effectively to user needs. Combining solid principles, appropriate design patterns, and proper documentation is key to creating high-quality systems.

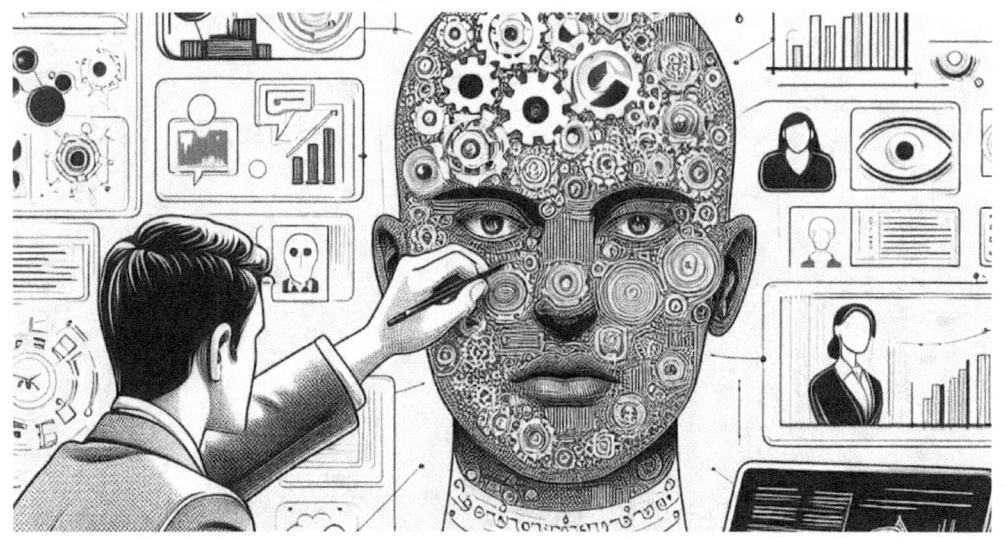

CHAPTER 5

SOFTWARE ARCHITECTURE

Software architecture is the fundamental structure of a software system, defining how its components are organized and communicate. This chapter explores the key concepts and patterns that help software architects design effective and scalable solutions.

5.1. FUNDAMENTAL CONCEPTS OF SOFTWARE ARCHITECTURE

Software architecture is a conceptual framework that defines the structure and organization of a software system. It plays a critical role in software development by laying the foundation upon which components are built and their interactions defined. Below are the fundamental concepts that form the basis of software architecture.

5.1.1. Components

Components are the individual building blocks of a software system. Each component has a specific function and can be considered a modular unit encapsulating its own logic, data, and behavior. Components can include:

- **Modules**: Groupings of functions and procedures forming a cohesive part of the system, e.g., an authentication module managing user logins.

- **Services**: Standalone functions that can be invoked by other components, e.g., a payment service processing transactions.

- **Databases**: Data stores enabling the persistence and retrieval of information.

- **User Interfaces:** Elements facilitating interaction between the user and the system.

Components should be designed to promote reusability and separation of concerns, making the system easier to maintain and scale.

5.1.2. Connectors

Connectors are mechanisms enabling communication and interaction between system components. They act as intermediaries facilitating data exchange and control flow between different parts of the system. Types of connectors include:

• **Communication Protocols:** Standards defining how data is transmitted between components, e.g., HTTP, WebSocket, MQTT.

• **Message Queues:** Systems enabling asynchronous communication between components, such as RabbitMQ or Apache Kafka. These allow messages to be sent without requiring both components to be available simultaneously.

• **APIs (Application Programming Interfaces):** Sets of rules enabling different software to communicate. APIs define methods and data exchange formats.

Choosing appropriate connectors is crucial to ensure efficient and reliable communication, which directly impacts software quality.

5.1.3. Architectural Styles

Architectural styles are general patterns that define the organization and relationships between components in a software system. Each style has unique characteristics and advantages, and selecting the right style is vital for project success. Examples include:

• **Layered Architecture:** Organizes the system into hierarchical layers, each with a specific responsibility. Higher layers communicate with lower layers through well-defined interfaces. This approach promotes separation of concerns and simplifies maintenance.

• **Service-Oriented Architecture (SOA):** In this style, system components are independent services communicating through well-defined interfaces, enabling service reuse and integration across applications.

• **Microservices**: A modern approach dividing an application into small, independent services that can be deployed and scaled separately, offering flexibility and agility in development.

• **Event-Driven Architecture:** Components communicate via

events, enabling high scalability and responsiveness to system changes. This style is ideal for distributed and real-time systems.

5.1.4. Impact on Quality, Performance, and Maintainability

Software architecture involves strategic decisions impacting various aspects of the system:

- **Quality**: A well-designed architecture ensures software quality by promoting consistency, reusability, and scalability.

- **Performance**: The organization and communication of components directly affect system performance. For instance, architectures minimizing latency and optimizing resource use significantly enhance the user experience.

- **Maintainability**: Thoughtful architectural design simplifies software maintenance, enabling changes and improvements without negatively affecting the overall system.

In summary, software architecture is a cornerstone of developing complex software systems. Understanding the basics of components, connectors, and architectural styles empowers developers to make informed decisions that positively affect the quality, performance, and maintainability of their applications.

5.2. COMMON ARCHITECTURAL PATTERNS

In software development, architectural patterns are recurring solutions to common problems in system design. Each pattern provides a structured approach to addressing specific challenges, enabling developers to build more effective and maintainable applications. Below are some of the most common architectural patterns:

5.2.1. Model-View-Controller (MVC)

The Model-View-Controller (MVC) pattern is widely used in application development, especially for web applications. This pattern separates an application into three main components:

- **Model**: Represents business logic and data management. It is responsible for retrieving, storing, and manipulating application data, ensuring consistent information.

- **View**: Handles the user interface, presenting information from the model to the user and sending user interactions to the controller.

- **Controller**: Acts as an intermediary between the model and the view, processing user input, updating the model, and notifying the view of changes.

MVC facilitates maintenance and scalability, allowing developers to work on individual components without affecting the entire system. It also promotes code reuse and separation of concerns, resulting in cleaner, more organized applications.

5.2.2. Layered Architecture

Layered architecture divides the system into hierarchical layers, each with a specific responsibility. Typical layers include:

- **Presentation Layer:** Manages the user interface and interaction, displaying information and receiving user input.

- **Business Layer:** Contains the application's business logic, processing data and applying necessary rules.

- **Data Access Layer:** Handles database interactions and other storage systems, providing a consistent interface for the business layer to access data.

This pattern promotes separation of responsibilities and simplifies change management. For instance, developers can modify the presentation layer without impacting business logic or data access.

5.2.3. Microservices

Microservices architecture is a modern approach that distributes an application into small, independent services. Each microservice is responsible for a specific functionality and can be developed, deployed, and scaled independently. Key features include:

- **Independence**: Microservices can be developed using different programming languages and technologies, offering flexibility in tool selection.

- **Scalability**: Services can scale independently, optimizing resource usage based on demand.

- **Resilience**: Failure of one microservice does not necessarily impact the entire application, improving system availability.

However, this architecture introduces challenges such as managing multiple services and ensuring efficient communication, often through REST APIs or events.

5.2.4. Service-Oriented Architecture (SOA)

Service-Oriented Architecture (SOA) uses services as the primary components, enabling communication between applications and systems. Key features include:

- **Interoperability**: Services can communicate across different platforms and languages, seamlessly integrating legacy and new applications.

- **Reusability**: Services are designed for reuse in various contexts, reducing duplication in development.

- **Decoupling**: Services are loosely coupled, allowing modification or replacement without affecting other system parts.

In SOA, services may use various technologies and standards, such as SOAP or REST, to communicate over networks. This approach is ideal for enterprise environments where integrating multiple systems is crucial.

5.2.5. Conclusion

Choosing the right architectural pattern depends on factors such as project requirements, team size, and available technologies. Understanding these patterns and their advantages allows developers to make informed decisions that influence project success and software quality. Each pattern presents unique opportunities and challenges, and combining them may provide the most effective solution for specific application needs.

5.3. SOFTWARE ARCHITECTURE MODELING

Software architecture modeling is a crucial process that involves creating visual and conceptual representations of a system to facilitate understanding, analysis, and communication of its structure and components. This process is not only essential for software architects but also benefits all project stakeholders, including developers, project managers, and clients. Below are the most relevant aspects and tools associated with software architecture modeling.

5.3.1. Visual Representations of Architecture

Diagrams are key tools in software architecture modeling. Some of the most commonly used include:

- **Class Diagrams**: Mainly used in the context of object-oriented programming, these diagrams represent the system's classes, their attributes, methods, and the relationships between them. They are fundamental for understanding data structures and business logic.

- **Component Diagrams**: These diagrams show how a system's components are organized and interrelated. They include details about interfaces and dependencies, facilitating the identification of integration and communication points within the system.

- **Flow Diagrams:** Represent the flow of control and data in a system, helping to visualize how inputs and outputs are processed. They are useful for describing complex processes and the logic behind decisions.

- **Deployment Diagrams:** Used to represent the physical distribution of software components on specific hardware. They include information about servers, databases, and networks, which is crucial for understanding the system's infrastructure.

5.3.2. Benefits of Architecture Modeling

Software architecture modeling offers numerous benefits essential for software development and management:

- **Visualization:** Diagrams provide a clear and comprehensible representation of how the system's components are organized. This helps all stakeholders achieve a shared understanding of the architecture and facilitates communication between teams. Good visualization allows quick identification of areas of interest, such as performance bottlenecks or potential failure points.

- **Documentation:** Architectural models act as a historical record of the architectural decisions made during software development. This documentation is invaluable for future reference, especially during system maintenance or when onboarding new team members. It also provides context to understand design and technology choices.

- **Analysis**: Through modeling, the impacts of proposed changes to the architecture can be evaluated before implementation. This enables the identification of potential issues, such as excessive complexity or unnecessary dependencies, helping to reduce risks and costs associated with development. Moreover, it allows for simulations to predict system behavior under different conditions and configurations.

5.3.3. Architecture Modeling Tools

Several tools and modeling languages can aid in creating these diagrams and models, such as:

- **UML (Unified Modeling Language):** A standard language providing a set of graphical notations to describe a system's design aspects. UML is widely used in software architecture modeling due to its versatility and ability to represent different system perspectives.

- **Archimate:** A specific language for modeling enterprise architectures, allowing for consistent descriptions of a system's structure and behavior.

- **PlantUML:** A tool for creating diagrams from text, facilitating documentation in agile development environments.

- **Microsoft Visio, Lucidchart, and Draw.io:** Graphical tools for creating customized and visual diagrams for documentation and modeling.

5.3.4. Best Practices in Architecture Modeling

Some best practices for effective modeling include:

- **Maintain Simplicity:** Avoid overloading diagrams with details to keep them easily understandable.

- **Update Models:** Ensure that models reflect system changes over time.

- **Engage Stakeholders:** Include team members and other stakeholders in the modeling process to ensure alignment with the architectural vision.

- **Use a Common Language:** Adopt a modeling approach that all project participants understand to improve communication and avoid misunderstandings.

5.3.5. Conclusion

Software architecture modeling is an essential activity that helps structure and communicate the complexity of software systems. Through visual representations, it allows teams to understand and document a system's architecture, assess its implications, and facilitate informed decisions about its development and evolution. Implementing a rigorous and well-documented approach to architecture modeling not only improves software quality but also contributes to the overall success of the project.

5.4. EVALUATION AND SELECTION OF ARCHITECTURES

The evaluation and selection of architectures is a critical process in software engineering that requires a systematic and strategic approach. This process aims to identify the most suitable architecture for a specific system, considering various factors that may influence its performance, sustainability, and alignment with business objectives. Below are the key aspects involved in evaluating and selecting architectures.

5.4.1. Key Factors in Architecture Evaluation

1. System Requirements:

• **Functional Needs**: These refer to the specific capabilities the system must offer, such as user management, data processing, or integration with other applications. Understanding these requirements is crucial to choosing an architecture that adequately supports the desired functionality..

• **Non-Functional Needs:** Include aspects like performance, availability, security, maintainability, and usability. These non-functional requirements can be decisive in selecting an architecture, as they influence how the system behaves in real-world scenarios. For instance, if a system requires high availability, a microservices architecture might be more suitable than a monolithic one.

2. Scalability:

• Scalability refers to the ability of a system to handle an increase in workload or number of users without compromising its performance. When evaluating architectures, it is essential to consider how each option allows for horizontal or vertical scaling.

- **Horizontal Scalability:** Involves adding more machines or instances to handle the load. This approach is common in microservices architectures, where each service can scale independently.

- **Vertical Scalability:** Refers to increasing resources (like CPU or memory) of a single instance. Some architectures are better suited for vertical scalability but may become limited as demands grow.

3. Costs:

- The cost evaluation includes both initial implementation and long-term maintenance costs. This encompasses not only the monetary costs, but also the time and human resources required to develop, implement, and maintain the architecture..

- **Implementation Costs:** Include expenses for hardware, software, personnel training, and development time. A cost-benefit analysis is essential to determine if the chosen architecture justifies the investment.

- **Maintenance Costs:** Involve the effort needed for updates, bug fixes, and adaptations to changing requirements. A more complex architecture may require greater maintenance efforts, increasing long-term costs.

4. Risks:

- Identifying and evaluating the risks associated with different architectures is a critical part of the selection process. This includes analyzing potential points of failure, security vulnerabilities, and implementation complexity.

- **Technical Risks:** Such as dependence on specific technologies that may lack support or become obsolete.

- **Management Risks:** Involve a lack of skills within the team to implement and maintain the selected architecture, potentially leading to delays and additional costs.

- **Change Risks:** If a significant architectural change is required later, this can result in high costs and negative impacts on the project.

5.4.2. Evaluation and Selection Process

The evaluation and selection of architectures can follow a structured process that includes:

1. Requirements Gathering:

• Conduct meetings with stakeholders to understand the system's needs and expectations.

2. Alternative Identification:

• Research and generate a list of potential architectures that could meet the system's requirements.

3. Option Evaluation:

• Use decision matrices or scoring models to assess each architecture based on key factors.

• Comparar las arquitecturas frente a una serie de criterios establecidos (por ejemplo, coste, escalabilidad, requisitos funcionales, etc.).

4. Proof of Concept (PoC):

• Develop prototypes or proofs of concept for the most promising architectures to evaluate their performance and feasibility.

5. Decision-Making:

• Based on the evaluation and PoC results, select the architecture that best aligns with the project requirements and goals.

6. Documentation:

• Document the decisions made, along with the reasons behind each choice, for future reference and as part of the knowledge management process.

5.4.3. Conclusions

The evaluation and selection of architectures is a vital process that significantly impacts a software project's success. By considering system requirements, scalability, costs, and associated risks, an informed decision can be made to optimize the software's performance and sustainability throughout its lifecycle. A well-chosen architecture not only improves the final product's quality but also contributes to client satisfaction and team efficiency.

5.5. MICROSERVICES-BASED ARCHITECTURE

Microservices-based architecture is a software design approach that breaks down complex applications into small, independent services that can be developed, deployed, and scaled autonomously. This paradigm has gained popularity in recent years due to its ability to handle the complexity of modern applications and its alignment with agile methodologies and DevOps. Below, we detail its benefits, challenges, and key considerations.

5.5.1. Benefits of Microservices-Based Architecture

1. Scalability:

• **Independent Scaling:** Each microservice can be scaled independently according to demand. For instance, if a user management service experiences increased load, only that service needs to be scaled without affecting others.

• **Resource Optimization:** This approach allows organizations to optimize their infrastructure resources by allocating more capacity only to the services that require it during high-demand periods, thereby improving operational efficiency.

2. Maintainability:

• **Independent Teams:** Microservices enable the creation of independent development teams that can work on different services without interference. This facilitates the implementation of new features and bug fixes without impacting the entire application.

• **Reduced Complexity:** Breaking down a monolithic application into smaller, manageable components reduces code complexity. Each microservice has its own codebase, simplifying testing, maintenance, and understanding of the system.

3. Flexibility:

• **Diverse Technologies:** Microservices allow the use of different technologies and programming languages for each service. Teams can choose the best tool for the specific task at hand, leading to more efficient development and easier adoption of new technologies when needed.

• **Ease of Adopting New Tools:** The implementation of new tools and technologies can be simpler in a microservices environment, as each service can be updated or replaced independently.

4. Continuous Deployment:

• Microservices promote the implementation of continuous integration and continuous delivery (CI/CD) practices. Since each microservice can be deployed independently, updates and new functionalities can be released quickly and easily without interrupting the entire application.

5.5.2. Challenges of Microservices-Based Architecture

1. Service Communication Management:

• Communication between microservices can be complex and may require appropriate network protocols (such as REST, gRPC, or event-based messaging). Managing this communication and synchronizing data between services can be a significant challenge.

• **Latency and Failures:** The need for inter-service communication introduces the potential for network latency and failures. Implementing resilience strategies, such as circuit breakers and retry patterns, is crucial to address these issues.

2. Orchestration Complexity:

• As more microservices are added, orchestration becomes more complex. Deployment, scaling, and monitoring needs must be effectively managed to ensure that all services work together as expected.

• **Orchestration Tools**: Tools like Kubernetes are required to manage the lifecycle of microservices, which can increase the learning curve and operational complexity.

3. Monitoring and Debugging:

- The distributed nature of microservices makes monitoring and debugging more challenging. Identifying issues across multiple services can be complicated, requiring advanced monitoring and tracing tools.

- **Data Consistency**: Maintaining data consistency across multiple microservices is a challenge. Strategies such as eventual consistency and distributed transaction management must be carefully considered and planned.

4. Security:

- Security in a microservices environment can be more difficult to manage than in a monolithic application. Each microservice may have different access points that need to be secured, and implementing a consistent security policy is crucial.

- **Authentication and Authorization**: Implementing centralized mechanisms for authentication and authorization, such as OAuth2 or OpenID Connect, can help manage security more effectively.

5.5.3. Conclusions

Microservices-based architecture offers a powerful and flexible approach to modern software development, enabling organizations to respond quickly to market needs and improve operational efficiency. However, it also presents significant challenges that require careful planning, appropriate tools, and robust management and monitoring practices. With a strategic approach, the implementation of microservices can result in highly scalable and maintainable systems that adapt to an ever-evolving technological landscape.

5.6. SERVERLESS ARCHITECTURE

Serverless architecture, also known as "Function as a Service" (FaaS), is a design model that allows developers to build and run applications without worrying about server management or the underlying infrastructure. This approach emphasizes letting developers focus on writing code and business logic, while the cloud service provider handles all operational aspects related to infrastructure. Below are the key features, benefits, drawbacks, and considerations of serverless architecture.

5.6.1. Features of Serverless Architecture

1. On-Demand Execution:

- **Event-Driven:** In a serverless environment, functions are executed in response to events, such as HTTP requests, database changes, message queues, and other triggers. This means functions only run when needed, optimizing resource usage.

- **No Provisioning:** Developers do not need to provision or manage servers. The cloud provider handles all infrastructure, allowing teams to focus on development and deployment.

2. Automatic Scalability:

- Load Adaptation: Serverless infrastructure automatically scales based on workload. During demand spikes, the system can spin up additional instances of functions within seconds, and when demand decreases, it automatically reduces resource usage.

- Variable Traffic Handling: This model is especially effective for applications with variable or unpredictable traffic patterns, where on-demand scaling is crucial.

3. Cost Efficiency:

- **Pay-As-You-Go:** Instead of paying for fixed resources or idle servers, the serverless model charges organizations only for the time functions are executed, resulting in significant savings, particularly for sporadic or fluctuating workloads.

- **No Infrastructure Costs:** By eliminating server maintenance, companies reduce operational and infrastructure expenses, allowing resources to be used more efficiently.

5.6.2. Benefits of Serverless Architecture

1. Reduced Development Time:

- Developers can focus on business logic instead of infrastructure management, accelerating development time and enabling quicker deployment of new features.

- Functions can be developed and deployed independently, facilitating iteration and agile methodologies.

2. Flexibility and Agility:

- Serverless architecture allows businesses to quickly adapt to market changes or demand fluctuations, as functions can be modified and deployed without infrastructure concerns.

- It supports experimentation by enabling developers to test new ideas without significant infrastructure investment.

3. Simplified Infrastructure Management:

- Cloud service providers handle the setup, provisioning, management, and security of infrastructure, letting developers concentrate on creating value through their code.

5.6.3. Challenges of Serverless Architecture

1. Event and Function Design:

- While serverless architecture offers many benefits, it requires careful event and function design. Developers must clearly define triggers and how functions interact with other services.

- **Development Complexity**: Managing multiple functions and their interactions can introduce complexity in development and debugging.

2. Execution Limitations:

- Many serverless platforms impose limits on function execution time, which may not be suitable for tasks requiring intensive or long processing.

- **State and Dependency Management:** Serverless functions are inherently stateless. Developers must manage application state through other services, complicating the design.

3. Monitoring and Traceability:

- The distributed nature of serverless architecture can make monitoring and traceability difficult. Implementing proper monitoring and logging solutions is essential to track function behavior and performance.

- **Debugging Challenges**: Debugging individual functions can be tricky, as execution contexts may vary, and interdependencies between functions may complicate problem identification.

4. Security Issues:

- While cloud providers handle much of the security, serverless applications can still be vulnerable to attacks. Proper security practices and secure development methodologies are critical.

- **Access Management**: Managing permissions and access is vital to protect resources in a serverless environment, as each function may require different levels of access.

5.6.4. Key Considerations When Implementing Serverless Architecture

1. Choosing the Right Provider:

- Evaluate various cloud service providers (e.g., AWS Lambda, Google Cloud Functions, Azure Functions) and their features, limitations, and pricing before selecting one.

- Compatibility with other services and ease of integration are key factors to consider when choosing a provider.

2. Design Planning:

- A robust architectural design is crucial for successful serverless implementation. This includes defining events and functions, managing their communication, and establishing a data management strategy.

- Using appropriate design patterns and considering resilience management are essential.

3. Testing and Monitoring:

- Establishing a robust testing environment is vital to ensure code quality before deployment. Unit and integration tests should be part of the development lifecycle.

- Implement monitoring solutions and alerts to track the performance and health of functions for effective serverless application management.

5.6.5. Conclusion

Serverless architecture represents an innovative approach to application development that can enhance efficiency and reduce operational costs. By allowing developers to focus on code and business logic rather than infrastructure management, this model is well-suited for modern applications with variable workloads. However, to maximize its benefits, understanding its challenges and careful planning in design and implementation are essential. With best practices and a strategic approach, serverless architecture can transform how applications are developed and managed today.

5.7. EVENT-DRIVEN ARCHITECTURES (EDA)

Event-Driven Architectures (EDA) are a design approach that enables software systems to react to events in real time, promoting asynchronous communication between system components. This architecture is particularly useful in contexts that require high interactivity, flexibility, and scalability. Below, we explore the characteristics, benefits, and challenges of event-driven architecture.

5.7.1. Characteristics of Event-Driven Architecture

1.   Component Decoupling:

•   Independence: In an event-driven architecture, components (or services) operate independently, meaning one component does not need to know another's implementation details to interact. They communicate through an event system, facilitating system evolution and maintenance.

•   Asynchronous Interaction: Events are generated and consumed asynchronously, allowing systems to respond to events without blocking other processes. This results in better resource utilization and optimized performance.

2.   Improved Resilience:

•   **Event Persistence:** If a component fails, the generated events can be stored in a queue system or an event database, allowing them to be processed later once the component becomes available again. This enhances the system's fault tolerance.

•   **Handling Load Spikes**: The ability to store events enables the system to manage load spikes without compromising functionality. Events can be queued and processed as resources become available.

3. Facilitating Scalability:

•   **Horizontal Scaling:** Components can be scaled independently based on the volume of events they handle. This allows applications to grow and adapt to changes in demand without redesigning the entire architecture.

•   **Real-Time Event Handling:** Event-driven architecture is ideal for applications requiring real-time processing, such as data analysis, system monitoring, and Internet of Things (IoT) applications.

5.7.2. Benefits of Event-Driven Architecture

1. Flexibility and Adaptability:

•   The separation of components and event-based communication enable organizations to quickly adapt their systems to business or technological changes. This results in greater agility for implementing new features or integrating new technologies.

•   Applications can evolve more smoothly, as changes to one component do not directly affect others.

2. Performance Optimization:

•   By enabling asynchronous communication, event-driven architecture can reduce latency in request processing, improving user experience.

•   Events can be processed in parallel, maximizing resource utilization and reducing response time.

3. Support for Real-Time Processing:

•   Event-driven architectures are ideal for applications requiring real-time analysis and decision-making, such as e-commerce platforms, financial monitoring systems, and social media applications.

•   They enable the integration of real-time data sources, facilitating applications that respond quickly to changing market conditions.

5.7.3. Challenges of Event-Driven Architecture

1. Design Complexity:

•   Designing event-based systems can be more complex than

traditional architectures, as it involves creating mechanisms to effectively generate, consume, and manage events.

- Managing event flows and coordinating between components can become challenging, especially in large, distributed systems.

2. Monitoring and Debugging:

- Monitoring event-driven systems can be difficult, as events may flow through multiple components. This requires implementing proper monitoring and tracing tools to identify issues in the system.

- Debugging can be harder in an environment where business logic is distributed among multiple services reacting to events.

3. Consistency Management:

- Maintaining data consistency in an event-based system can be challenging, especially when events occur asynchronously. Developers must implement appropriate strategies to manage data coherence and integrity.

- Distributed transactions can be difficult to handle, potentially leading to inconsistent states if not managed correctly.

5.7.4. Common Use Cases for Event-Driven Architecture

1. Real-Time Analytics Systems:

- Used in platforms requiring real-time processing and analysis of large data volumes, such as social media analytics, financial system monitoring, and web traffic analysis.

2. IoT Applications:

In applications involving multiple connected devices, event-driven architecture allows data to be collected, processed, and analyzed in real time to make informed decisions.

3. Monitoring and Alert Systems:

- Implemented in systems that generate alerts in response to critical events, such as IT infrastructure monitoring systems where quick responses to performance or security issues are required.

5.7.5. Conclusion

Event-driven architectures provide a powerful approach to designing and implementing systems requiring interactivity and real-time responsiveness. By promoting component decoupling, improving resilience, and facilitating scalability, this approach aligns well with modern software development needs. However, addressing associated challenges, such as design complexity and data consistency management, is crucial for ensuring successful implementation. With careful planning and the right tools, event-driven architectures can provide a solid foundation for building efficient and scalable applications.

5.8. SCALABILITY AND PERFORMANCE IN SOFTWARE ARCHITECTURES

Scalability and performance are fundamental aspects of software architecture as they determine a system's ability to handle increased load and user numbers without degrading the user experience. A well-designed architecture must not only function properly under normal conditions but also adapt to fluctuating demand and future requirements. Below are key strategies to achieve scalability and performance in software architectures.

5.8.1. Vertical Scalability

Vertical scalability, also known as "scaling up," involves increasing the resources of a single server or instance by upgrading existing hardware. This can include:

- **Increasing CPU Capacity:** Enhancing the server processor to handle more simultaneous operations.

- **Adding RAM:** Expanding memory to allow more applications and processes to run in memory, reducing reliance on secondary memory (hard disk).

- **Storage Upgrades:** Switching to faster solid-state drives (SSDs) to improve data access speed.

-Advantages:

- **Simplicity:** Easier to implement than horizontal scalability as it doesn't require changes to the application architecture.

- **Reduced Complexity:** Maintaining a single instance reduces the need to manage communication between multiple servers.

-Disadvantages:

- **Physical Limitations**: There is a limit to the resources that can be added to a single server, potentially leading to bottlenecks.

- **Cost**: Hardware upgrades can be expensive, especially in high-availability environments where downtime must be minimized.

5.8.2. Horizontal Scalability

Horizontal scalability, or "scaling out," involves adding more servers or instances to the system to distribute the load. This approach is widely used in microservices architectures and cloud environments. Key considerations include:

- **Load Balancing:** Implementing a load balancer to distribute requests among multiple servers, ensuring no server becomes overloaded.

- **Server Replication:** Cloning application instances to handle load and improve availability.

-Advantages:

- **Unlimited Scalability:** In theory, as many servers as needed can be added to handle growth.

- **Redundancy and High Availability:** Load distribution across multiple servers enhances system resilience; if one fails, others can continue operating.

-Disadvantages:

- **Management Complexity:** Requires more infrastructure management and solutions for server communication and consistency.

- **Operational Costs:** Involves higher costs for maintaining and monitoring multiple instances.

5.8.3. Performance Optimization

Performance optimization ensures an application operates efficiently even under high loads. Techniques include:

- **Caching:** Using systems like Redis or Memcached to store query results or frequently accessed data, reducing database load and improving response times.

- **Load Balancing:** Distributing traffic among multiple servers to prevent overload, enhancing overall performance and availability.

- **Data Compression:** Compressing data before transmitting it across the network to reduce loading time and improve application speed.

- **Query Optimization:** Improving database queries and using indexes to accelerate data retrieval.

5.8.4. Scalability Evaluation and Planning

Evaluating and planning scalability from the early stages of architectural design is crucial. Best practices include:

1. **Load Analysis:** Conducting load tests to understand system behavior under various traffic levels, identifying bottlenecks and weaknesses.

2. **Scalability Limit Definitions:** Establishing performance metrics and clear thresholds indicating when scaling is necessary.

3. **Prototyping and Simulations:** Building prototypes and simulations to explore different scalability and performance configurations before deployment.

4. **Continuous Monitoring:** Using monitoring tools to observe real-time performance, enabling proactive adjustments before significant issues arise.

5.8.5. Conclusion

Scalability and performance are critical components of a robust software architecture. By considering both vertical and horizontal scalability and performance optimization strategies, software architects can design systems that meet current demands and are prepared for future growth. Early evaluation and planning, along with proactive infrastructure management, are essential to ensure applications operate efficiently and effectively in a constantly evolving environment.

5.9. SECURITY IN SOFTWARE ARCHITECTURE

Security is a critical consideration in software architecture, as vulnerabilities can have devastating consequences for systems, data, and organizational reputation. Incorporating security practices from the early stages of architectural development not only prevents attacks but also ensures compliance with regulations and security standards. Below are key practices to ensure security in software architecture.

5.9.1. Principle of Least Privilege

The principle of least privilege ensures that system components, services, and users have only the permissions necessary to perform their functions. This includes:

- **Access Restrictions**: Limiting access to sensitive resources and functions only to those who truly need it, implemented via role and permission management.

- **Permission Audits:** Regularly reviewing granted permissions to ensure there are no unnecessary or excessive accesses.

- **Separation of Duties:** Dividing critical functions among different roles to reduce the risk of errors or abuse, such as in audits where one person should not have full control over all functions.

-Benefits:

- **Risk Reduction:** Minimizes the attack surface by limiting the chances of exploiting a compromised component.

- **Change Control:** Facilitates tracking and managing permission changes over time.

5.9.2. Input Validation

Input validation is essential to protect against various attacks such as SQL injection, Cross-Site Scripting (XSS), and other injection types. Key aspects include:

- **Data Sanitization**: Cleaning and disinfecting user input to remove harmful characters or data. This includes removing HTML tags, scripts, and special characters that could be used in attacks.

- **Type and Format Validation**: Ensuring input data matches the expected type (e.g., numbers, emails, dates) and format.

- **Whitelist Usage**: Implementing whitelists of acceptable input rather than blacklists of unacceptable input to increase security by stricter restrictions.

-Benefits

- **Attack Prevention**: Reduces the likelihood of attacks exploiting uncontrolled input, maintaining application integrity and security.

- **Improved User Experience**: Proper input validation also enhances user experience by preventing input errors and providing clear error messages.

5.9.3. Encryption

Encryption is a fundamental technique for protecting sensitive data both at rest (stored) and in transit (moving). Best practices include:

- Data-at-Rest Encryption: Securing databases and files containing sensitive information using robust encryption algorithms (e.g., AES), ensuring data cannot be read even if storage devices are accessed physically.

- Data-in-Transit Encryption: Using secure protocols (e.g., HTTPS and TLS) to encrypt client-server communication, protecting data from interception during transmission.

- Key Management: Implementing effective key management policies to ensure cryptographic keys are stored and used securely, including regular key rotation and the use of hardware security modules (HSMs).

-Benefits:

- **Sensitive Data Protection:** Ensures confidential information is safeguarded from unauthorized access, theft, and breaches.

- **Regulatory Compliance:** Many data security regulations (e.g., GDPR, HIPAA) require data encryption, aiding in compliance and avoiding penalties.

5.9.4. Integrating Security into the Development Lifecycle

Security must be an integral part of the software development lifecycle (SDLC), not an afterthought. Strategies include:

1. **Code Reviews:** Conducting regular security-focused code reviews to detect vulnerabilities before deployment.
2. **Security Testing:** Performing penetration tests and security assessments during development and pre-release to identify and address vulnerabilities.
3. **Training and Awareness:** Educating developers and staff on best security practices and associated risks to foster a culture of security within the organization.

5.9.5. Conclusion

Incorporating security measures into software architecture from the start is essential to prevent vulnerabilities and protect system integrity. By applying the principle of least privilege, validating inputs, and encrypting data, software architects can build more secure and resilient systems. Security is a shared and ongoing responsibility, and its integration into the software development lifecycle is crucial for the success and sustainability of any application.

5.10. SOFTWARE ARCHITECTURE DOCUMENTATION

Software architecture documentation is a crucial aspect that enables development teams to understand and maintain the system effectively over time. Well-structured and clear documentation not only aids current developers but also facilitates onboarding new team members and improves collaboration. Below are the key elements that should be included in architecture documentation.

5.10.1. Component Description

Detailed documentation of system components is essential to understand how they interact and work together. This section should include:

- **Component Identification**: A list of all system components, such as modules, services, libraries, and databases. Each component should have a clear and descriptive name.

- **Functions and Responsibilities:** For each component, provide a description of its functions and responsibilities within the system. This includes what it does, how it contributes to the system, and its importance in the overall application flow.

- **Interactions and Dependencies:** Detail how the components communicate with each other. This includes identifying APIs, protocols, and data formats used in interactions, as well as any external dependencies that may affect the component's functioning.

- **Performance Considerations:** Include information about the expected performance of each component and any known limitations, which can help in scalability planning and optimization.

-Benefits:

- **Design Clarity:** Facilitates understanding of the system design and the role of each component.

- **Efficient Maintenance:** Provides guidance for developers who need to modify or update components in the future.

5.10.2. Architectural Diagrams

Architectural diagrams are key visual tools that represent the system structure in a comprehensible manner. This section may include:

- **Component Diagram:** Shows how different system components are related and the interfaces through which they communicate.

- **Data Flow Diagram:** Represents how data flows through the system, identifying data sources, destinations, and the processes involved in manipulating the data.

- **Deployment Diagram:** Illustrates how components are deployed in the infrastructure, including servers, networks, and other necessary resources.

- **Sequence Diagrams:** Represent interactions between components over time, showing the order in which interactions occur.

-Benefits:

- **Clear Visualization:** Helps developers and stakeholders understand the system architecture quickly.

- **Improved Communication:** Diagrams are effective tools for discussing architecture with non-technical stakeholders, such as managers and clients.

5.10.3. Architectural Decisions

Recording architectural decisions is crucial for the system's long-term development. This section should include:

- **Key Decision Records:** Document important decisions made during architectural design, including choices of patterns, technologies, and tools.

- **Rationale Behind Decisions:** Explain why certain decisions were made, considering factors such as performance, scalability, maintainability, and alignment with business requirements.

- **Considered Alternatives:** Include a summary of alternatives that were considered and why they were discarded. This can be helpful for future reviews or to better understand the context of the decisions.

- **Potential Impact**: Evaluate how architectural decisions might affect the system in the future, which can be critical for planning system evolution.

-Benefits:

- **Transparency**: Provides a clear record of how and why the architecture was developed, facilitating audits and reviews.

- **Future Guidance**: Helps developers understand the context of past decisions when implementing changes or adding new functionalities.

5.10.4. Conclusion

Good software architecture documentation is vital for ensuring the sustainability and understanding of the system throughout its lifecycle. By including detailed component descriptions, clear architectural diagrams, and a comprehensive record of architectural decisions, you create a solid foundation that facilitates collaboration, maintenance, and software evolution. Documentation is not just a resource for the present but a valuable tool that can influence the success of future developments and system updates.

5.11. SERVICE-ORIENTED ARCHITECTURE

Service-Oriented Architecture (SOA) is an architectural approach that uses independent and well-defined services to facilitate communication and integration between different applications. SOA is based on the idea that applications can be decomposed into service components that are reusable and can interact efficiently. Below are detailed explanations of SOA's key characteristics and benefits, as well as its challenges and considerations.

5.11.1. Interoperability

- **Definition**: Interoperability is the ability of different services, developed on diverse platforms and technologies, to communicate and collaborate. In a SOA environment, services are designed to function independently of underlying programming languages, operating systems, or platforms.

- **Implementation**: This is achieved using open standards like SOAP (Simple Object Access Protocol) and REST (Representational State Transfer), enabling communication between services through common network protocols.

5.11.2. Reusability

- **Definition**: Reusability refers to the capability of using existing services across multiple applications and contexts. This not only reduces redundancy in development but also accelerates the delivery of new functionalities.

- **Benefit**: By creating modular services that encapsulate business logic, teams can focus on building new features instead of reinventing the wheel, improving development efficiency and reducing costs.

5.11.3. Flexibility

- **Definition**: Flexibility refers to the ability to adapt and evolve the application architecture agilely. In a SOA system, services can be added, modified, or removed without affecting the system as a whole.

- **Advantage**: This feature is especially valuable in business environments where requirements change rapidly, as it allows organizations to respond effectively to new market demands.

5.11.4. Benefits of SOA

1. **Simple Integration:** SOA facilitates the integration of various applications and systems, both internal and external, which is especially useful for companies using multiple platforms and technologies.

2. **Improved Productivity:** By enabling service reuse, development teams can focus on building new features, resulting in greater productivity and efficiency.

3. **Ease of Maintenance:** Since services are decoupled, any change to a specific service does not directly affect others, reducing the risk of introducing errors and simplifying maintenance.

4. **Scalability:** SOA allows for independent scaling of services, which is crucial for handling increased workloads without restructuring the entire architecture.

5. **Adaptability to Change:** The ability to quickly adapt or replace services makes SOA ideal for organizations that need to continuously evolve in a dynamic business environment.

5.11.5. Challenges and Considerations in SOA

- **Implementation Complexity**: Designing and implementing a service-oriented architecture can be complex, especially for organizations without prior experience in this approach. Careful design and planning are required.

- **Service Management**: As more services are created, managing versions, monitoring performance, and ensuring availability becomes a critical challenge.

- **Performance**: Communication between services over a network can introduce latencies, which may affect overall system performance. It is essential to optimize interactions and minimize unnecessary service calls.

- **Security**: Ensuring security in a SOA environment can be challenging, as security measures must be implemented for each service and in the communication between them.

5.11.6. Conclusion

Service-Oriented Architecture (SOA) provides a powerful and flexible framework for building modern, scalable software systems. By focusing on reusability, interoperability, and flexibility, SOA enables organizations to quickly adapt to changing business needs and facilitates the integration of various applications and systems. However, addressing the challenges associated with its implementation and management is essential to maximize benefits and ensure a robust and efficient architecture.

5.12. SOFTWARE ARCHITECTURE PRACTICES FOR HIGH AVAILABILITY SYSTEMS

High availability (HA) refers to a system's ability to remain operational and accessible for extended periods, minimizing downtime. This is crucial for mission-critical applications where service continuity is paramount. Achieving high availability requires the implementation of several architectural practices that strengthen system resilience. These practices are detailed below.

5.12.1. Redundancy

- **Definition**: Redundancy involves duplicating critical components within the architecture to prevent functionality loss in the event of failures. This applies to various system elements, including servers, databases, networks, and storage.

- Implementation:

- **Duplicated Servers**: Use multiple servers that can perform interchangeably. If one fails, another can take over without interrupting service.

- **Data Backups:** Implement real-time or scheduled backups of databases and critical data, storing them in geographically distinct locations to protect against local disasters.

- **Network Components:** Employ redundant switches, routers, and network links to eliminate single points of failure in the network infrastructure.

5.12.2. Load Balancing

•   **Definition**: Load balancing involves distributing workloads across multiple servers or resources to ensure none are overwhelmed, which could affect performance and availability.

- Implementation:

•   **Load Balancers**: Use hardware or software load balancers to direct user traffic equitably to available servers. This not only enhances availability but also optimizes performance.

•   **Dynamic Scalability**: Implement auto-scaling techniques that add or remove servers in real time based on demand. This ensures sufficient resources are available during peak loads.

•   **Balancing Algorithms:** Use different balancing algorithms, such as round-robin, least connections, or IP hash, depending on traffic characteristics and application needs.

5.12.3. Monitoring and Alerts

•   **Definition**: Continuously monitoring system performance and availability is critical to detecting issues before they affect users.

- Implementation:

•   **Monitoring Tools:** Employ solutions that provide complete visibility into the infrastructure and applications. This includes monitoring server health, application performance, and network metrics.

•   **Real-Time Alerts:** Set up alerts to notify administrators about potential issues, such as server crashes, unusual load spikes, or high latency. This allows rapid response, minimizing downtime.

•   **Trend Analysis:** Implement historical performance analyses to identify patterns and predict future issues. This aids in capacity planning and resource optimization.

5.12.4. Proactive Maintenance

•   **Definition**: Regular maintenance and system updates help prevent failures.

- Implementation:

- **Resilience Testing:** Periodically simulate failure scenarios to ensure backup and recovery systems function properly.

- **Scheduled Updates:** Plan and execute software and hardware updates during defined maintenance windows to minimize user impact.

5.12.5. Deployment Across Multiple Availability Zones

- **Definition:** Use multiple data centers in different geographic locations to ensure that a failure in one zone does not affect global service availability.

- Implementation:

- **Data Replication:** Implement real-time data replication between different data centers to ensure information is always accessible.

- **Automatic Failover:** Configure failover systems to automatically switch to an alternate data center in the event of an outage.

5.12.6. Conclusion on High Availability Practices

High availability architectural practices are essential to ensuring services remain accessible to users. By implementing redundancy, load balancing, continuous monitoring, and proactive maintenance, organizations can minimize downtime and quickly respond to performance and availability issues. These practices not only improve system resilience but also enhance the user experience, fostering trust in the applications and services provided.

5.13. CHAPTER CONCLUSIONS

Software architecture is a critical discipline that impacts all aspects of software development. From choosing architectural patterns to considering scalability, performance, and security, every architectural decision significantly affects system success. Understanding these concepts and applying best practices will enable software architects to create robust, efficient, and adaptable systems that meet the changing needs of users and the market.

CHAPTER 6
CODING PRINCIPLES

Coding is the process of writing instructions in a programming language to make a computer perform specific tasks. This chapter explores the fundamental principles that guide effective coding, covering everything from basic concepts to advanced practices.

6.1. CODING FUNDAMENTALS

Coding is the process of writing instructions in a programming language to make a computer perform specific tasks. Mastering the fundamentals of coding is crucial for developing efficient and maintainable programs. These fundamentals encompass several essential aspects that guide the software development process:

6.1.1. Syntax

- **Definition**: Syntax in a programming language refers to the set of rules that specify how instructions should be written and organized in that language. Each language has its own syntax, dictating the structure of variables, functions, operators, and statements.

-Importance:

- **Error Prevention**: Understanding syntax helps avoid compilation or runtime errors, as even a minor mistake like a missing semicolon can cause a program to fail.

- **Readability**: Adhering to proper syntax makes the code easier to read and understand, which is crucial when working in teams.

-Examples:

- In Python, the syntax for defining a function is def function_name():.

- In JavaScript, code blocks are enclosed in curly braces {}.

6.1.2. Semantics

- **Definition**: Semantics refers to the meaning of the instructions written in a programming language. While syntax focuses on the correct structure of code, semantics emphasizes the behavior that results from it.

-Importance:

- **Expected Behavior**: Understanding semantics ensures developers can anticipate how their programs will behave under different scenarios, meeting established requirements.

- **Efficient Debugging**: When a program behaves unexpectedly, knowledge of semantics helps identify and fix logical errors.

-Examples:

- In C++, the expression a = b + c means that the value of b plus c is assigned to a. Syntax defines how the expression is written, while semantics defines the operation performed.

- In Python, the semantic meaning of x.append(y) is adding the element y to the end of the list x.

6.1.3. Control Structures

- **Definition**: Control structures are instructions that determine the flow of execution in a program, enabling certain sections of code to run based on conditions or repetitions.

-Common Types:

- **Conditionals**: Execute code blocks if specific conditions are met. Examples include if, else, and switch in various languages.

- **Loops**: Facilitate the repetition of code blocks while a condition is met. Common examples are for, while, and do-while.

- **Exception Handling**: Manage errors and exceptions during program execution, using constructs like try, catch, and finally in Java and Python.

-Importance:

- **Execution Efficiency:** Using loops instead of repeating code manually can reduce code length and improve efficiency.

- **Logical Flow Control:** Conditional structures allow programs to make dynamic decisions based on varying inputs and scenarios.

6.1.4. Variables and Data Types

- **Definition:** Variables are containers for storing values, and data types determine the class of values they can store, such as numbers, text strings, and booleans.

-Importance:

- **Efficient Memory Usage**: Choosing the right data type optimizes memory usage and improves program performance.
- **Data Manipulation:** Variables enable flexible manipulation of different data types, essential for program logic.

Examples:

- In Java, int is used for integers, while String is used for text strings.
- In JavaScript, let and const define variables with different scopes.

6.1.5. Functions and Modularity

- **Definition**: Functions are reusable code blocks that perform specific tasks. Modularity refers to dividing a program into smaller, manageable modules.

-Importance:

- **Code Reusability:** Functions eliminate duplication by encapsulating common tasks that can be called in different parts of a program.
- **Maintainability:** Breaking code into functions and modules enhances clarity and simplifies maintenance.

-Examples:

- In Python, a function is defined with def function_name():.
- In JavaScript, a function can be defined as function functionName() {}.

6.1.6. Algorithms

- **Definition**: An algorithm is a set of instructions that describe how to solve a problem or perform a specific task efficiently.

Importance:

- **Optimization**: Well-designed algorithms reduce a program's execution time and resource usage.

- **Problem-Solving:** Algorithms decompose complex problems into simpler steps executable by a machine.

-Examples:

- Search algorithms, such as binary search.
- Sorting algorithms, such as quicksort and mergesort.

6.1.7. Conclusion

Mastering the fundamentals of coding is essential for any software developer, as they form the foundation for building robust and efficient applications. The combination of precise syntax, a deep understanding of semantics, and the appropriate use of control structures allows developers to create programs that meet technical requirements while remaining easy to maintain and scale. Coding, like any other skill, improves with continuous practice and exploration of diverse languages and programming paradigms.

6.2. MOST USED PROGRAMMING LANGUAGES

In software development, the choice of programming language is crucial as it affects the efficiency, scalability, and development time of a project. Each language has unique characteristics that make it suitable for different types of applications and environments. Some of the most commonly used languages include:

6.2.1. Python

-Features:

• Renowned for its simplicity and syntax, which is close to natural language, making it easy for beginners to learn.

• Supports multiple programming paradigms, such as object-oriented programming (OOP) and functional programming.

• Extensive standard library and a vast number of third-party libraries, enabling the resolution of complex problems with less code.

-Applications:

• **Data Science and Machine Learning:** Libraries like NumPy, pandas, scikit-learn, and TensorFlow have made Python the go-to language for data analysis and machine learning model development.

• **Web Development:** Frameworks such as Django and Flask simplify the creation of robust and scalable web applications.

• **Automation and Scripting:** Popular for creating scripts that automate repetitive tasks.

• **Advantages**: Flexibility, large community, and abundant documentation.

- **Disadvantages**: It can be slower than other languages due to runtime interpretation.

6.2.2. JavaScript

-Features:

- An interpreted language primarily executed in browsers, though its server-side use has grown with Node.js.
- The essential language for developing interactive and dynamic web applications.
- Supports object-oriented and functional programming.

-Applications:

- **Frontend Development:** Used alongside HTML and CSS to create user interfaces for web applications.
- **Backend Development:** With Node.js, JavaScript has become a popular choice for server-side development, enabling the use of a single language across the stack.
- **Mobile Application Development**: Frameworks like React Native allow for building native mobile applications using JavaScript.
- **Advantages**: Large community, versatility, and the ability to develop full-stack applications with one language.
- **Disadvantages**: Handling asynchronous operations and callbacks can be challenging for beginners.

6.2.3. Java

- Características:

-Features:

- An object-oriented programming language compiled into bytecode and executed on the Java Virtual Machine (JVM).
- Known for its "write once, run anywhere" capability, thanks to JVM portability.
- Strongly typed, reducing errors and enhancing security in large

applications.

-Applications:

• **Enterprise Applications**: Widely adopted for enterprise-level applications due to its robustness and support for frameworks like Spring.

• **Mobile Development:** The primary language for Android app development until Kotlin's introduction.

• **Embedded Systems and Backend:** Used in high-performance servers and systems requiring high availability.

•   **Advantages**: Stability, portability, and a solid ecosystem of tools.

•   **Disadvantages**: More verbose syntax compared to modern languages, leading to longer code.

6.2.4. C#

-Features:

• A language developed by Microsoft, part of the .NET platform.

• Object-oriented, with modern features that facilitate clean and efficient code.

• Closely integrated with Microsoft's ecosystem of tools and services, such as Visual Studio and Azure.

-Applications:

• **Desktop Applications:** Ideal for creating native Windows applications.

• **Game Development:** The primary language for the Unity game engine, widely used for 2D and 3D game creation.

• **Web Applications:** High-performance web applications can be developed with ASP.NET.

•   **Advantages:** Strong compatibility with Microsoft's services and a thriving game development community.

•   **Disadvantages**: Dependence on the Microsoft ecosystem and limited portability outside of it.

6.2.5. C++

-Features:

• A low-level programming language offering detailed control over memory management and hardware.

• Supports object-oriented, generic, and metaprogramming.

• Enables resource optimization, making it ideal for performance-critical applications.

-Applications:

• **Operating Systems:** Used in developing operating systems like Windows and Linux.

• **Video Games and Graphics Engines:** Widely used in game engines like Unreal Engine for leveraging hardware capabilities.

• **High-Performance Software:** Applications requiring memory efficiency, such as databases and scientific simulations.

•   **Advantages**: High efficiency and control over hardware.

•   **Disadvantages**: Steeper learning curve and higher risk of errors like memory leaks due to manual memory management.

6.2.6. Other Popular Languages

• **Kotlin**: A modern and concise language gaining popularity for Android development, offering interoperability with Java and advanced features.

• **Swift**: Developed by Apple for creating iOS and macOS applications, known for its speed and user-friendly syntax.

• **Go** (Golang): Created by Google, it is famous for its efficiency and capability to handle high-performance and concurrent systems, making it popular in microservices development.

6.2.7. Language Selection

The choice of programming language depends on several factors, such as the project type, technical requirements, learning curve, community, and available tools. Some aspects to consider include:

• **Project Objective:** For instance, C# with Unity might be preferred for game development, while Python is better for data analysis.

- **Target Platform:** Languages like Swift and Kotlin are optimal for iOS and Android mobile development, respectively.

- **Performance Requirements**: C++ and Rust are ideal for applications requiring fine control over system resources.

- **Developer Availability:** Languages with large communities like JavaScript and Python make it easier to hire developers and access learning resources.

Understanding the strengths and weaknesses of each language is crucial to making informed decisions, optimizing the software development process, and ensuring the use of appropriate tools for each situation.

6.3. ALGORITHMS

An algorithm is a set of well-defined steps to solve a problem or perform a task systematically. They are the foundation of programming and play a crucial role in the optimization and performance of applications. Understanding the principles and types of algorithms enables programmers to tackle complex problems efficiently and effectively. The key aspects of algorithms are outlined below:

6.3.1. Efficiency

- **Definition**: Algorithm efficiency refers to the measurement of how it utilizes resources such as runtime (speed) and memory space.

- **Temporal Analysis (Execution Time):** Evaluates how long an algorithm takes to execute based on the input size (n). It is typically expressed using Big O notation, which describes the worst-case scenario, such as $O(n)$, $O(\log n)$, $O(n^2)$, and others.

- **Spatial Analysis (Memory Usage):** Considers the amount of memory required by an algorithm, including variables, data structures, and temporary storage space.

- **Importance**: Choosing an efficient algorithm is crucial, especially when working with large datasets, as it can mean the difference between a solution running in seconds or hours.

6.3.2. Complexity

- **Temporal Complexity:** Measures how an algorithm's execution time changes as the input size increases. Examples:

- $O(1)$: Constant time; execution time does not change with input size.

- $O(n)$: Linear time; execution time grows linearly with input size.

- $O(n^2)$: Quadratic time; execution time grows quadratically, making it less efficient for large inputs.

- **Spatial Complexity:** Measures the memory usage of the algorithm based on the input size, including variables, arrays, and temporary structures.

- **Optimization:** Good algorithm design seeks to optimize both temporal and spatial complexity, which is essential in hardware-constrained environments and high-performance systems.

6.3.3. Types of Algorithms

Various types of algorithms solve different kinds of problems. Some of the most common include:

-Search Algorithms:

- **Linear Search:** Scans a list or array from start to finish to find a specific element. Complexity: $O(n)$.

- **Binary Search:** Requires a sorted list and repeatedly divides it in half to find the element. Complexity: $O(\log n)$.

- **Graph Search Algorithms:** Includes BFS (Breadth-First Search) and DFS (Depth-First Search) for traversing nodes and edges in a graph.

-Sorting Algorithms:

- **Bubble Sort:** Successive comparisons between adjacent elements. Complexity: $O(n^2)$.

- **Quick Sort:** Uses the "divide and conquer" technique to divide and sort recursively. Average complexity: $O(n \log n)$.

- **Merge Sort:** Divides the list into smaller parts, sorts them, and merges them. Complexity: $O(n \log n)$.

-Recursive Algorithms:

- Use self-calling techniques to solve smaller problems of the same type, such as calculating factorials or Fibonacci sequences.

- Proper recursion handling is crucial to avoid stack overflows and ensure efficient performance.

-Dynamic Programming Algorithms:

- Solve problems by breaking them into overlapping subproblems and storing partial solutions to avoid redundant calculations.

- Classic examples include the "knapsack problem" and finding the longest common subsequence (LCS).

- Enhance efficiency, reducing complexity from $O(2^n)$ to $O(n^2)$ or $O(n*m)$.

-Greedy Algorithms:

- Make locally optimal choices with the hope of finding a globally optimal solution.

- Useful in problems like coin change, minimum spanning trees (Prim's and Kruskal's algorithms), and activity selection.

- Their simplicity and speed are advantages, but they do not always guarantee optimal solutions.

6.3.4. Algorithm Design and Optimization

-Divide and Conquer:

- Divide the problem into smaller subproblems, solve them recursively, and combine the solutions. Examples: Quick Sort and Merge Sort.

- Especially useful for problems that can be decomposed into independent tasks.

-Backtracking:

- Explores all possible solutions to a problem by making decisions and backtracking when a solution proves unviable.

- Applied in combinatorial problems like the n-queens problem or maze solving.

-Memoization and Caching:

- Stores results of already-solved subproblems to avoid repeated calculations, enhancing the performance of recursive algorithms.

6.3.5. Algorithm Analysis

- **Big O Notation:** Provides a way to describe the asymptotic behavior of an algorithm's execution time as input size grows.

- **Best Case:** The most favorable behavior of the algorithm.

- **Worst Case:** The least favorable behavior, important to ensure efficiency in all scenarios.

- **Average Case:** The expected average performance, useful for algorithms with significantly variable performance.

- **Benchmarking**: Measures the real execution time of an algorithm on different inputs to understand its practical performance, especially useful for comparing solutions.

6.3.6. Importance of Algorithms in Software Development

- **Resource Optimization:** Well-designed algorithms allow applications to consume fewer resources, critical in memory- and processing-constrained environments.

- **Scalability**: Efficient algorithms ensure that applications can handle large data volumes and users without performance degradation.

- **Complex Problem Solving:** Enable developers to address computation-intensive problems like scientific simulations, data analysis, and image processing.

- **Improved User Experience:** Efficient search and sorting algorithms reduce wait times in user interfaces, enhancing the usability of applications.

A strong understanding of algorithms and their design not only helps programmers write more efficient code but also enables them to make strategic decisions about the best ways to approach and solve complex problems in software development.

6.4. PROGRAMMING LOGIC

Programming logic is an essential skill that enables developers to approach problems in a structured and effective way using programming. It goes beyond knowing a specific programming language, focusing on applying logical principles and algorithms to break down problems, identify patterns, and create robust solutions. Strong programming logic leads to applications that are not only functional but also efficient and maintainable. Below are the key elements of programming logic:

6.4.1. Decomposition

-Definition:

Decomposition involves breaking down a complex problem into smaller, manageable subproblems. This helps understand each part of the problem and tackle it progressively.

-Advantages:

- **Clarity**: Improves understanding of the entire problem by analyzing it in parts.

- **Code Reusability:** Allows for creating modular and reusable solutions, useful in software development.

- **Maintainability**: Simplifies code maintenance and modification, as changes can be made to specific modules without impacting the entire system.

-Examples:

- **Developing a web application:** Breaking it into user interface creation, server-side data management, and connecting the two.

- **Creating a video game:** Dividing tasks into character control logic, game physics, and level design.

6.4.2. Pattern Recognition

-Definition:

Pattern recognition means identifying common problems that have been solved previously and applying known solutions to address new challenges.

-Advantages:

- **Efficiency**: Reuse proven solutions instead of reinventing the wheel.
- **Error Reduction**: Reduces the likelihood of mistakes by using established design patterns.

-Types of Patterns:

- **Design Patterns:** General reusable solutions for common software design problems, such as Singleton, Observer, or Factory patterns.
- **Algorithmic Patterns:** Standard solutions for algorithmic issues, like binary search for sorted lists or dynamic programming for optimization problems.

-Examples:

- Recognizing that a data organization problem can be solved using a binary tree.
- Applying the MVC (Model-View-Controller) design pattern to structure web and mobile applications.

6.4.3. Flow Control

-Definition:

Flow control refers to how the execution of a program is directed based on specific conditions and control structures. It is crucial for decision-making and repeating tasks within a program.

-Key Control Structures:

- **Conditionals (if, else, switch)**: Execute different blocks of code depending on whether a condition is true or false.

- **Example**: Using an if statement to verify if a user has entered the correct password before granting access.

- **Loops (for, while, do-while)**: Repeat the execution of a block of code as long as a specific condition is met.

-Example: Using a for loop to iterate over a list of products and calculate the total price.

- **Control Exit Structures (break, continue):** Modify loop flow, such as exiting a loop early or skipping to the next iteration.

-Importance:

- **Flexibility**: Enables dynamic responses to various situations.

- **Precise Control:** Developers can handle tasks within a program accurately, essential for optimizing performance and efficiency.

6.4.4. Abstraction

-Definition:

Abstraction is the process of simplifying problems by focusing on relevant features and hiding unnecessary details. In programming, it translates to creating functions, classes, or modules that encapsulate specific behaviors.

-Advantages:

- **Modularity**: Facilitates the creation of code organized into independent components.

- **Reusability**: Abstractions allow functions or classes to be reused across different parts of an application.

- **Complexity Reduction**: Simplifies development by isolating complex logic into functions or modules.

-Examples:

- Writing a function to encapsulate database connection logic so the rest of the code doesn't need to handle connection details.

- Using classes to represent problem entities, such as an Employee class in a personnel management system.

6.4.5. Algorithmic Thinking

-Definition:

Algorithmic thinking involves structured problem-solving to design algorithms that address specific problems. It requires identifying necessary steps, their execution order, and potential edge cases.

-Key Components:

- **Solution Planning:** Analyzing the problem and designing a series of steps or a flowchart to represent the solution before coding.
- **Optimization**: Finding the most efficient way to solve the problem, using minimal resources and time.

-Examples:

- Designing an algorithm to find the shortest path between two points on a map.
- Creating an algorithm to analyze large datasets and identify user behavior patterns.

6.4.6. Solving Complex Problems

-Definition:

Programming logic allows developers to tackle complex problems by breaking them into manageable steps. This is essential for creating robust applications that adapt to various situations and demands.

-Examples:

- Developing an application to process bank transactions, considering different types of operations and security validations.
- Implementing a recommendation system that analyzes user behavior to suggest relevant products or content.

-Importance of Developing Strong Programming Logic

- **Efficiency in Development:** Programmers with strong logic quickly identify the best way to solve a problem, reducing development time.

- **Code Quality:** Well-applied logic leads to cleaner, more understandable, and maintainable code, resulting in higher-quality software.

- **Adaptability**: A solid foundation in programming logic makes it easier to learn new languages and technologies, as the underlying principles remain consistent.

- **Real-Time Problem Solving**: Critical when debugging or resolving issues in real-time, requiring quick and structured thinking.

Mastering programming logic is essential for any programmer aspiring to create effective and efficient solutions. By excelling in problem decomposition, pattern recognition, flow control, and algorithmic thinking, developers can handle everything from simple tasks to the most complex challenges in software development. This skill is fundamental not only for writing code but also for designing systems that work reliably and efficiently.

6.5. BASIC DESIGN PATTERNS

Design patterns are proven and reusable solutions to recurring problems in software development. They serve as templates that can be adapted to solve specific design problems in different contexts. Using design patterns facilitates writing cleaner, more structured, and maintainable code while improving communication among developers by providing a common language. Below are some of the most widely used basic design patterns:

6.5.1. Singleton

- **Description**: The Singleton pattern ensures that a class has only one instance throughout the application and provides a global access point to that instance. It is useful when a single object is needed to coordinate actions across the system.

-Common Applications:

- **Configuration management**: A single instance storing application settings.

- **Database connections:** Ensures only one active database connection to prevent concurrency issues.

-Advantages:

- **Access control:** Simplifies access to global resources.

- **Memory efficiency:** Saves resources by avoiding multiple instances.

- **Example**: In a game, a Singleton could manage the global game state, such as user preferences or sound settings.

- **Description**: The Factory Method pattern defines an interface for creating objects but allows subclasses to decide which class to instantiate. This promotes object creation without specifying the exact class that will be created.

-Common Applications:

•   **Creating complex objects:** When object creation is complex and varies by context.

•   **Interoperability**: Helps applications adapt to future changes without relying on a specific class.

-Advantages:

•   **Decoupling**: Separates object creation from its use, simplifying maintenance and extensibility.

•   **Scalability**: Allows developers to add new object types without altering existing code.

•   **Example:** In a payment application, a Factory Method could create different payment methods (e.g., credit card, PayPal, bank transfer) based on user choice.

6.5.3. Observer

•   **Description**: The Factory Method pattern defines an interface for creating objects but allows subclasses to decide which class to instantiate. This promotes object creation without specifying the exact class that will be created.

-Common Applications:

•   **Creating complex objects**: When object creation is complex and varies by context.

•   **Interoperability**: Helps applications adapt to future changes without relying on a specific class.

-Advantages:

•   **Decoupling**: Separates object creation from its use, simplifying maintenance and extensibility.

•   **Scalability**: Allows developers to add new object types without altering existing code.

- **Example**: In a payment application, a Factory Method could create different payment methods (e.g., credit card, PayPal, bank transfer) based on user choice.

6.5.4. Decorator

- **Description**: The Decorator pattern allows adding additional functionality to an object dynamically without altering its structure. It serves as an alternative to inheritance, enabling behavior extension through composition.

-Common Applications:

- **User interfaces:** Adding features like borders, shadows, or background colors to UI components.
- **Data processing:** Adding behaviors like compression or encryption to data streams.

-Advantages:

- **Flexibility**: Enables adding functionalities without changing the base code.
- **Behavior combination**: Multiple decorators can be combined to create objects with various features.
- **Example**: In a notification system, a notification object could be decorated with additional functionality, such as sending via email or SMS.

6.5.5. Strategy

- **Description**: The Strategy pattern defines a family of algorithms and allows each one to be interchangeable. Algorithms are encapsulated in separate classes, enabling flexible behavior changes without modifying the code that uses them.

-Common Applications:

- **Fee calculation:** Switching the fee calculation strategy based on shipping methods.
- **Sorting systems**: Selecting different sorting strategies depending on data size.

-Advantages:

- **Maintainability**: Each algorithm is isolated, simplifying modifications.

- **Extensibility**: New strategies can be added easily without altering existing code.

- **Example**: In a video game, different AI strategies (aggressive, defensive, exploratory) can be dynamically assigned to a character based on difficulty levels.

6.5.6. Adapter

- **Description**: The Adapter pattern allows two incompatible interfaces to work together. It acts as a bridge between two classes that would otherwise be unable to interact.

Common Applications:

- **Third-party libraries:** Enables the use of libraries that lack a compatible interface.

- **Data conversion:** Adapts different data formats between systems.

-Advantages:

- **Code reuse:** Facilitates reusing existing classes without modifying them.

- **Interoperability**: Integrates software components with different interfaces.

- **Example**: In a media application, an Adapter could convert an audio library's format to another format supported by the main player.

6.5.7. Model-View-Controller (MVC)

- **Description**: Though more of an architectural pattern, MVC is fundamental for organizing applications with user interfaces. It separates an application into three main components:

- **Model**: Manages data and business logic.
- **View**: Displays the data visually.
- **Controller**: Acts as an intermediary between the view and model,

handling user interactions.

-Common Applications:

•   **Web development**: Used in frameworks like Django, Ruby on Rails, and ASP.NET to structure application logic.

-Advantages:

•   **Responsibility separation:** Simplifies application maintenance and scalability.

•   **Reusability**: Views and controllers can change without affecting the underlying model.

•   **Example**: In an e-commerce application, the model handles product data, the view displays product lists and cart information, and the controller manages user interactions with the cart.

6.5.8. Importance of Design Patterns

•   **Facilitate Collaboration**: By providing a common language, design patterns improve communication among developers.

•   **Promote Best Practices**: They encapsulate years of experience solving common problems, encouraging good practices from the outset.

•   **Enhance Code Quality:** Applying design patterns results in cleaner, more readable, and maintainable code.

Design patterns are a powerful tool in a software developer's arsenal. When used appropriately, they enable the creation of more robust, adaptable, and maintainable solutions, reducing development complexity and ensuring efficient system design.

6.6. CODE OPTIMIZATION

Code optimization is the process of refining and enhancing a program to make it run faster, consume fewer resources, and execute more efficiently. While prioritizing code clarity and readability is essential, proper optimization can be crucial in large-scale systems or applications requiring high performance. Optimization practices include:

6.6.1. Eliminating Redundancies

- **Description**: Identifying and removing duplicate or unnecessary code is one of the simplest ways to optimize a program. This not only improves performance but also enhances code maintainability and readability.

-Common Practices:

- **Refactoring**: Reorganizing code to make it cleaner and more efficient.
- **Reusable Functions:** Extracting repeated code blocks into reusable functions or methods.
- **Example:** If a mathematical operation is repeated in several places, encapsulating it in a function can reduce code size and improve consistency.

6.6.2. Efficient Use of Data Structures

- **Description**: Selecting the right data structure can significantly impact a program's performance. Proper data structures allow for faster operations and reduced memory usage.

-Common Practices:

- **Choosing the Right Structure**: For instance, using a HashMap for quick lookups instead of an ArrayList when key-based access is needed.

- **Memory Optimization:** Using memory-efficient structures, such as linked lists, to avoid overhead from large arrays.

- **Example:** In a social media application, using a set to store unique user IDs can be more efficient than a list, as it avoids duplicates and enables faster lookups.

6.6.3. Profiling and Identifying Bottlenecks

- **Description**: Profiling involves analyzing code to pinpoint areas that consume the most resources or execution time. Profiling tools help identify bottlenecks, such as slow functions or excessive memory usage.

-Common Practices:

- **Execution Time Analysis:** Measuring the time each part of the code takes to identify areas needing optimization.

- **Memory Usage Monitoring**: Detecting memory leaks and oversized objects.

- **Example**: In a web application, profiling might reveal slow database queries, which could be addressed by optimizing SQL statements or adding indexes.

6.6.4. Algorithm Optimization

- **Description**: Choosing the right algorithm for each task is crucial for code efficiency. A suboptimal algorithm can make an application slow and resource-intensive, especially with large datasets.

-Common Practices:

- **Reducing Time Complexity:** Opting for algorithms with better time efficiency, such as moving from an $O(n^2)$ sorting algorithm to an $O(n \log n)$ one.

- **Optimal Search and Sorting Algorithms:** Using algorithms like binary search instead of linear search for ordered data.

- **Example**: For searching an element in a sorted list, binary search ($O(\log n)$) is much faster than sequential search ($O(n)$).

6.6.5. Efficient Memory Usage

- **Description**: Optimizing memory usage is essential to prevent applications from consuming unnecessary resources, which is especially critical for mobile devices or systems with limited resources.

-Common Practices:

- **Avoiding Unnecessary Object Creation**: Reusing object instances whenever possible, particularly in loops.

- **Releasing Resources:** Ensuring proper cleanup of resources like database connections, open files, and memory-heavy variables.

- **Example**: In mobile app development, managing object lifecycles effectively helps prevent memory leaks that could slow down or crash the app.

6.6.6. Parallelism and Concurrency

- **Description**: Leveraging modern processors 'ability to perform multiple tasks simultaneously can significantly enhance a program's performance. This is achieved through threads and parallel processes.

-Common Practices:

- **Multithreading:** Distributing intensive tasks across multiple threads to execute processes concurrently.

- **Asynchronous Processing**: Using asynchronous operations for I/O tasks to prevent blocking the program flow.

- **Example**: In an image processing application, parallel threads can handle each image simultaneously, reducing overall processing time.

6.6.7. Minimizing Costly Operations

- **Description**: Identifying and minimizing time-consuming operations, such as disk access, network operations, or complex mathematical computations, can improve overall performance.

-Common Practices:

- **Result Caching:** Storing the output of complex calculations to avoid recalculating them repeatedly.

- **Batching**: Grouping I/O operations to reduce overhead.

- **Example**: In a data analysis application, caching intermediate results instead of repeatedly querying the database can dramatically speed up performance.

6.6.8. Following Good Programming Practices

- **Description**: Optimization is not just about specific code tweaks but also about adhering to good practices from the beginning of development. This includes writing clean, modular, and maintainable code.

-Common Practices:

- **Code Simplification**: Avoiding unnecessarily complex structures and methods.
- **Modularization**: Dividing code into small, specific functions or methods for easier optimization.
- **Example**: Instead of writing a single, extensive method performing multiple tasks, breaking it into smaller functions makes it easier to identify and optimize performance-impacting sections.

6.6.9. The Importance of Code Optimization

- **Enhanced User Experience:** Optimized code reduces application load and response times, resulting in a better user experience.
- **Lower Infrastructure Costs:** Efficient resource usage enables applications to run on lower-capacity servers, saving infrastructure costs.
- **Scalability**: Optimized code makes it easier to scale applications as the user base grows, as fewer resources are required per user.
- **Sustainable Maintenance**: Efficient, well-structured code is easier to maintain and update, reducing the risk of future errors and simplifying the addition of new features.

Code optimization is a continuous process that must be balanced with readability and clarity. Premature optimization, which complicates program structure without a clear understanding of performance needs, should be avoided. However, when done correctly, optimization can transform a system from merely functional to outstandingly performant.

6.7. SECURE PROGRAMMING PRACTICES

Secure programming focuses on creating software that is resistant to attacks, minimizing vulnerabilities that could be exploited by attackers. Given the increase in cyberattacks and strict privacy regulations, implementing secure programming practices is essential to protect both applications and user data. Key practices include:

6.7.1. Input Validation

- Description: Validating user input is crucial to prevent code injection attacks, such as SQL injection and Cross-Site Scripting (XSS). Validation ensures that the provided data is correct and in the expected format.

-Common Practices:

- Data Sanitization: Clean inputs to remove harmful characters that could be used in an attack.

- Whitelist Usage: Accept only predefined and expected values instead of trying to block suspicious ones.

- Example: When processing a login form, it is essential to validate that the username does not contain special characters that could alter the SQL query.

6.7.2. Session Handling

- Description: Sessions are mechanisms used to maintain the user's state while interacting with an application. Protecting these sessions is critical to prevent session hijacking and identity spoofing.

-Common Practices:

- Secure Cookies: Configure cookies with Secure and HttpOnly flags to prevent interception by third parties.

- Session Expiry: Set expiration times for inactive sessions to reduce the risk of attackers exploiting an open session.

- CSRF Protection: Use CSRF tokens to ensure that requests originate from the same application.

- Example: In a banking application, ensuring that a user's session expires after a few minutes of inactivity can prevent an attacker from accessing the account if the user leaves their device unattended.

6.7.3. Data Encryption

- Description: Encryption is the conversion of data into a format that can only be read by someone with the encryption key. It is essential for protecting sensitive information both at rest (stored) and in transit (moving between client and server).

-Common Practices:

- TLS/SSL: Use TLS/SSL encryption to secure data transmission between client and server, protecting against Man-in-the-Middle attacks.

- Database Encryption: Encrypt sensitive data in the database, such as passwords and personal information, using robust algorithms like AES.

- Secure Password Storage: Never store passwords in plaintext; instead, use hash functions like bcrypt or Argon2.

- Example: In an e-commerce application, encrypting users 'credit card information before storing it in the database ensures that, even if the database is compromised, the data will be inaccessible without the decryption key.

6.7.4. Error and Exception Management

- Description: Improper error handling can reveal internal system details that attackers could exploit. It is important to handle exceptions securely and provide error messages that do not expose the system's internal structure.

-Common Practices:

•	Hide Technical Details: Error messages displayed to the user should not include technical information such as stack traces or SQL query details.

•	Error Logging: Maintain detailed logs of errors and exceptions for analysis without compromising the application's security.

•	Example: In an authentication system, if an error occurs when validating a user, the error message should not indicate whether the problem was with the username or password, as this could facilitate brute-force attacks.

6.7.5. Access Control and Authorization

•	Description: Implementing appropriate access controls ensures that users can only access the information and functionalities they are authorized to use. This is crucial for protecting sensitive data and preventing unauthorized access.

-Common Practices:

•	Roles and Permissions: Assign roles to users and control access to different parts of the application based on these roles.

•	Authorization Checks: Validate that the user has the necessary permissions before performing critical actions, such as modifying data or accessing resources.

•	Example: In a business management application, an employee with the "user" role should not have access to financial reports, which are restricted to administrators.

6.7.6. API Security

•	Description: APIs are common entry points for applications and services, making it essential to secure their usage. This includes authentication, authorization, and request rate limiting.

-Common Practices:

•	Strong Authentication: Implement protocols like OAuth2 for secure user authentication.

•	Rate Limiting: Limit the number of requests a client can make to the API within a given period to prevent abuse and DoS attacks.

- JSON/XML Validation: Ensure that data received via the API is in the expected format and does not contain malicious payloads.

- Example: In an application using an API for payment processing, authentication with OAuth2 ensures that only authorized users can perform transactions.

6.7.7. Dependency Management and Updates

- Description: Software dependencies, such as libraries and frameworks, can contain vulnerabilities that attackers might exploit. Keeping these dependencies updated and applying security patches is crucial to reduce risks.

-Common Practices:

- Vulnerability Monitoring: Use tools like Dependabot or Snyk to detect vulnerable dependencies.

- Secure Versions: Prefer stable and well-supported versions of libraries.

- Disable Unused Features: Remove or disable unused library features to reduce the attack surface.

- Example: In a web application using an authentication library, updating to the latest version ensures protection against known vulnerabilities.

6.7.8. Security by Design

- Description: Security should not be an afterthought but an integral component from the beginning. This approach, known as "Security by Design," involves considering security at every stage of software development.

-Common Practices:

- Threat Modeling: Identify potential threats and vulnerabilities during the project's initial phases.

- Code Review: Conduct regular code audits to identify vulnerabilities and improve code quality.

- Penetration Testing: Perform active security tests to identify possible weaknesses.

- Example: When designing a new feature in a banking application, the development team conducts a threat analysis to identify potential security risks and takes preventive measures before implementation.

6.7.9. Importance of Secure Programming

Implementing secure programming practices is vital to protect the confidentiality, integrity, and availability of data and systems. Furthermore, secure programming helps comply with privacy and security regulations, such as GDPR in Europe and CCPA in California. Adopting these practices from the outset of development not only reduces attack risks but also strengthens user and customer trust in the application, creating a safer and more reliable environment.

6.8. TECHNICAL DEBT (CODE DEBT)

Technical debt is a concept that describes the consequences of taking shortcuts in software development, such as opting for quick and lower-quality solutions to meet deadlines or accelerate product launches. While these decisions may address immediate issues and enable faster releases, the price to pay is often the accumulation of problems that affect code quality and long-term maintainability. Similar to financial debt, if not addressed promptly, these decisions can generate "interest," making software evolution more challenging and future improvements costlier.

6.8.1. What is Technical Debt?

Technical debt arises when a suboptimal development solution is chosen with the intention of correcting it later. Over time, this debt accumulates, meaning the effort and time required to make corrections and improvements increase significantly. This can lead to code that is difficult to read, modify, and extend, ultimately affecting the speed and efficiency of the development team.

6.8.2. Common Types of Technical Debt

- **Poorly Documented Code**: When code is not well-documented, understanding its logic and purpose becomes more challenging for developers, especially those who were not involved in its creation. This can make adding new features or fixing bugs more time-consuming.

- **Example**: A developer writes a complex function without adding comments to explain its logic. Months later, another developer spends hours trying to understand how it works before making the necessary changes.

- **Consequence**: Lack of adequate documentation hampers

teamwork and delays maintenance tasks.

- **Outdated Dependencies:** Many applications rely on third-party libraries. If these libraries are not regularly updated, they may fall behind in terms of security, performance, and compatibility. Outdated dependencies represent a form of technical debt that can become problematic when trying to scale the system or adapt to new technologies.

- **Example**: An application uses an outdated version of an authentication library. Updating the library requires changes across multiple parts of the system, so the development team postpones the update. However, the old library contains known security vulnerabilities that could put users at risk.

- **Consequence:** Outdated dependencies can compromise system security and limit the ability to implement new features.

- **Lack of Automated Testing:** Skipping unit tests, integration tests, and other forms of automated testing to speed up development can create significant technical debt. Without tests, identifying bugs or regressions when making code changes becomes difficult.

- **Example**: A development team skips unit tests to meet a tight deadline. When a new feature is released, several undetected bugs emerge, requiring significant time to resolve unexpected issues.

- **Consequence**: Lack of testing increases the risk of introducing errors into the code, raising maintenance costs and complicating the delivery of stable releases.

6.8.3. Impact of Technical Debt

Technical debt can significantly affect the software's lifespan and the development team's productivity. Notable effects include:

- **Increased Maintenance Costs:** As technical debt accumulates, the cost of maintaining and updating the software rises. Simple modifications can become complex tasks requiring extensive refactoring.

- **Slower Development Speed:** Technical debt makes incorporating new features slower and more laborious. Each new feature must work with existing code, which may be difficult to modify due to accumulated problems.

- **Reduced Software Quality:** Code burdened with technical debt is more prone to bugs, performance issues, and security vulnerabilities. This can lead to poor user experiences and a negative perception of the product.

6.8.4. Managing Technical Debt

Effectively managing technical debt is crucial for maintaining software quality and sustainability over the long term. Strategies to manage and reduce technical debt include:

- **Identification and Assessment:** Recognizing and measuring technical debt is the first step. This involves reviewing code, identifying problematic areas, and assessing the debt's impact on future development.

- **Evaluation Techniques:** Use static code analysis tools like SonarQube to detect common issues such as excessive complexity, code duplication, and unsafe practices.

- **Continuous Refactoring:** Refactoring involves improving code without changing its external behavior. Continuous refactoring during development helps keep code clean and reduces the accumulation of technical debt.

- **Example**: A development team dedicates a small percentage of each sprint to improving code that needs refactoring. This helps them maintain clean code without significantly affecting deadlines.

- **Prioritization**: Not all technical debt can or should be addressed immediately. It is important to prioritize areas with the highest risk or impact on the project. This might include addressing critical outdated dependencies or refactoring hard-to-maintain functions.

- **Management Method**: Classify technical debt into categories like "High," "Medium," and "Low" to determine which issues should be tackled first.

- **Incorporating Technical Debt into Planning**: Include technical debt reduction in project planning and development sprints to ensure time is allocated to this aspect. This could involve assigning specific tasks for refactoring or improving automated tests.

- **Example**: During sprint planning, the team allocates 10% of the total time to addressing technical debt, such as updating a dependency or improving test coverage.

6.8.5. Benefits of Managing Technical Debt

- **Improved Stability and Maintainability:** Reducing technical debt makes software easier to maintain and update. This enhances the team's ability to add new features without introducing additional problems.

- **Reduced Security Risks:** Updating dependencies and improving code quality helps mitigate vulnerabilities and security risks, protecting both the application and user data.

- **Increased Team Productivity:** Clean, well-maintained code allows developers to work more efficiently as they can more easily understand and modify the code.

6.8.6. Conclusion: Technical Debt as a Strategic Investment

While often viewed negatively, technical debt can be used strategically if managed properly. Sometimes, incurring technical debt in early development stages is a logical decision to quickly reach the market. However, ignoring technical debt for too long can jeopardize the software's viability. Recognizing the importance of balancing development speed with code quality is key to ensuring the health and longevity of a software project.

6.9. CODE REFACTORING

Refactoring is a fundamental process in software development that involves modifying the internal structure of existing code to improve its quality without altering its observable behavior. Through refactoring, the goal is to make the code clearer, more efficient, and easier to maintain, ultimately reducing development costs and enhancing system stability. Incorporating refactoring into the workflow can significantly impact the health of a software project.

6.9.1. What is Refactoring?

Refactoring means "restructuring" the code to improve its design and organization while keeping its original functionality intact. This involves modifying how the code is written to make it cleaner and more organized without changing what it does. The idea is that the final code should produce the same output or result but be easier to understand, maintain, and expand.

- **Basic Example:** Suppose a developer has a function with a generic and unclear name, like *function1()*, that performs a specific task, such as calculating the area of a circle. Refactoring might involve renaming the function to something more descriptive, like *calculateCircleArea()*, without modifying its internal logic. While the functionality remains unchanged, the code is now more readable and its purpose evident.

6.9.2. Benefits of Refactoring

- **Improved Readability:** Code that is hard to read and understand can become problematic when adjustments are needed or new developers join the team. Refactoring makes the code more comprehensible, facilitating future maintenance and modification.

- **Example**: Renaming unclear variables such as x, y, or temp to more meaningful names like length, width, or temporaryResult.

- **Removal of Dead Code:** As a project evolves, some functions, variables, or classes may no longer be used. Dead code not only takes up unnecessary space but can also cause confusion and errors if modified accidentally. Refactoring involves identifying and removing these unused sections of code.

- **Example**: A project that has evolved over time might include functions that are no longer called from anywhere in the code. Refactoring helps identify and eliminate such functions, keeping the project clean.

- **Enhanced Maintainability:** Well-structured code is easier to update and expand with new functionalities. Refactoring allows developers to detect repetitive patterns and replace them with reusable functions, reducing the amount of code and simplifying system modifications.

- **Example**: If multiple parts of the code use the same logic to validate an email address, that logic can be extracted into a single reusable function. This way, any future changes to the email validation process only require updating one function instead of multiple code fragments.

6.9.3. When to Refactor Code

Refactoring should be a continuous process rather than something left for the end of a project. Specific times when refactoring is especially useful include:

- **Before Adding New Features**: Refactoring before adding a new feature can make the code easier to adapt to changes, reducing the effort needed to implement the new functionality.

- **After Fixing Bugs:** Once a bug has been fixed, refactoring the code can make it more understandable and help prevent the issue from reoccurring.

- **During Code Reviews:** Code reviews are an excellent opportunity to spot areas of the code that could benefit from refactoring, revealing parts that can be improved.

6.9.4. Common Refactoring Techniques

- **Renaming Variables and Functions:** Rename elements in the code to make their purposes more precise. This helps other developers quickly understand what each part of the code does.

- **Before:** a = b * c
- **After:** rectangleArea = base * height
- **Extracting Functions:** When a block of code performs a specific task, moving it to a separate function with a descriptive name is a good practice. This simplifies code reading and reuse.
- **Before:**

*total = price * quantity*

if total > 100:

   *total = total * 0.9*

- **After:**

total = calculateDiscount(price, quantity)

- **Removing Duplicate Code:** If the same block of code appears in multiple parts of a program, refactor it into a reusable function or class. This not only reduces code quantity but also simplifies maintenance.
- **Example:** Extracting repetitive form validation logic into a single reusable function for a web application.
- **Simplifying Complex Conditions:** Nested control structures like multiple if or switch statements can make code hard to follow. Refactoring these structures using functions or design patterns like polymorphism can enhance clarity.
- **Before:**

if type == 'A':

   # Logic for type A

elif type == 'B':

   # Logic for type B

- **After:** Use a function dictionary or a base class with subclasses to encapsulate logic for each type.

6.9.5. Long-Term Benefits of Refactoring

- **Reduced Future Errors:** Clean and organized code is less prone to errors, as inconsistencies are easier to spot and problems are easier to fix before they escalate.

- **Facilitates Collaboration:** In development teams, refactoring improves collaboration, enabling all members to understand and work on the code more effectively. This is especially important in large-scale projects where clarity and consistency are crucial for productivity.

- **Improved Performance**: Although refactoring doesn't always aim to directly improve system performance, simplifying and optimizing code can lead to better resource utilization, resulting in faster and lighter applications.

6.9.6. Conclusion: Refactoring as an Integral Part of Development

Refactoring should not be viewed as a tedious task but as an investment in software quality. Adopting a mindset of continuous improvement and regularly dedicating time to refactoring ensures that code remains flexible and adaptable over time. This not only simplifies the integration of new features but also contributes to creating robust software that is prepared for the future.

6.10. UNIT TESTING IN CODING

Unit testing is a fundamental technique in software development that involves writing automated tests to verify the functionality of individual units of code, such as functions, methods, or classes. Each test focuses on a specific part of the code, ensuring it behaves correctly under various conditions. This approach is essential for ensuring software quality and enables safer, more reliable development.

6.10.1. What Is Unit Testing?

Unit testing focuses on evaluating small pieces of code in isolation. Through this process, automated tests are run on units of code to verify that they produce the expected results for given inputs. Since these tests are automated, they can be executed every time the code is modified, ensuring that changes do not introduce errors elsewhere in the system.

- **Basic Example:** Suppose we have a function called sum(a, b) that returns the sum of two numbers. A unit test for this function might verify that sum(2, 3) returns 5, sum(-1, 1) returns 0, and so on.

6.10.2. Advantages of Unit Testing

- **Early Error Detection:** Unit tests help identify problems in the code before integrating it into the complete system. This saves developers time and effort by catching errors early in the development process.

- **Example**: If the logic of a mathematical function is changed, unit tests can immediately indicate if the change introduces a bug, before the code is used by other parts of the application.

- **Code Documentation:** Unit tests also serve as living documentation, clearly specifying how each function or class is expected to behave. This is especially useful for new developers joining a project who need to quickly understand how the code works.

- **Example:** By reading a unit test, a developer can quickly deduce that a multiply(a, b) function should return 0 if one of the arguments is 0.

- **Facilitates Refactoring:** With a suite of unit tests, developers can make changes to the code with greater confidence, knowing that if something breaks, the tests will catch it. This makes it easier to refactor code to improve its structure without fear of introducing new errors.

- **Example**: If a developer optimizes a function for better performance, unit tests ensure the updated version behaves the same as the original.

6.10.3. Best Practices for Unit Testing

To maximize the benefits of unit tests, follow these practices:

- **Write Simple and Isolated Tests:** Each unit test should focus on a single functionality. This ensures that, if a test fails, the issue can be quickly identified.

- **Example**: Instead of testing multiple tasks within a single function, write separate tests for each aspect of the function's functionality.

- **Use Assertions**: Assertions are the checks used in unit tests to compare the actual result of a function with the expected result. Proper use of assertions ensures tests detect any discrepancies.

- **Example**: If *assertEqual(sum(2, 3), 5)* fails, the test indicates that the sum function is not returning the expected value.

- **Automate and Run Tests Frequently**: Unit tests should be executed automatically whenever the code changes. This ensures that any unexpected changes are immediately detected, maintaining code integrity.

- **Example**: Configure a continuous integration (CI/CD) environment to automatically run all unit tests every time a commit is made to the repository.

6.10.4. Types of Unit Tests

- **Behavioral** Tests: Verify that a function behaves correctly for various inputs, ensuring expected outcomes.

- **Example**: Test that a function calculating product discounts always returns a positive value and doesn't allow discounts over 100%.

- **Exception Tests:** Ensure a function handles errors and exceptions properly. This helps verify that the code doesn't break with invalid inputs.

- **Example**: Test that a function dividing two numbers throws an exception when dividing by zero.

- **Edge Case Tests:** Evaluate a function's behavior with boundary values to ensure it handles extreme cases correctly.

- **Example**: Test that a function accepting age as a parameter throws an error if the provided age is less than 0 or greater than 120.

6.10.5. Popular Unit Testing Tools

Several tools simplify writing and running unit tests for different programming languages. Some of the most popular ones are:

- **JUnit (Java):** The standard for unit testing in Java, allowing easy test definition, organization, and execution.

- **pytest (Python):** Provides a simple yet powerful syntax for writing tests in Python, with automatic test execution and detailed reports.

- **Jest (JavaScript):** Widely used for testing JavaScript applications, especially in frontend development and React projects.

- **xUnit (.NET):** Ideal for writing unit tests for .NET and C# applications.

Each of these tools is designed to integrate seamlessly with its respective language and environment, offering features such as automatic test execution and reporting.

6.10.6. Practical Example of Unit Testing

Here's a simple example of a unit test in Python using pytest for a function that sums two numbers:

 # Function to be tested

```python
def sum(a, b):
    return a + b

# Unit test
def test_sum():
    assert sum(2, 3) == 5
    assert sum(-1, 1) == 0
    assert sum(0, 0) == 0
    assert sum(1.5, 2.5) == 4.0
```

In this example:

- The sum function is the unit of code being tested.
- The test_sum function contains several assertions to verify that the sum function returns the expected results for various cases.
- If any assertion fails, pytest will report the error, indicating the specific case where the function doesn't behave correctly.

6.10.7. Conclusion: The Value of Unit Testing in Software Development

Implementing unit testing is a crucial practice that significantly contributes to software quality. By detecting errors early, providing code documentation, and enabling confident refactoring, unit tests become an indispensable tool for developers. Although it may seem like an initial time investment, the automation of these tests and the assurance of robust, reliable code more than compensate for the effort.

6.11. PROGRAMMING STYLES

Programming styles are approaches and conventions that guide how code is written and organized. Each style has its characteristics, advantages, and disadvantages, and choosing the right approach can significantly impact the clarity, maintainability, and efficiency of the code. Below, we will explore some of the most common programming styles:

6.11.1. Functional Programming

Functional programming is a paradigm that treats computation as the evaluation of mathematical functions and avoids changing state or mutable data. This style is based on key concepts such as:

- **First-Class Functions**: Functions are treated as first-class citizens, meaning they can be assigned to variables, passed as arguments, and returned from other functions. This allows for greater flexibility in programming.

- **Immutability**: Data is not modified after its creation. Instead, new data is generated from existing data, minimizing side effects and making the code more predictable and easier to understand.

- **Pure Functions**: A function is considered pure if its output depends solely on its inputs and it has no side effects, such as modifying external variables or program state.

- **Example**: Functional programming can be seen in languages like Haskell or in the use of higher-order functions in JavaScript:

```
const sum = (a, b) => a + b;

const result= sum(2, 3); // result: 5
```

Functional programming is especially useful in concurrent and parallel systems because immutability and the absence of side effects simplify handling multiple threads of execution.

6.11.2. Object-Oriented Programming (OOP)

Object-oriented programming is a paradigm based on the concept of "objects," which encapsulate both data and behavior. The fundamental principles of OOP include:

•   **Encapsulation**: Data and methods that operate on that data are grouped within a single object. This hides complexity and provides a simpler interface for interacting with the object.

•   **Inheritance**: Allows the creation of new classes that inherit properties and behaviors from existing classes. This promotes code reuse and the creation of class hierarchies.

•   **Polymorphism**: Enables different classes to respond to the same interface in various ways. This can be achieved through method overloading or implementing interfaces.

•   **Example**: A classic example of OOP is creating a Car class:

class Car:

   def __init__(self, brand, model):

      self.marca = brand

      self.model = model

   def drive(self):

      print(f"Driving un {self.brand} {self.model}")

my_car = Car("Toyota", "Corolla")

my_car.drive() # Output: Driving a Toyota Corolla

OOP is particularly effective in large and complex projects, as it helps organize code and facilitates system maintenance and scalability.

6.11.3. Imperative Programming

Imperative programming is a style that relies on using sequential instructions to modify the program's state. It focuses on how tasks are performed, using a series of commands or statements to achieve a goal. Its characteristics include:

- **Sequence of Instructions:** Code is written as a sequence of steps that the program must follow to achieve a specific result.
- **Control Flow:** Uses control structures like loops, conditionals, and jumps to direct program execution.
- **Mutability:** Often allows variables to change state over time, which can introduce complexity and make it harder to track the state.
- **Example**: An algorithm that calculates the sum of numbers from 1 to 10:

sum = 0

for i in range(1, 11):

   sum += i

print(sum) # Output: 55

Imperative programming is widely used and serves as the foundational approach for many programming languages, such as C and Java.

6.11.5. Considerations for Choosing a Programming Style

When selecting a programming style, several factors should be considered:

- **Project Requirements:** Some projects may benefit more from a functional approach, while others may require the flexibility of OOP.
- **Team Experience:** The team's familiarity with a particular style can influence the decision. A team experienced in OOP may prefer that approach, while one experienced in functional programming may opt for that style.
- **Maintainability and Scalability:** The choice of programming style can impact how easily software can be maintained and scaled as it

evolves.

6.11.6. Conclusion

Programming styles are valuable tools that influence how code is written and organized. Understanding the characteristics and benefits of each style enables developers to make informed decisions when tackling programming challenges. By choosing the right style, developers can improve the clarity, efficiency, and maintainability of the code, resulting in higher-quality software that is easier to manage over time.

6.12. ERROR AND EXCEPTION HANDLING

Error and exception handling is a fundamental aspect of software development, enabling the creation of robust and reliable applications. Effective error management not only prevents abrupt software crashes but also improves user experience by providing helpful information about potential issues. Below are some key strategies for error and exception handling:

6.12.1. Using Try-Catch Blocks

Try-catch blocks are a common structure in many programming languages for managing exceptions. This technique attempts to execute a block of code and, if an exception occurs, captures it to prevent the program from halting.

- General Syntax:

try:

   # Code that might raise an exception

except ExceptionType:

   # Code to handle the exception

- **Example**:

try:

   resultado = 10 / 0   # This generates a division by zero exception

except ZeroDivisionError:

   print("Error: Cannot divide by zero.")

Using try-catch blocks allows the program to continue running even when an error occurs. This is particularly important in critical applications where service interruptions are unacceptable.

6.12.2. Error Logging

Error logging is essential for troubleshooting and maintaining software. Keeping a record of errors helps developers and system administrators analyze recurring issues and track errors over time.

- **Implementation**: Use libraries or logging tools to store information about errors, including:
    I. Error type
    II. Error message
    III. Date and time of the error
    IV. Environment information (e.g., software version, system configuration)
- Example:

import logging

logging.basicConfig(filename='errors.log', level=logging.ERROR)

try:
  # Code that might fail
  resultado = 10 / 0
except ZeroDivisionError as e:
  logging.error(f"Division by zero error: {e}")

Error logging not only aids in diagnosing problems but also provides valuable insights for future system improvements.

6.12.3. Clear Error Messages

Providing clear and concise error messages is crucial for helping users understand what went wrong and how to resolve it. A good error message should be:

- **Informative**: Clearly explain the issue.

- **User-Friendly:** Use plain language and avoid technical jargon whenever possible.

- **Instructive**: Offer suggestions on how to resolve the issue or where to find more information.

- Example:

```
try:
    # Code that might raise an error
    result = int(input("Enter a number: "))
except ValueError:
    print("Error: Please enter a valid number.")
```

Clear error messages improve user experience, reduce support inquiries, and simplify issue resolution.

6.12.4. Error Handling Strategies

In addition to the practices mentioned above, implementing additional strategies can enhance error management:

- **Retries:** In some cases, an error may be temporary (e.g., network issues). Implementing a retry mechanism can improve system resilience.

- **Graceful Degradation**: Design the system to degrade functionality in a controlled way rather than failing completely. For example, if an external service is unavailable, provide cached information instead of an error.

- **Pre-Validation:** Perform validations before executing critical operations. For instance, check if a file exists before attempting to open it.

6.12.5. Conclusion

Error and exception handling is an essential component of quality software development. By implementing effective error management strategies, developers can create more robust and failure-resistant applications, enhancing user experience and ensuring system stability. A proactive approach to error management not only minimizes the impact of issues but also provides a framework for continuous software improvement.

6.13. CODE DOCUMENTATION

Code documentation is a fundamental aspect of software development that contributes to the understanding, maintenance, and evolution of a project over time. Good documentation not only helps current developers but also facilitates the onboarding of new team members and improves collaboration in software development. Below are the key components of code documentation:

6.13.1. Code Comments

Comments are annotations within the source code that explain the logic, purpose, and functionality of specific sections. Their purpose is to provide clarity on how the code works and why certain decisions were made.

-Types of Comments:

- Inline Comments: Used to explain a specific line of code.

x = x + 1 # Incrementa x en 1

- **Block Comments**: Provide a broader description of a code block.

 # This function calculates the area of a circle

*# using the formula: area = pi * radius^2*

def calculate_circle_area(radius):

   *return 3.14 * radius * radius*

-Best Practices:

- Keep comments updated to match the code.
- Avoid redundant comments that do not add extra information.
- Use comments to explain the "why" behind design decisions, not just the "what."

6.13.2. External Documentation

In addition to code comments, maintaining external documentation that provides broader project context is essential. This documentation can include:

- **Installation Guides:** Instructions for setting up the development environment and running the application.
- **API Specifications:** Descriptions of endpoints, parameters, and expected responses when working with an API.
- **System Architecture:** Diagrams and descriptions explaining the system's structure, including its main components and their interactions.
- **Libraries and Dependencies:** A list of libraries used in the project, their purposes, and instructions for installing them.

6.13.3. Usage Examples

Providing usage examples is crucial for helping other developers understand how to use the implemented functions or classes. These examples can include:

- **Code Samples**: Code snippets demonstrating how to use a function or class in a practical context.

```
# Example of using the calculate_circle_area function
radius = 5
area = calculate_circle_area(radius)
print(f"The area of the circle with radius {radius} is {area}.")
```

- **Test Cases:** Examples showing how the code behaves with different input types, illustrating proper usage and limitations.

6.13.4. Importance of Documentation

Good documentation provides numerous benefits:

- **Eases Onboarding:** New team members can quickly understand the code and its structure, reducing the learning curve.

- **Enhances Collaboration:** Well-documented code allows developers to collaborate more effectively by providing a clear framework for how the system works and its components interact.

- **Reduces Error Risks:** Clear documentation helps prevent misunderstandings and errors by facilitating precise comprehension of the code.

- **Simplifies Maintenance:** Software projects often evolve and require changes. Proper documentation enables these changes to be made more efficiently and with a lower risk of introducing errors.

6.13.5. Conclusion

Code documentation is an integral part of software development that should not be underestimated. Investing time in creating and maintaining clear and accessible documentation is crucial for the long-term success of any software project. By following best documentation practices, developers can ensure their code is understandable, maintainable, and adaptable to future needs.

6.14. INDUSTRY CODING STANDARDS

6.14.1. Naming Conventions

Naming conventions dictate how elements in the code, such as variables, functions, classes, and other identifiers, should be named. These conventions enhance code readability and comprehension. Key aspects include:

• Consistency: Maintain a coherent naming scheme throughout the project. For example, if camelCase is chosen for variable names, this format should be used consistently across the codebase.

 # Example of camelCase

totalAmount = 100

userName = "John"

• Clarity: Names should be descriptive and clearly reflect the function or purpose of the element. For example, instead of using generic names like temp, use temperatureInCelsius for greater clarity.

• Class and Function Formatting: Classes typically follow PascalCase, while functions and variables often use camelCase or snake_case, depending on the language and organizational conventions.

6.14.2. Formatting Styles

Code formatting refers to the visual presentation of code, playing a crucial role in its readability. Some formatting guidelines include:

• Indentation: Consistent indentation helps delineate code blocks, which is especially critical in languages like Python where indentation is part of the syntax. Uniform use of spaces or tabs is recommended, avoiding a mix of both.

def calculate_area(base, height):

　　*return (base * height) / 2   # Indented with 4 spaces*

- Use of Spaces: Guidelines for using whitespace (e.g., after commas, around operators) improve code clarity.

 # Recommended use of spaces

result = a + b

- Code Organization: Sections of code should be logically organized, with comments separating different sections for easier navigation.

 # Initialization section

initialize_variables()

 # Calculation section

calculate_results()

6.14.3. Security Recommendations

Code security is a critical aspect that should not be overlooked. Security recommendations are practices that help protect code from vulnerabilities and attacks. These include:

- Input Validation: Ensure all input data is validated and sanitized before processing to prevent attacks such as SQL injection and Cross-Site Scripting (XSS).
- Error Handling: Implement proper error handling to avoid exposing sensitive information through error messages.
- Use of Secure Libraries: Keep libraries and dependencies up to date and use only those that are well-known and reliable.

6.14.4. Importance of Coding Standards

Adherence to coding standards brings numerous benefits:

- Improves Software Quality: Following consistent and well-defined coding practices reduces errors and enhances code quality.

- Facilitates Collaboration: Standards allow multiple developers to work on the same code without confusion, as everyone adheres to the same rules and conventions.

- Increases Maintainability: Well-structured and documented code is easier to maintain, reducing the time and cost associated with future modifications and bug fixes.

- Streamlines Continuous Integration: By adhering to coding standards, the continuous integration process becomes smoother, as automated tools can analyze and validate code more effectively.

6.14.5. Conclusion

Coding standards are an essential component of software development that influence the quality, security, and maintainability of code. Adopting and following these standards benefits both individual developers and teams while contributing to the long-term success of software projects. Implementing best coding practices leads to more robust and reliable applications, better suited to evolving business and market needs.

6.15. CONTINUOUS INTEGRATION AND ITS RELATIONSHIP WITH CODING

Continuous Integration (CI) is a fundamental practice in modern software development aimed at improving code quality and team efficiency. This methodology involves frequently merging code changes into a shared repository, enabling early problem detection and fostering effective collaboration. Below, we detail the key components and benefits of Continuous Integration in relation to coding.

6.15.1. What Is Continuous Integration?

Continuous Integration is a development approach that promotes frequent integration of code changes, often multiple times a day. This process is accompanied by the automation of testing and other development tasks, such as application building and deployment. Developers work on separate branches and merge their changes into the main branch once they are ready. This approach helps maintain the codebase in a stable state.

6.15.2. Benefits of Continuous Integration

Implementing Continuous Integration provides several significant advantages:

-Early Error Detection

- Automated Testing: Frequent integration triggers automated tests, ensuring that errors introduced by new changes are detected almost immediately. This facilitates identifying and resolving issues before they escalate, reducing the cost of fixing errors. Minor issues can be resolved quickly compared to problems that emerge later in the development cycle.

-Ease of Collaboration

•   Conflict-Free Teamwork: CI allows teams to work simultaneously on different features or fixes. Frequent merges minimize code conflicts that may arise when multiple developers work on the same part of the project. This not only eases collaboration but also improves communication among team members, keeping everyone informed about recent changes in the codebase.

-Faster Delivery

•   Accelerated Development Cycle: Continuous Integration accelerates the development cycle by automating testing, building, and deployment processes. As a result, new features and bug fixes can be delivered to end users more quickly. This is especially valuable in agile environments where customer expectations may change rapidly, and time-to-market is critical.

6.15.3. Continuous Integration Tools

To implement CI, development teams often use CI tools that streamline the automation process. Some popular tools include:

•   Jenkins: An open-source tool that allows developers to automate building and testing processes.

•   Travis CI: Integrated with GitHub, it enables automatic testing whenever changes are made to the repository.

•   CircleCI: Provides a fast and flexible CI/CD environment that integrates with various platforms and services.

•   GitLab CI/CD: Part of the GitLab platform, it offers native support for Continuous Integration and Continuous Delivery.

6.15.4. Enhancements in Software Quality

Integrating CI into the coding workflow brings significant improvements in software quality:

•   Cleaner, More Efficient Code: Continuous feedback from automated tests encourages developers to write clean and efficient code, knowing that every change will be promptly verified.

- Reduction in Technical Debt: CI promotes a disciplined development approach, helping teams address issues as they arise rather than allowing them to accumulate, reducing technical debt over time.

6.15.5. Continuous Integration and Team Culture

Adopting Continuous Integration involves not only technical changes but also a cultural shift within the team. Open communication, collaboration, and a willingness to embrace feedback are essential for CI's success. Creating an environment where mistakes are seen as learning opportunities motivates developers to adopt rigorous coding practices and work together to enhance software quality.

6.15.6. Conclusion

Continuous Integration is a fundamental practice that transforms the software development process, enabling teams to detect errors more quickly, collaborate more effectively, and deliver high-quality software at a faster pace. Incorporating CI into the coding workflow is critical not only for improving software quality but also for fostering an agile and adaptable development environment that better meets market and user needs.

6.16. Chapter Conclusions

Coding principles form the foundation of quality software development. From understanding programming fundamentals and logic to implementing best practices in security and optimization, every aspect of coding impacts the final product's quality. By following these principles and applying effective techniques, developers can create software that not only functions well but is also sustainable, secure, and easy to maintain over time.

CHAPTER 7

CLEAN CODE PRINCIPLES

The concept of "Clean Code" refers to a set of practices and principles that guide developers in creating readable, maintainable, and efficient code. This chapter explores the fundamentals of clean code and provides guidelines for achieving high-quality software.

7.1. FUNDAMENTALS OF CLEAN CODE

The fundamentals of clean code are essential principles that guide developers in producing high-quality software. These principles not only aim for functional code but also ensure it is easy to read, understand, and maintain over time. Below are the key principles that form the foundation of clean code.

7.1.1. Readability

Readability is one of the most critical aspects of clean code. Readable code enables other developers (or even the original author at a later time) to quickly grasp the logic and purpose of the code. To achieve high readability:

- **Consistent Coding Style:** Maintaining a uniform coding style throughout a project helps developers anticipate how the code is structured. This includes consistent use of indentation, naming conventions, and control structures.

- **Helpful Comments:** While code should be as self-explanatory as possible, comments can provide additional context. However, it's important to avoid unnecessary or redundant comments. Comments should explain why something is done, not what is being done, as the latter should be evident from the code itself.

- **Descriptive Names:** Using clear and descriptive names for variables, functions, and classes is fundamental. Names should communicate the intent of the code, making its purpose easier to understand without delving into its implementation.

7.1.2. Simplicity

Simplicity in code is key to avoiding unnecessary complexity. Simple code is easier to understand and less prone to errors. To maintain simplicity:

- **Avoid Complexity:** Always question if the solution is as simple as possible. Complex solutions tend to introduce more opportunities for errors and are harder to maintain.

- **Minimize Dependencies:** Code that relies on numerous libraries or modules can become convoluted and difficult to follow. Aim to reduce dependencies to the essentials.

- **Modularity:** Dividing code into small, well-defined modules or functions makes problems easier to address. Each module should do one thing and do it well, avoiding the temptation to bundle multiple functionalities into a single unit of code.

7.1.3. Single Responsibility

The Single Responsibility Principle states that each function or class should have a single responsibility. This means:

- **Specialized Functions and Classes:** Each function should perform a single task or calculation. This not only makes the code easier to understand but also enhances reusability. If a function performs multiple tasks, it becomes harder to test and maintain.

- **Ease of Testing:** Structuring code so that each component has a single responsibility simplifies the creation of unit tests. Each unit can be tested independently, contributing to more reliable software.

- **Simplified Maintenance**: By applying this principle, developers can make changes to one part of the system without worrying about unintended consequences in other parts. This is especially crucial in long-term projects where requirements may evolve over time.

7.1.4. Importance of These Principles

Adhering to these principles is essential not only for code quality but also for the overall health of the project. Clean code is easier to maintain, allowing development teams to focus on implementing new features and improving the software instead of dealing with confusing and complex code.

7.1.5. Conclusion

The fundamentals of clean code—readability, simplicity, and single responsibility—are pillars in creating software that not only works but can also be managed and improved over time. These principles should be embraced and promoted at all levels of development to foster a more productive and efficient work environment and to ensure the code is accessible and understandable to any team member who needs to interact with it in the future.

7.2. NAMING AND CONVENTIONS

Naming and coding conventions are fundamental aspects that directly influence code readability and comprehension. These elements are essential to facilitate collaboration among developers, improve software maintainability, and minimize the learning curve for new team members. Below are some recommendations and practices related to naming and coding conventions.

7.2.1. Descriptive Names

Using descriptive names is one of the most effective practices for enhancing code clarity. Names should clearly reflect the function or purpose of variables, functions, and classes. Some guidelines include:

- **Reflect Functionality:** A good name should clearly indicate what the element does. For instance, calculateAverage() is descriptive and communicates its purpose immediately, while function1() is vague and provides no useful information.

- **Use Verbs and Nouns:** For functions, begin with a verb indicating the action, such as getData(), saveFile(), or sendEmail(). For variables, use nouns that describe the content or purpose, like numberOfUsers or taskList.

- **Avoid Cryptic Abbreviations:** While abbreviations may seem convenient, they often hinder understanding. Opt for full, clear names that might be longer but convey meaningful information.

7.2.2. Consistency

Consistency in naming is crucial for maintaining readability throughout a project. Key considerations include:

- **Naming Conventions:** Choose a naming style and apply it uniformly across the codebase. Common options include:

camelCase: variableName, calculateAverage()).

snake_case: variable_name, calculate_average().

PascalCase: ClassName, ExampleClass.

- **Establish Style Guidelines:** Document chosen conventions in a style guide accessible to all developers. This ensures uniformity and reduces confusion.

- **Uniform Verb Tenses:** If a specific tense (e.g., present) is used for functions, apply it consistently across the project. This creates a sense of uniformity that enhances code readability.

7.2.3. Use of Comments

Comments are valuable tools for understanding code but must be used effectively:

- **Explanatory Comments:** Use comments to clarify sections of code that may be complex or non-obvious. Explain why a decision was made rather than simply describing what the code does.

- **Avoid Obvious Comments:** Comments should not be redundant with the code. If a code snippet is self-explanatory, avoid adding a comment that merely repeats its functionality.

- **Function Documentation:** Consider using documentation comments (docstrings) to describe the purpose of functions, their parameters, and their return values. This is particularly useful in languages that support this feature, such as Python.

7.2.4. Benefits of Good Naming and Conventions

Adhering to good naming and convention practices offers numerous benefits:

- **Improved Communication:** Well-named code facilitates communication among developers, as everyone can quickly grasp the intent behind the code.

- **Accessibility:** New team members can more easily onboard and understand the existing codebase.

- **Maintainability**: Readability and clarity make it easier to implement changes, add new features, and fix bugs.

7.2.5. Conclusion

Naming and conventions are essential aspects of software development that should be considered from the beginning of a project. A good naming system, consistency in conventions, and effective use of comments not only enhance code quality but also foster collaboration and productivity among developers. By establishing and following these practices, you can create clean, accessible code that endures and evolves over time.

7.3. ELIMINATING REDUNDANCY

Code redundancy refers to the duplication of logic, structures, or data, which can lead to confusion, errors, and increased maintenance time. Eliminating redundancies not only improves code clarity but also facilitates its evolution and reduces the risk of introducing errors during modifications. Below are some effective strategies to achieve cleaner, more efficient code.

7.3.1. DRY Principle (Don't Repeat Yourself)

The DRY principle is a fundamental tenet in software development. This concept suggests avoiding the duplication of information or logic whenever possible. Ways to apply this principle include:

- **Reusable Functions:** Instead of copying and pasting code blocks, encapsulate repetitive logic into functions. For example, if a specific validation logic appears in multiple places, create a validateData() function to be called wherever needed.

- **Classes and Objects:** Use object-oriented programming to create classes that encapsulate common properties and behaviors. For instance, instead of having multiple classes for different user types, create a base User class with shared attributes and methods.

- **Centralized Configuration:** Rather than duplicating configurations across multiple locations, centralize them in a single file or module. This ensures any changes are made in one place and reflected throughout the system.

7.3.2. Modularization

Modularization involves dividing code into independent modules or components that encapsulate specific functionality. This practice offers multiple benefits:

- **Encapsulation of Functionality:** Each module should handle a single responsibility, making it easier to understand and maintain. For instance, one module might manage authentication, while another handles user management.

- **Ease of Testing:** Encapsulated functionalities in modules make unit testing more effective, as each module can be tested independently.

- **Ease of Integration:** Well-designed modules can be reused across different projects or contexts, reducing the need to rewrite code and minimizing redundancy.

7.3.3. Leveraging Libraries and Frameworks

Utilizing existing libraries and frameworks is an effective way to eliminate redundancy and accelerate development. Recommendations include:

- **Identify Existing Solutions:** Before implementing functionality, research whether libraries or frameworks provide the needed features. For example, instead of writing your own form management system, consider using libraries like Formik or React Hook Form in React applications.

- **Contribute to the Community:** When creating a solution that could be useful to others, consider turning it into a library that can be shared. This not only helps the community but also reduces redundancy in the software ecosystem.

7.3.4. Continuous Review and Refactoring

Eliminating redundancy is not a one-time effort but an ongoing process. Practices for maintaining code quality include:

- **Code Reviews:** Conduct code reviews where other developers analyze the code to identify potential redundancies or duplications. This also fosters a learning and collaborative environment within the team.

- **Regular Refactoring:** Schedule refactoring sessions to review existing code, improve its structure, and eliminate redundancies introduced over time.

7.3.5. Benefits of Eliminating Redundancy

Removing redundancy in code provides several significant advantages:

- **Improved Readability:** Code free of duplications is easier to read and understand, facilitating onboarding of new developers.

- **Ease of Maintenance:** Less redundancy means fewer places to make changes, reducing the likelihood of errors when modifying code.

- **Optimized Performance:** In some cases, eliminating redundant code can improve system performance by reducing unnecessary processing.

7.3.6. Conclusion

Eliminating redundancy is a key principle in creating clean, efficient code. By following practices such as the DRY principle, modularization, and leveraging existing libraries, developers can build more maintainable and comprehensible systems. This not only improves software quality but also fosters team collaboration and optimizes the development process over time.

7.4. CODE ORGANIZATION

7.4. Code Organization

Code organization is essential to ensure readability, maintainability, and scalability. Well-organized code not only facilitates understanding and work for current developers but also makes it easier for new team members to integrate into the project. Below are several best practices for achieving effective code organization.

7.4.1. File Structure

The file structure of a project should be logical and easy to understand, reflecting the software's architecture and functionality. Guidelines to achieve this include:

• **Folders by Functionality**: Organize code into folders representing different functionalities or system modules. For example, in an e-commerce project, separate folders could be created for products, users, orders, and payments. This structure helps developers quickly locate relevant code.

• **Clear Folder and File Names:** Use descriptive names for folders and files that clearly indicate their content. For instance, models.py for data models or controllers.py for controller logic in an MVC application.

• **Naming Conventions:** Adopt and follow common naming conventions, such as using PascalCase for class names and snake_case for file and function names, to maintain consistency and ease navigation.

7.4.2. Separation of Concerns

Separation of concerns is a fundamental programming principle that involves dividing code into distinct sections, each responsible for a specific functionality. This can be achieved through:

- **Independent Modules:** Create modules focused on specific tasks, such as data validation, database access, or session management. This prevents a single file or module from becoming a "cocktail" of different logics and responsibilities.

- **Architectural Layers:** Implement architectural patterns like MVC (Model-View-Controller) or MVVM (Model-View-ViewModel), where each layer has a clear and defined role. This not only improves organization but also enables more agile development and efficient testing.

7.4.3. Logical Grouping

Grouping related functions and classes can enhance code navigability and cohesion. Strategies for logical grouping include:

- **Related Classes and Methods:** Keep classes and methods that work together in the same file or module. For example, if you have a User class, methods related to user management, like registerUser() or validateUser(), should be within the same module.

- **Domain-Based Organization:** In larger projects, consider grouping code by business domains. For example, all components related to inventory management could be in a module called inventory, while billing components could be grouped in another module called billing.

7.4.4. Documentation and Comments

Ensuring the code organization is well-documented is also key:

- **Structure Documentation:** Include a README file or style guide explaining the project structure and how it is organized. This can be helpful for new developers joining the project.

- **Code Comments:** Use comments to explain design decisions, the logic behind certain groupings, and any conventions being used. This helps others and serves as a reminder for the future.

7.4.5. Advantages of Good Code Organization

Proper code organization offers several benefits:

- **Ease of Navigation:** Developers can quickly and efficiently locate and modify specific parts of the software, speeding up development and reducing frustration.

- **Improved Maintainability:** With a clear and logical structure, identifying problems and implementing changes become much more manageable, facilitating long-term software maintenance.

- **Scalability:** As the project grows, good code organization allows new functionalities to be added without complicating the existing structure. This is crucial for projects intended to evolve over time.

7.4.6. Conclusion

Code organization is a critical aspect of software development that impacts the quality, maintainability, and scalability of a project. By following practices such as a logical file structure, separation of concerns, and logical grouping of functions, developers can create a more accessible and efficient environment. Ultimately, good code organization contributes to more agile development and higher-quality software.

7.5. CODE MAINTENANCE

Code maintenance is a crucial aspect of software development that involves ensuring code remains clean, accessible, and efficient over time. As projects grow and evolve, it is common for code to become outdated or difficult to manage, potentially leading to performance issues and increased technical debt. To prevent these problems and ensure code sustainability, certain key practices must be followed.

7.5.1. Code Reviews

Code reviews are a valuable tool for maintaining software quality. This process involves having other team members review code before it is merged into the main codebase. The advantages of implementing code reviews include:

- Early Problem Detection: Reviews help identify errors and vulnerabilities in the code before they become larger issues. This is essential for preventing the accumulation of technical debt.

- Quality Improvement: Through constructive feedback, developers can learn from each other's mistakes and apply better practices in their code.

- Collaboration Promotion: Code reviews foster a culture of collaboration among developers, enabling knowledge and technique sharing.

- Consistency in Style: Reviews help ensure code adheres to team-agreed conventions and standards, resulting in cleaner and more consistent code.

7.5.2. Continuous Documentation

Documentation is an integral part of code maintenance. As code evolves, keeping documentation updated to reflect the system's current state is vital. This can include:

- Updating Technical Documentation: Every significant change in the code or system architecture should be reflected in the technical documentation to remain a reliable source of information.

- Process Documentation: Maintain records of development processes, decisions made, and lessons learned over time. This facilitates maintenance and serves as a guide for future developers joining the team.

- Usage Examples: Including examples of how to use the most important functions and classes in the documentation helps other developers better understand the code.

7.5.3. Automated Testing

Implementing automated testing is a key strategy for ensuring code continues to function correctly after changes or updates. Automated tests may include:

- Unit Tests: These tests focus on small code units, such as functions or methods, ensuring each part of the system works as expected. Unit tests are essential for detecting errors early in development.

- Integration Tests: These tests verify that different system modules or components function correctly together. They ensure interactions between various parts of the code do not cause unexpected problems.

- Regression Tests: Whenever code changes are made, regression tests ensure existing functionalities continue to operate as expected. This is crucial for maintaining software stability over time.

7.5.4. Regular Refactoring

Refactoring is the process of restructuring existing code without changing its functionality. This is important for code maintenance because:

- Improves Readability: As code evolves, it can become confusing and complex. Regular refactoring helps keep code clean and easy to understand.

- Eliminates Dead Code: Over time, it is common to accumulate unused code fragments. Refactoring allows identifying and removing dead code, reducing complexity and improving performance.

- Adapts to New Requirements: As project requirements change, refactoring allows adapting the code to new needs without compromising quality.

7.5.5. Proactive Maintenance Strategy

Proactive maintenance involves anticipating problems before they occur. This can be achieved through:

- Performance Monitoring: Use monitoring tools to identify bottlenecks and performance issues in real time. This enables corrective measures before problems impact end users.

- Regular Maintenance Planning: Establish a schedule for code reviews, documentation updates, and automated testing. This ensures maintenance is consistently performed and not indefinitely postponed.

- Continuous Team Training: Encourage team training and professional development to ensure everyone is up to date on best practices and new technologies.

7.5.6. Conclusion

Code maintenance is a continuous process requiring constant attention and effort. By implementing practices like code reviews, continuous documentation, and automated testing, development teams can ensure code remains clean, accessible, and efficient over time. This proactive approach not only improves software quality but also contributes to the project's long-term sustainability, allowing it to evolve and adapt to the changing needs of businesses and users.

7.6. PRACTICAL EXAMPLES

Practical examples are essential to understanding and applying clean code principles. They allow developers to see how theory translates into practice, illustrating both common coding errors and effective solutions. Below are two examples: one that demonstrates unclean code and another showing how that code can be refactored to adhere to clean code principles.

7.6.1. Unclean Code

Let's consider a code snippet that calculates the average of scores but is poorly structured and hard to read. This example highlights bad programming practices:

```
def f1(a):
    s = 0
    for i in a:
        s += i
    return s / len(a)

print(f1([5, 10, 15, 20, 25]))
```

-Problems with Unclean Code:

- Non-descriptive names: The function f1 and the variable a provide no insight into their purpose. Names should clearly reflect their functionality.
- Lack of error handling: There's no validation to handle cases

where the input list is empty, potentially resulting in a division-by-zero error.

- No comments: The logic behind the calculation isn't explained, making the code harder to understand for other developers.

7.6.2. Clean Code

Now, let's refactor this code to make it more readable and aligned with clean code principles:

```python
def calculate_average(scores):
    if not scores:
        raise ValueError("The scores list cannot be empty")
    total_sum = sum(scores)
    return total_sum / len(scores)


# Usage example
try:
    average = calculate_average([5, 10, 15, 20, 25])
    print(f"The average is: {average}")
except ValueError as e:
    print(e)
```

-Improvements in Clean Code:

- Descriptive names: The function calculate_average and the variable scores clearly indicate their purpose, improving readability.
- Error handling: Validation ensures that an exception is raised if the list is empty, enhancing code robustness.
- Use of built-in functions: The sum() function simplifies the calculation, making the code more concise.

- Comments and exception handling: A try-except block gracefully handles exceptions, improving the user experience.

7.6.3. Example Comparison

Comparing these two code snippets reveals several key points:

- Readability: Clean code is easier to read and understand, facilitating team collaboration and onboarding of new developers.
- Maintainability: By adhering to principles like descriptive names and error handling, the code becomes easier to maintain over time. Future developers can make changes with less risk of introducing bugs.
- Software Quality: Implementing good coding practices contributes to higher-quality software with fewer bugs and better performance.

7.6.4. Conclusion

These practical examples are valuable tools for developers to understand the difference between clean and unclean code. By visualizing the effects of applying clean code principles, programmers can internalize the importance of following best practices and ultimately improve the quality of the software they produce. Adopting these principles benefits developers in their daily work and contributes to the sustainability and scalability of software in the long term.

7.7. CODE SIMPLIFICATION TECHNIQUES

Code simplification is fundamental to creating high-quality software. It involves applying a series of techniques and approaches to reduce code complexity, improving readability, maintainability, and testability. Below are some of the most effective techniques for achieving simpler and cleaner code.

7.7.1. Use Short Functions

One of the most effective techniques for simplifying code is keeping functions short and focused on a single task. Functions that perform multiple tasks or have too many lines of code can become difficult to understand and maintain.

Example:

```
def process_data(data):
    # Non-simplified function
    for d in data:
        # Complex logic for filtering and processing data
        if d > 0:
            print(f"Positive data: {d}")
        elif d < 0:
            print(f"Negative data: {d}")
        else:
```

print("Zero data")

Refactoring:

```
def print_data(d):
    if d > 0:
        print(f"Positive data: {d}")
    elif d < 0:
        print(f"Negative data: {d}")
    else:
        print("Zero data")

def process_data(data):
    for d in data:
        print_data(d)
```

7.7.2. Avoid Complex Logic

Complex logic can be hard to follow and understand. Breaking down complex decisions into simpler steps makes the code more accessible and easier to modify. This approach also facilitates unit testing, as individual parts of the logic can be tested separately.

Example:

```
def calculate_discount(price, discount_percentage):
    if price > 100 and discount_percentage > 0:
        return price - (price * (discount_percentage / 100))
    else:
        return price
```

Refactoring:

```
def is_discount_applicable(price, discount_percentage):
    return price > 100 and discount_percentage > 0


def calculate_discount(price, discount_percentage):
    if is_discount_applicable(price, discount_percentage):
        return price - (price * (discount_percentage / 100))
    return price
```

7.7.3. Minimize Nesting

Deeply nested control structures (like loops and conditionals) can make code difficult to read. Reducing nesting levels makes it easier to follow the program's flow. This can be achieved by using early returns or extracting parts of the logic into separate functions.

Example:

```
def process_list(lst):
    for element in lst:
        if element > 0:
            if element % 2 == 0:
                print(f"Even element: {element}")
```

Refactoring:

```
def is_even(n):
    return n % 2 == 0


def process_list(lst):
    for element in lst:
```

    if element > 0 and is_even(element):

        print(f"Even element: {element}")

7.7.4. Benefits of Code Simplification

- **Better understanding:** Simpler code is easier to read and understand, enabling new and experienced developers to follow the application flow without difficulty.

- **Ease of maintenance:** With simpler functions and logic, developers can make changes or add new features without fear of breaking existing functionality.

- **Fewer errors**: By reducing complexity and code quantity, the likelihood of introducing errors is minimized, resulting in more robust software.

- **Testing efficiency:** Short functions and simple decisions allow for more effective unit tests, helping identify and fix bugs before they reach production.

7.7.5. Conclusion

By applying these simplification techniques, developers can create cleaner, more efficient code. Simplicity not only enhances readability but also contributes to the long-term sustainability of software. In a world where software evolves constantly, maintaining simple and manageable code is key to the continuous success of development projects. Implementing these practices from the start can significantly improve the quality of delivered software.

7.8. CONTINUOUS REFACTORING

Continuous refactoring is a systematic and proactive approach aimed at constantly improving and optimizing code without altering its functionality. This process is fundamental in the software development lifecycle, based on the premise that as a project evolves, the code must also adapt to remain efficient, readable, and maintainable. Below are the key aspects and benefits of implementing continuous refactoring.

7.8.1. Continuous Improvement

A core principle of continuous refactoring is the constant enhancement of the code. As new features are developed or project requirements change, it is essential to update the code to align with these new demands. This involves:

- **Adapting to Changes:** As new needs arise or requirements shift, code can become outdated or inefficient. Continuous refactoring allows teams to adjust the code to remain relevant and functional.

- **Modernizing Technologies:** Over time, technologies and best practices evolve. Continuous refactoring provides opportunities to update libraries, frameworks, and technologies used in the project, resulting in more efficient and maintainable code.

7.8.2. Identifying Issues

Continuous refactoring is not only about improving existing code but also about identifying and addressing potential issues before they become significant obstacles. This includes:

- **Proactive Analysis:** Regular code reviews and applying clean code principles allow developers to spot design problems, inefficient implementations, or areas that could benefit from simplification.

- **Resolving Technical Debt:** Continuous refactoring enables the management and reduction of technical debt by addressing areas of code that do not meet current standards or require significant improvements.

7.8.3. Team Satisfaction

Clean, well-structured code enhances software quality and positively impacts the morale and collaboration of the development team. Benefits include:

- **Improved Collaboration:** Clear and understandable code facilitates teamwork, knowledge sharing, and joint efforts on new features or improvements without fear of introducing errors.

- **Stress Reduction:** A clean and organized codebase reduces developers 'cognitive load, leading to a healthier and less stressful work environment, ultimately boosting overall productivity.

7.8.4. Strategies for Continuous Refactoring

To effectively implement continuous refactoring, teams can adopt various strategies:

- **Regular Code Reviews:** Scheduled code reviews allow developers to receive feedback and identify overlooked issues during implementation.

- **Automated Testing:** Integrating unit and integration tests into the development workflow ensures that changes made during refactoring do not affect existing functionality.

- **Scheduled Refactoring Time:** Allocating specific time in the development cycle to focus on refactoring helps maintain this practice as a priority.

7.8.5. Conclusion

Continuous refactoring is an essential practice in modern software development, enabling teams to adapt to changes while maintaining high-quality code. By fostering a culture of constant improvement, developers can ensure their code not only meets current requirements but is also sustainable and easy to maintain in the long term. This proactive approach enhances software quality and promotes a more collaborative and fulfilling work environment for all team members.

7.9. CHAPTER CONCLUSIONS

The principles of clean code are essential for creating software that is readable, maintainable, and efficient. By adhering to guidelines on naming, redundancy elimination, organization, and maintenance, developers can produce high-quality code that not only meets the project's immediate requirements but is also sustainable over time. Implementing these principles improves software quality and fosters a more collaborative and satisfying development environment.

CHAPTER 8
VERSION CONTROL

Version control is an essential practice in modern software development, enabling the management and tracking of changes in code over time. This chapter covers the key concepts of version control, focusing on Git—the industry's most popular tool—and the use of remote repositories and collaboration strategies.

8.1. INTRODUCTION TO VERSION CONTROL IN SOFTWARE

Version control is a fundamental component of modern software development, allowing teams to manage and monitor changes made to code in a structured and efficient manner. As software projects grow more complex and collaborative, the need for a robust version control system becomes evident. Below are the goals and benefits of implementing version control in software.

8.1.1. Tracking Changes

One of the most critical functions of version control is the ability to track and record all changes made to the source code. This includes:

- **Comprehensive History:** Every modification, whether a new feature, bug fix, or improvement, is saved in a version control system, creating a complete project history. This allows developers to see what changes were made, when, and by whom.

- **Change Breakdown:** Version control systems provide tools to view a detailed breakdown of each change, helping developers understand how the code evolves over time. This is especially useful for code reviews and audits.

8.1.2. Collaboration

Version control facilitates collaboration among developers, which is critical in team environments where multiple people may work on the same project simultaneously. Key features include:

- **Parallel Work:** With branches in version control systems, developers can work on different features or fixes in parallel without interfering with each other's work, promoting a more agile and efficient workflow.

- **Change Merging:** Once a task is completed, changes made in a branch can be merged into the project's main branch. Version control systems efficiently handle these merge processes, resolving conflicts when multiple developers modify the same code sections.

8.1.3. Restoring Previous Versions

Another critical advantage of version control is the ability to restore previous versions of the project. This is vital in cases of errors or the need to revert to an earlier state of the code. Benefits include:

- **Error Correction:** If a new change introduces an error, developers can easily revert to a previous version where the issue did not exist. This minimizes downtime and allows teams to maintain workflow continuity.

- **Exploring Alternatives:** Version control allows developers to experiment with different implementations. If one approach does not yield the desired results, they can revert to an earlier version and test a new solution without losing prior work.

8.1.4. Code Integrity and Development Efficiency

Version control not only manages changes but also plays a vital role in ensuring code quality and integrity:

- **Quality Assurance:** By maintaining a change history, teams can audit code quality and review the evolution of the codebase, identifying problematic patterns and implementing long-term solutions.

- **Productivity Improvements:** With a well-implemented version control system, developers can work more efficiently and in an organized manner, leading to higher productivity and shorter delivery times.

8.1.5. Conclusion

In summary, version control is an indispensable tool for software development, providing an organized structure for managing code changes. It facilitates collaboration, allows recovery of previous versions, and enhances code integrity and quality. In agile and dynamic development environments, version control is a cornerstone of efficiency and project success.

8.2. GIT

Git is a distributed version control system that has become the de facto standard in the software industry. Its design and functionality make it highly effective for managing code in projects of any scale, from small scripts to complex, collaborative applications. Below are some of Git's most notable features and its impact on software development.

8.2.1. Distributed Version Control System

One of Git's key characteristics is its distributed nature:

- **Complete Local Copies:** Unlike centralized version control systems, which rely on a single main repository, Git allows each developer to have a complete copy of the project's history on their local machine. This ensures that all changes, versions, and commits are accessible at any time, even without an internet connection.

- **Increased Flexibility:** This approach enables developers to work independently in their own branches without affecting the main repository. This is especially useful for large teams where multiple developers can work on different features simultaneously.

8.2.2. Storage Efficiency and Speed

Git is designed to be efficient in terms of storage and speed:

- **Incremental Storage:** Git uses a storage model that saves changes incrementally, meaning it only stores the differences (or "deltas") between versions. This significantly reduces the disk space needed to maintain the project's history.

- **Fast Operations:** Due to its design, many Git operations—such as creating branches, switching between them, and merging changes—are extremely fast. This enhances the developer experience by enabling shorter and more efficient work cycles.

8.2.3. Basic Git Commands

Git offers a set of basic commands that allow developers to manage a project's version history easily and effectively. Some of the most commonly used commands include:

- **git init:** Initializes a new Git repository in the current directory, the first step in starting version control for a new project.

- **git add:** Adds specific files or changes to the staging area, enabling developers to select precisely what they want to include in the next commit.

- **git commit:** Saves changes to the repository history. Each commit can include a message describing the changes, helping maintain a clear and understandable development record.

- **git push:** Sends local commits to a remote repository, essential for sharing changes with team members and keeping the remote repository updated.

- **git pull:** Fetches and merges the latest changes from a remote repository into the local copy, ensuring all team members work with the most current code version.

8.2.4. Integration with Collaboration Tools

Git's popularity has led to the development of numerous collaboration tools that seamlessly integrate with it. Some of the most notable tools include:

- **GitHub:** One of the most widely used platforms for hosting Git repositories, offering collaboration features such as issue tracking, pull requests, and code reviews.

- **GitLab:** Similar to GitHub, GitLab provides a comprehensive suite of development and collaboration tools, including continuous integration (CI) and continuous deployment (CD), making it ideal for teams looking to optimize workflows.

- **Bitbucket:** Offers functionalities similar to GitHub and GitLab, with a particular focus on integration with other Atlassian tools such as Jira and Confluence for project management.

8.2.5. Conclusion

In summary, Git is a powerful and flexible version control system that has revolutionized the way developers manage source code. Its ability to enable efficient collaboration, incremental storage, and fast operations has made it an indispensable tool in modern software development. Mastering Git is essential for any developer looking to improve productivity and collaboration in software projects.

8.3. GITHUB AND REMOTE REPOSITORIES

GitHub is one of the most popular and widely used platforms in modern software development. It serves as a hosting service for Git repositories and provides a robust set of features that facilitate collaboration and project management. Below are the key features of GitHub and its impact on teamwork.

8.3.1. Remote Repositories

Remote repositories on GitHub are fundamental for collaborative work:

• **Cloud Storage:** GitHub allows developers to store their code in a cloud-based environment, ensuring that the code is accessible from anywhere, anytime, as long as there's internet access.

• **Multi-Level Access:** Storing code in remote repositories facilitates collaboration among multiple developers. Access permissions can be configured to grant different levels of control, from read-only access to the ability to make changes.

• **Backup and Security:** Storing code on GitHub provides a secure backup, reducing the risk of data loss due to local hardware failures or human errors.

8.3.2. Collaboration Tools

GitHub offers various tools that promote effective collaboration:

• **Pull Requests:** This feature allows developers to request a review of their changes before they are merged into the main branch. Pull requests are a structured way to discuss changes and receive feedback, ensuring code quality.

• **Code Reviews:** Alongside pull requests, GitHub enables team members to conduct code reviews, enhancing code quality and promoting knowledge sharing among team members.

• **Inline Comments:** GitHub allows reviewers to leave specific comments on lines of code within a pull request, facilitating detailed discussions on specific changes. This improves communication and helps clarify doubts.

8.3.3. Automation and CI/CD

GitHub integrates with continuous integration and continuous delivery (CI/CD) tools to enhance workflow efficiency:

• **GitHub Actions:** This tool allows developers to create automated workflows triggered by repository events, such as pushes or pull requests. It simplifies tasks like testing, building software, and deployment.

• **Third-Party Integrations:** GitHub can connect with various CI/CD services like Travis CI, CircleCI, and Jenkins, enabling teams to set up integration and delivery pipelines that run automatically with every code change.

8.3.4. Project Management

GitHub is more than just a version control tool; it offers features for effective project management:

• **Issues:** GitHub provides an issue tracking system for logging and managing tasks, bugs, and feature requests. Each issue can have labels, assignments, and comments to organize work efficiently.

• **Projects:** GitHub's "Projects" feature allows teams to organize tasks and workflows using Kanban boards, helping visualize project progress and manage tasks effectively.

8.3.5. Community and Resources

GitHub hosts a vast community of developers, offering valuable resources:

• **Open Source Projects:** GitHub is home to millions of open-source projects, allowing developers to explore, contribute to, and learn from existing projects. This enriches the developer experience and fosters a culture of collaboration and continuous improvement.

- **Documentation and Examples:** Many GitHub projects include detailed documentation and usage examples, making it easier for new developers to learn about the technologies and practices used.

8.3.6. Conclusion

In summary, GitHub is more than just a Git repository hosting service; it's a comprehensive platform that facilitates software project collaboration and management. With features that promote effective communication, process automation, and task organization, GitHub has become an essential tool for development teams of all sizes. Mastering GitHub not only enhances team efficiency but also contributes to the overall quality and success of software projects.

8.4. GIT WORKFLOW

A well-defined Git workflow is essential for managing code changes and collaborating effectively on development projects. A basic workflow enables developers to organize their work and maintain a clear change history. Below are the key steps in a typical Git workflow.

8.4.1. Cloning the Repository

Cloning is the first step when working on an existing project:

- **Create a Local Copy:** Using the git clone command, developers can create a complete copy of a remote repository on their local machine, including all files, change history, and branches, allowing offline work and independent changes.

- **Initial Setup**: Cloning the repository also sets up the connection between the local and remote repositories, making synchronization easier.

8.4.2. Creating and Switching Branches

Branches are fundamental for developing new features or fixing bugs without affecting the main code:

- **Branch Usage:** The git branch command allows developers to create new branches. For example, creating a branch for a new feature ensures that changes won't affect the main branch until merged.

- **Branch Switching:** Using the git checkout command, developers can switch between branches, enabling simultaneous work on multiple features while keeping work organized.

- **Merging Changes:** Once a feature is completed and tested in a separate branch, it can be merged back into the main branch using git merge, ensuring the main branch is always up-to-date.

8.4.3. Committing Changes

Effectively saving changes is crucial for maintaining a clear history:

• **Staging Changes:** The git add command stages selected changes for the next commit, allowing developers to group related changes and ensure only desired changes are saved.

• **Creating a Commit:** With git commit, developers save their work locally along with a descriptive message explaining the changes. Clear commit messages provide context, making the project history easier to understand.

8.4.4. Integrating Changes

Once changes are made and saved locally, they need to be synchronized with the remote repository:

• **Pushing Changes:** The git push command uploads local commits to a remote repository, updating the cloud repository and allowing other developers to see and use the changes.

• **Pulling Updates:** To stay in sync with other developers 'work, use git pull, which downloads the latest changes from the remote repository and integrates them into the active local branch.

8.4.5. Conflict Resolution

Conflicts are inevitable in collaborative environments:

• **Merge Conflicts:** When two developers make changes to the same part of the code and try to merge their branches, Git may encounter a conflict. Resolving these conflicts manually by selecting which changes to keep is essential before completing the merge.

• **Using Tools:** Git provides tools to help developers resolve conflicts, and platforms like GitHub offer visual interfaces to simplify the process.

8.4.6. Best Practices

Implementing a Git workflow effectively involves following best practices:

• **Frequent Commits:** Committing frequently with small changes rather than large blocks makes tracking and reviewing history easier.

• **Descriptive Commit Messages:** Clear and descriptive commit messages help other developers quickly understand the nature of the changes.

• **Keeping Branches Updated:** Regular synchronization with the remote repository and keeping branches up-to-date minimizes conflicts and ensures work aligns with team progress.

8.4.7. Conclusion

A well-defined Git workflow is essential for collaborative software development. By following these steps, teams can manage code changes effectively, ensure smooth collaboration, and maintain a clear and organized change history. Proper Git usage helps developers work more efficiently and contributes to the overall quality of the project.

8.5. GIT BRANCHING STRATEGIES

Git branching strategies are essential for efficiently managing code development in software projects. Each strategy has its own approach and benefits, and the most suitable choice depends on factors like project complexity and team dynamics. Below are some of the most common branching strategies.

8.5.1. Git Flow

Git Flow is one of the most popular strategies for large and complex projects. It is based on creating multiple specific branches that facilitate version control and organized development:

- **Main Branches:** It includes two permanent branches: main (or master), containing the production code, and develop, which is the development branch where all new features are integrated.

- **Feature Branches:** For each new functionality, a feature branch is created from develop. These branches are generally named feature/feature-name. Once the feature is completed, it is merged back into develop.

- **Release Branches:** When a stable state is reached in develop, a release branch (release/version-number) is created to prepare a new version. This branch allows for minor adjustments and bug fixes before the final release.

- **Hotfix Branches:** If a production issue needs fixing, a hotfix branch (hotfix/issue-name) is created from main. Once the issue is resolved, it is merged into both main and develop.

- **Benefits:** Git Flow provides a clear structure that allows different types of work to be handled in parallel, minimizing conflicts and facilitating a more organized development cycle.

8.5.2. GitHub Flow

GitHub Flow is a simpler and more agile strategy, ideal for projects requiring continuous deployment and rapid iterations. It uses a main branch and feature branches:

- **Main Branch:** The main branch should always be in a deployable state, meaning any commit on this branch should be safe for production deployment.

- **Feature Branches:** Developers create feature branches to work on new functionalities or fixes, naming them feature/feature-name.

- **Pull Requests:** Once a feature is complete, the developer opens a pull request (PR) to merge the feature branch into main. Team members review the code, provide feedback, and, once approved, the branch is merged.

- **Deployment:** After merging the feature branch into main, it can be automatically deployed to production.

- **Benefits:** GitHub Flow is highly flexible and encourages collaboration, allowing teams to make frequent and rapid changes. It's ideal for teams implementing continuous integration and continuous delivery practices.

8.5.3. Trunk-Based Development

Trunk-Based Development emphasizes constant work on the main branch (trunk), promoting frequent integrations and avoiding long-lived branches:

- **Continuous Integration:** All developers work on the main branch, committing frequently and integrating small changes rather than working on long-lived branches.

- **Short-Lived Branches:** If a feature branch is necessary, it should be short-lived, aiming for quick merges back into the main branch.

- **Frequent Deployment:** By working in the main branch with continuous integration, the code remains ready for deployment, enabling faster release cycles.

- **Benefits:** This approach minimizes complexity and merge conflicts since code is integrated constantly. It also fosters a culture of collaboration and communication among team members.

8.5.4. Choosing the Right Strategy

Choosing the right branching strategy depends on several factors:

- **Project Complexity:** Large, complex projects may benefit from Git Flow, while smaller projects can opt for GitHub Flow or Trunk-Based Development.

- **Team Culture:** Team dynamics and preferred workflows also influence the strategy choice.

- **Deployment Requirements:** For frequent, fast deployments, GitHub Flow or Trunk-Based Development are ideal options.

8.5.5. Conclusion

Branching strategies are valuable tools that help teams manage software development in an organized and efficient manner. Selecting the right strategy not only improves code quality but also facilitates team collaboration and communication. Implementing a structured branching approach is essential for the success of any development project.

8.6. GIT INTEGRATION WITH CI/CD TOOLS

Integrating Git with CI/CD (Continuous Integration and Continuous Delivery) tools is essential for modernizing and optimizing the software development workflow. This integration automates previously manual processes, saving time, reducing human errors, and enhancing overall software quality. Below are some key benefits and aspects of this integration.

8.6.1. Test Automation

Test automation is a cornerstone of CI/CD, and its integration with Git makes the process more efficient:

• **Automatic Test Execution:** When a developer pushes changes or creates a pull request, tools like Jenkins, GitHub Actions, or GitLab CI can automatically trigger a set of predefined tests, ensuring that changes don't break existing functionality.

• **Diverse Testing:** Automated tests can include unit, integration, and end-to-end tests. Running different types of tests with each commit helps catch issues early in development.

• **Quick Feedback:** Developers receive near-instant notifications about test results, allowing for quick fixes and accelerating the feedback loop.

8.6.2. Continuous Deployment

Continuous deployment ensures that code can be deployed to production at any time, with Git integration playing a crucial role:

• **Deployment Automation:** CI/CD tools can automatically deploy changes to production or testing environments once all defined tests pass, reducing time between development and software availability.

• **Deployment Criteria:** Tools allow specific deployment criteria, such as pull request approval or successful test completion, ensuring that only validated code is deployed.

- **Multi-Environment Deployment:** CI/CD tools facilitate deploying the same code to different environments (development, testing, production), ensuring consistent behavior.

8.6.3. Notifications and Reports

Effective communication is crucial in development teams, and CI/CD tools provide functionalities to enhance this:

- **Automatic Notifications:** Teams can receive notifications about build and test statuses via email, instant messaging, or integrations with platforms like Slack, keeping everyone informed in real-time.

- **Detailed Reports:** CI/CD tools generate automatic reports with information on test statuses, code coverage, and build performance, which are valuable for continuous evaluation and informed decision-making.

- **Change History:** Git integration with CI/CD allows tracking changes and their impact on software performance, helping identify trends and areas for improvement.

8.6.4. Workflow Improvement

Git integration with CI/CD tools transforms how development teams work together:

- **Effective Collaboration:** Automation and visibility improve collaboration among developers, QA, and operations, as everyone can see project status and ongoing changes.

- **Time Savings:** Automating repetitive tasks allows developers to focus on critical activities, like designing new features and solving complex issues.

- **Higher Code Quality:** Automated testing and controlled deployments maintain high code quality, resulting in more reliable and maintainable software.

8.6.5. Conclusion

Git integration with CI/CD tools is a fundamental component of modern software development strategies. This combination accelerates development and deployment processes while improving product quality. As teams adopt these practices, they become more agile and responsive to changing requirements and customer expectations. Implementing CI/CD with Git is, therefore, a key investment for any team aiming to enhance efficiency and effectiveness in software development.

8.7. CHAPTER CONCLUSIONS

Version control is a fundamental practice in modern software development, enabling teams to manage changes, collaborate efficiently, and ensure code quality. Git, combined with platforms like GitHub, simplifies version management and collaboration. Branching strategies and CI/CD integration further enhance workflow organization and delivery speed. Implementing a solid version control workflow is crucial for any software project, regardless of size or complexity.

CHAPTER 9
SOFTWARE TESTING

Software testing is a crucial part of the development cycle, ensuring that the system functions as expected and meets established requirements. This chapter covers different types of tests, automation, software quality management, and strategies to ensure application robustness and performance.

9.1. TYPES OF SOFTWARE TESTING: UNIT, INTEGRATION, FUNCTIONAL

Software testing is essential to ensure the quality and correct functioning of an application. Each type of test has a specific focus and objective, contributing to different aspects of software behavior. Below are some of the most common types of tests described in detail:

9.1.1. Unit Testing

Unit tests form the foundation of the testing process, focusing on validating the smallest units of code in isolation:

- **Purpose:** Their goal is to ensure that each individual component, such as a function, method, or class, operates correctly and predictably. Each unit test verifies a small part of the code's behavior to catch errors early in development.

- **Common Tools:** Various tools facilitate unit test creation, such as JUnit for Java, pytest for Python, and Jest for JavaScript. These tools provide an automated environment for running tests.

- **Benefits:** Unit tests help identify issues in specific components without needing to test the entire system. This makes it easier to locate errors and contributes to more agile development, allowing for refactoring with greater confidence.

- **Practical Example:** Imagine a Python function that calculates the area of a triangle. A unit test could verify if the function returns the correct value for a given set of bases and heights.

9.1.2. Integration Testing

Integration tests focus on validating how different modules or components interact with each other, ensuring proper communication between them:

- **Purpose:** While unit tests validate isolated components, integration tests ensure that those components work properly when combined. This is particularly important in applications with multiple dependencies and components.

- **Scope:** They can test interactions between two or more code modules, database integration, external API connections, or how different microservices interact.

- **Benefits:** Integration tests catch issues that arise from combining components, such as interface incompatibilities or communication problems, ensuring seamless cooperation between different parts of the application.

- **Practical Example:** In an e-commerce system, integration tests could validate how the user authentication module interacts with the shopping module, ensuring that an authenticated user can complete a transaction correctly.

9.1.3. Functional Testing

Functional tests verify that the software meets expected requirements and functionalities from the user's perspective:

- **Purpose:** Their goal is to ensure that each system functionality works as specified. Unlike unit tests, functional tests focus on the end results presented to the user rather than the internal code structure.

- **Methodology:** They rely on test cases representing real use scenarios. Each case describes an input, an action, and the expected outcome. If the system produces the expected result, the test passes; otherwise, it fails.

- **Benefits:** They ensure that the software meets user expectations, which is critical for customer satisfaction and product acceptance. Functional tests are useful for verifying complete workflows and user experiences.

- **Practical Example:** In an online banking application, a functional test could verify that the fund transfer process between accounts works correctly, ensuring funds are deducted from one account and credited to another as per user instructions.

-Importance of Combining Different Types of Tests

Each type of test plays a crucial role in software quality assurance:

- Unit Tests ensure that basic components are reliable and error-free, providing a solid foundation for the rest of the development.

- Integration Tests detect issues not visible at the component level, ensuring proper collaboration between parts.

- Functional Tests validate the final user experience, ensuring the product meets business requirements and customer expectations.

Combining these tests creates a comprehensive quality assurance approach, detecting errors at different development levels and stages. This helps build stable, reliable software aligned with user needs.

9.2. TEST AUTOMATION: TOOLS AND STRATEGIES

Automation tools help execute tests systematically, facilitating error detection and ensuring the software works as expected after each change. Some of the most popular tools include:

•   **Selenium:** One of the most widely used tools for web application test automation. It simulates user actions like clicks and page navigation, making it easy to automate functional and UI (User Interface) tests. Selenium supports multiple programming languages and browsers.

•   **JUnit:** A standard tool in the Java ecosystem for automating unit tests. It provides a simple way to define test cases and group them into test suites. Additionally, it integrates well with CI/CD tools like Jenkins for automatic test execution with every code change.

•   **Cypress:** Especially useful for testing modern web applications, Cypress allows end-to-end (E2E) testing and is known for its ease of use and quick setup. Unlike Selenium, it runs tests directly in the browser, simplifying debugging and providing a more realistic testing environment.

•   **PyTest:** A powerful tool in the Python ecosystem for creating unit and integration tests. Its simple syntax and extensibility through plugins make it ideal for automating tests in projects of various scales.

•   **TestNG:** Similar to JUnit but with additional features such as test case prioritization, parallel execution, and support for complex integration tests. It is widely used in the industry for automating both unit and integration tests.

9.2.2. Automation Strategies

A well-defined automation strategy helps maximize test coverage and ensures efficient test execution. Common strategies include:

• **Test Pyramid:** This strategy suggests a balanced proportion of tests at different levels:

• **Unit Tests:** Form the base of the pyramid, as they are quick and cost-effective to run. They validate isolated code components, allowing early error detection.

• **Integration Tests:** Occupy the middle of the pyramid, verifying how different software modules interact, helping identify communication issues between components.

• **Functional/E2E Tests:** At the top of the pyramid, they validate complete application flows from the user's perspective. While useful, they tend to be slower and more expensive to maintain, so strategic use is recommended.

• **Continuous Integration (CI) Automation:** Integrating automated tests into the CI process using tools like Jenkins, GitHub Actions, or GitLab CI ensures that tests run automatically with every code change, detecting errors immediately.

• **Test-Driven Development (TDD):** A development methodology where tests are written before implementing code. This ensures code development guided by the need for each functionality to pass a series of validations from the start.

• **Automated Regression:** Running a set of tests whenever a change is introduced to ensure new features don't break existing behavior. This is essential in fast-evolving projects.

• **Data-Driven Testing:** Running the same tests with different datasets facilitates validation for various input scenarios, especially useful for applications handling multiple input-output scenarios.

9.2.3. Benefits of Test Automation

Automating software tests offers numerous benefits, directly impacting product quality and development efficiency:

• **Reduced Test Time:** Automated tests can be run quickly and repeatedly, significantly reducing the time needed to validate code changes.

- **Consistency and Accuracy:** Automated tests ensure consistent results each time they are run, reducing human error and ensuring precise validation.

- **Fast Feedback:** Integrating automated tests into CI/CD workflows provides developers with immediate feedback on the impact of their changes, accelerating problem identification and correction.

- **Scalability:** As software complexity grows, manual testing becomes unsustainable. Automation allows scalable testing processes, maintaining adequate coverage even in large, complex systems.

9.2.4. Test Automation Challenges

Despite its benefits, test automation presents challenges to consider:

- **Test Maintenance:** As software evolves, automated tests must be updated to reflect changes, requiring time and additional effort.

- **Learning Curve:** Effective use of automation tools may require specialized technical knowledge, posing a learning curve for teams.

- **Initial Cost:** Setting up automated test infrastructure and creating test cases can be costly in terms of time and resources, though long-term efficiency offsets this.

Test automation is a key investment in software development that enhances product quality and streamlines the development process. By implementing the right strategy and tools, development teams can ensure reliable software ready for production environments.

9.3. BLACK-BOX AND WHITE-BOX TESTING

Software testing can be divided into two main approaches: black-box testing and white-box testing. Each approach has its methodology and objectives, aimed at validating different aspects of the software. A balanced combination of both ensures application quality from various perspectives.

9.3.1. Black-Box Testing

Black-box testing focuses on verifying software functionality without requiring knowledge of the internal structure or underlying code. It ensures that the system meets specified functional requirements and responds correctly to input data. Key features and techniques include:

- **Functionality Validation:** Testers evaluate how the system responds to various use cases, ensuring functionalities work as expected. This includes verifying user interfaces, input data handling, and error management.

- **Equivalence Partitioning & Boundary Value Analysis:** These techniques reduce the number of test cases by identifying representative input data. Boundary value analysis tests upper and lower input limits, while equivalence classes group similar inputs expected to yield the same outcome.

- **Functional & Non-Functional Testing:** In addition to functionality, black-box testing covers non-functional aspects such as performance, security, and usability to ensure the system meets user quality standards.

9.3.2. White-Box Testing

White-box testing involves a deep understanding of the source code and internal logic. It focuses on validating the system's internal structure and ensuring the code follows expected logical paths. Key features and techniques include:

- **Code Coverage:** White-box testing ensures that all lines, decision branches, and conditions are executed at least once. Techniques include:

- **Statement Coverage:** Ensures every line of code is executed.

- **Branch Coverage:** Verifies all decision paths (e.g., if/else) are tested.

- **Condition Coverage:** Ensures all conditions in decision structures are tested as both true and false.

- **Logic & Internal Flow Verification:** Helps detect internal logic errors, such as infinite loops or incorrect calculations, particularly in critical algorithms.

- **Path Testing:** Focuses on identifying and testing all possible paths within the code. While achieving 100% coverage in complex systems is difficult, path testing highlights critical routes likely to contain errors.

9.3.3. Complementarity of Black-Box and White-Box Testing

Though distinct, both approaches are essential for comprehensive and effective test coverage:

- **Comprehensive Coverage:** Black-box testing ensures the system meets user expectations, while white-box testing verifies the internal code's robustness. This combination detects both visible errors and hidden performance or stability issues.

- **Collaborative Approach:** In development teams, QA testers typically perform black-box tests simulating user behavior, while developers conduct white-box tests using their code knowledge, fostering a collaborative quality assurance process.

- **Risk Reduction:** Combining both approaches minimizes critical production errors. For example, black-box tests may identify functional issues, while white-box tests reveal underlying logic problems causing them.

- **Adaptability:** Black-box testing is ideal for validating functional changes or new modules, while white-box testing is better for code refactoring and performance enhancements.

Together, these approaches ensure software is functional, robust, efficient, and free from internal issues, guaranteeing a high-quality user experience and long-term system reliability.

9.4. TEST CASE MANAGEMENT & SOFTWARE QUALITY

Test case management is a fundamental process for maintaining software quality throughout the development cycle. Through detailed planning and systematic execution of test cases, every aspect of the application is adequately evaluated, contributing to a robust and reliable final product.

9.4.1. Test Cases

Test cases are detailed documents that describe each scenario to be evaluated to validate the correct functioning of the software. A typical test case includes:

• **Scenario Description:** Defines the purpose of the test and the specific functionality to be evaluated, helping establish the context and objective of the test.

• **Inputs:** Details the specific data entered into the system during the test, including variables and values. This can range from valid data to inputs designed to evaluate how the system handles exceptional situations.

• **Steps to Follow:** Describes each step the tester must follow to conduct the test, facilitating process replicability and ensuring uniform execution of all tests.

• **Expected Results:** Specifies what should happen after the test is executed, detailing the expected outcomes for each set of inputs. This is essential to determine whether the test has been successful or if an error has been detected.

- **Actual Result and Test Status:** Once the test is executed, the actual result is documented and compared with the expected outcome. If they match, the test is marked as "successful"; if not, it is recorded as "failed," indicating that the issue needs to be investigated and resolved.

Well-structured test cases facilitate problem identification and ensure that every functionality is thoroughly reviewed before reaching end users.

9.4.2. Software Quality

Software quality is a broad concept encompassing several critical product aspects, such as the absence of errors, ease of use, performance, security, and stability. Key elements of software quality include:

- **Reliability**: Refers to the software's ability to function without failures over a specific time period. High reliability ensures the system can handle errors and exceptions in a controlled manner, reducing service interruptions.

- **Usability:** Measures how easily users can interact with the software and understand its functionalities. High-quality software not only functions correctly but is also intuitive and easy to use, enhancing the end-user experience.

- **Performance:** Evaluates how the software responds under different workloads and conditions. Performance tests, such as load and stress tests, help ensure the system maintains efficiency and response times in real-world usage scenarios.

- **Security:** Quality is also measured by the software's ability to protect sensitive user information and prevent vulnerabilities. Security tests are essential for identifying potential breaches and ensuring data integrity.

9.4.3. Test Case Management Tools

To ensure efficient test case management, many organizations use specialized tools that enable centralized organization, execution, and tracking of tests. Some popular tools include:

- **TestRail, Zephyr, and qTest:** These platforms allow for test case management, detailed reporting, and defect tracking during the testing phase.

- **Integration with CI/CD Tools:** Test case management tools can be integrated with CI/CD systems like Jenkins, GitLab CI, or GitHub Actions to automatically execute tests whenever a code change is made. This ensures that new implementations do not introduce errors that affect existing functionality.

- **Test Case Automation:** Many tools support integration with automation frameworks, facilitating the creation of scripts that replicate manual test cases automatically, improving process efficiency and reducing the time required for repetitive tests.

9.4.4. Importance of Effective Test Case Management

Efficient test case management offers several key benefits for maintaining software quality:

- **Comprehensive Test Coverage:** By documenting all possible test cases, it ensures that all software functionalities are validated, including less obvious or less frequently used ones, helping prevent unnoticed errors.

- **Traceability and Auditing:** Documenting test cases facilitates tracking which functionalities have been tested and which need more attention. This is particularly useful during audits or quality reviews, as it demonstrates that a rigorous testing process has been conducted.

- **Enhances Team Collaboration:** Well-defined test cases enable different testers, even those in various locations or new to the project, to quickly understand what needs to be evaluated and how. This improves collaboration and ensures a consistent testing approach across the team.

- **Reduction of Technical Debt:** Effective test case management helps identify problems early and allows developers to fix them before they become harder-to-manage technical debt. This contributes to maintaining clean code and a more easily maintainable product in the long term.

9.4.5. Ensuring Quality Before Delivery

Test case management focuses not only on finding errors but also on ensuring the product meets quality standards before release. This includes:

- **User Acceptance Testing (UAT):** Before the final delivery, acceptance tests are conducted to verify that the software meets the client's expectations and project requirements. Test cases designed for UAT are essential to ensure the product aligns with the end user's needs.

- **Quality Criteria Evaluation:** It is crucial to review the quality criteria established at the project's start, such as response times, regulatory compliance, and security features, and verify that the software meets them through specific tests.

Having effective test case management ensures that the software meets quality standards before being delivered to end users, minimizing the risk of production errors and ensuring a positive user experience. This not only increases customer satisfaction but also strengthens the reputation of the development team and the organization.

9.5. SECURITY AND PERFORMANCE TESTING

Security and performance testing are essential to ensure that software is robust, secure, and capable of handling the expected load of users and transactions. These tests ensure that the system not only functions correctly but is also prepared to face threats and meet speed and stability requirements.

9.5.1. Security Testing

Security testing focuses on identifying and mitigating potential vulnerabilities in the software. Its goal is to ensure that the application is not exposed to attacks that could compromise the integrity, confidentiality, and availability of information. Key aspects of security testing include:

- **Penetration Testing:** This involves simulating controlled attacks against the system to identify potential weak entry points. A security specialist attempts to exploit weaknesses, such as SQL injections, XSS (cross-site scripting) attacks, and configuration issues, to detect flaws before real attackers do.

- **Data Security Analysis:** This focuses on ensuring that sensitive data (such as user information, credentials, and financial transactions) is protected using encryption techniques and robust authentication mechanisms. These tests ensure that information is protected both in transit and at rest.

- **Code Security Review:** This involves analyzing the source code to detect potential vulnerabilities, such as improper error handling, lack of input validation, and session management issues. Static analysis tools like SonarQube are commonly used to identify security issues before the code is deployed.

- **Authentication and Authorization Testing:** These tests validate that the system properly implements access controls, ensuring that users can only access information and functionalities they are authorized to. This is critical to prevent unauthorized access to sensitive areas of the application.

- **API Security Testing:** If the system includes APIs (Application Programming Interfaces), they must undergo security testing to ensure that only authenticated users can access the endpoints, that requests are properly validated, and that data is transmitted securely.

These tests are critical for any application that handles sensitive data, such as personal or financial information, and are required to comply with regulations like GDPR, HIPAA, and other data privacy standards.

9.5.2. Performance Testing

Performance testing is essential to ensure that the software functions efficiently under different load conditions and maintains a good user experience even during periods of high demand. The main types of performance tests include:

- **Load Testing:** Simulates a specific number of users interacting with the system to evaluate how it performs under a normal or slightly higher-than-expected load. These tests identify the point at which the system begins to experience performance problems, such as slow response times or server errors.

- **Stress Testing:** Pushes the system to its limits by simulating a much higher load than expected to identify how it responds in extreme situations. The goal is to see whether the system crashes in a controlled manner or fails unpredictably, as well as to analyze how the system recovers after overload.

- **Scalability Testing:** Evaluates the system's ability to grow and handle increases in users or transactions efficiently. These tests help determine whether the system can scale vertically (by adding resources to a single server) or horizontally (by adding more servers).

- **Stability Testing (Soak Testing):** Involves running the system under continuous load for an extended period of time to identify issues that only appear after prolonged use, such as memory leaks or error accumulation.

- **Response Time Testing:** Measures the time it takes for the system to respond to specific requests, ensuring that the software meets established response time requirements. This is crucial for applications where speed is key, such as e-commerce and online financial services.

- **Use of Performance Testing Tools:** Tools like JMeter, Gatling, and LoadRunner are popular for conducting load and stress tests, allowing the simulation of thousands of users and analyzing detailed metrics on response times, CPU usage, memory consumption, and more.

9.5.3. Importance of Security and Performance Testing

Implementing security and performance testing is essential to ensure that software meets quality standards and can face the challenges of the production environment. These tests are especially critical in applications that:

- **Handle Sensitive Information:** Such as banking systems, healthcare applications, and e-commerce platforms, where privacy and data protection are paramount.

- **Require High Availability:** Mission-critical applications, such as emergency services or real-time monitoring systems, must be able to maintain performance even under high load conditions.

- **Offer Services at Scale:** Social media platforms, streaming systems, and applications with millions of users need performance testing to ensure they can handle demand efficiently.

- **Need to Comply with Regulations:** Security tests are necessary to meet information security and cybersecurity regulations, which require applications to be audited and verified to avoid data breaches.

The combination of security and performance testing not only helps identify vulnerabilities before they can be exploited but also ensures that the software maintains optimal performance under any circumstance. By integrating these tests into the development cycle, critical issues in production are minimized, and a better experience for end users is ensured. This also contributes to the company's reputation, demonstrating a commitment to the quality and security of the product.

9.6. A/B TESTING AND USABILITY

A/B testing and usability testing are key techniques in user-centered software development, as they allow for the validation of design decisions and ensure that the user experience (UX) is optimal. Through these tests, improvements can be made based on data, and insights can be gained into how users actually interact with the system, leading to a more effective and satisfying product.

9.6.1. A/B Testing

A/B testing is an experimentation methodology used to compare two versions of an application, webpage, or feature to determine which one is more effective based on certain key performance indicators (KPIs). These tests are especially valuable in digital marketing, conversion optimization, and user interface design.

-A/B Testing Process:

- **Defining the Objective:** A clear goal is identified, such as increasing conversion rates, improving time spent on the page, or reducing bounce rates.

- **Creating Variants:** Two versions of the same page or feature are created: version A (original) and version B (modified). Version B may include changes in design, text, colors, or element layout.

- **Traffic Division:** Users are randomly divided between both versions, with some seeing version A and others version B.

- **Data Collection and Analysis:** The collected data, such as conversion rates or clicks, are analyzed to determine which version best achieves the established goal.

- **Implementing the Best Variant:** Once the most effective version is identified, it is implemented permanently.

-Common Applications:

• **Optimizing Landing Pages:** A/B tests are used to identify which elements of a landing page (such as headings, call-to-action buttons, or images) generate the most conversions.

• **Improving User Flows:** Different paths within a user flow (e.g., the registration or checkout process) can be tested to see which is simpler and more engaging for users.

• **Personalizing Content:** A/B testing is also used to test the effectiveness of different personalized messages based on user type or market segment.

A/B testing allows for data-driven improvements and reduces the risk of implementing changes that do not generate the expected results. This leads to a more personalized experience that is tailored to the needs of users.

9.6.2. Usability Testing

Usability testing focuses on evaluating how intuitive and easy to use a system is from the perspective of the end user. These tests aim to identify issues that may hinder the user experience, ensuring that the software is accessible, clear, and efficient for those who use it.

-Usability Testing Methodology:

• **Selecting Representative Users:** Users who represent the target audience of the system are selected. This ensures that the test results reflect the issues that real users might face.

• **Usage Scenarios:** Specific tasks are designed for users to complete, such as registering, making a purchase, or searching for information. The scenarios must be realistic and reflect the activities users would carry out on the system.

• **Direct Observation:** Users are observed while interacting with the application, noting any problems they encounter, questions they have, and moments where they may get stuck.

• **Collecting Feedback:** In addition to observing, feedback is gathered from users about their experience, helping to understand how they perceive the interface and what aspects they find confusing or complicated.

-Types of Usability Testing:

• **Moderated Testing:** A moderator guides the user during the test, providing context and clarifying doubts without interfering with the user's decisions. This is useful for better understanding the reasoning behind the user's actions.

• **Unmoderated Testing:** Conducted remotely without a moderator, allowing the user to complete tasks independently. This provides a larger volume of data and observes behavior in a more natural environment for the user.

• **Remote Usability Testing:** Using digital tools, tests can be conducted with users in different regions, providing a more global perspective on how the application is perceived in different cultural contexts.

-Benefits of Usability Testing:

• **Early Problem Detection:** Usability tests help identify obstacles before the application is released to the general public, saving time and resources by addressing design issues early on.

• **Improved User Experience:** By understanding how users interact with the system, developers and designers can adjust the interface and workflows to be more natural and seamless.

• **Increased Satisfaction and Retention:** Intuitive, easy-to-use software increases user satisfaction, which in turn can improve user retention and reduce app abandonment rates.

9.6.3. Importance of A/B and Usability Testing

A/B testing and usability testing are complementary tools that help ensure that the system is not only functional but also offers an engaging and seamless user experience:

• **Continuous Optimization:** A/B testing allows for ongoing improvement through experimentation, adjusting specific elements of the interface or functionality to maximize results.

• **User-Centered Design:** Usability tests ensure that the system is designed with the needs and expectations of the end users in mind, which is crucial for the success of any digital product.

• **Risk Reduction:** Both tests help mitigate the risk of investing in design changes that may not be effective, enabling development teams to make data-driven decisions.

Together, these tests ensure that applications not only meet functional requirements but also provide an exceptional user experience, maximizing acceptance and market success. This is especially important in a highly competitive digital environment where usability and user satisfaction are key differentiators.

9.7. LOAD TESTING AND STRESS TESTING

Load testing and stress testing are essential for evaluating the performance and robustness of an application under different usage conditions. These tests help ensure that the software not only works well under normal use but also handles peak demand and extreme situations efficiently and securely.

9.7.1. Load Testing

Load testing focuses on analyzing the performance of a system when subjected to an increasing load until it reaches the expected levels of use in a real-world environment. This helps identify bottlenecks and adjust the system to ensure a smooth experience for users.

-Objectives of Load Testing:

• **Determining the Saturation Point:** Identifying when the system begins to show signs of performance degradation, such as slower response times or an increase in error rates.

• **Verifying the Support Capacity:** Ensuring that the system can handle the maximum expected load, such as the number of concurrent users or the volume of transactions per second.

• **Optimizing Performance:** Through load testing results, adjustments can be made to the infrastructure or code optimization to improve response speed and efficiency.

-Tools for Load Testing:

• **JMeter:** A popular open-source tool for load testing web applications, allowing simulation of a large number of concurrent users and analysis of response times.

• **LoadRunner:** An advanced tool used in corporate environments for load and performance testing, especially in complex applications and ERP systems.

- **Gatling:** Ideal for developers, Gatling allows programmatic load testing using scripts, facilitating automation and integration with CI/CD workflows.

9.7.2. Stress Testing

Stress testing goes a step further than load testing by pushing the system beyond its maximum capacity to evaluate its behavior under extreme conditions. The goal is to determine how the system fails and whether it can recover properly once the load conditions are reduced.

-Objectives of Stress Testing:

- **Identifying Failure Points:** Detecting the exact limits at which the system begins to fail, which is essential for identifying vulnerabilities or limitations in the software architecture.

- **Evaluating Recovery:** Verifying if the system can return to a stable state after facing an overload or if it remains in an error state requiring manual intervention.

- **Robustness and Resilience:** Ensuring that the software is robust and can handle unforeseen situations, such as a sudden increase in demand, avoiding unexpected crashes that affect users.

Common Use Cases for Stress Testing:

- **Promotional Events:** When a company launches a major marketing campaign, it's important to ensure the website or app can handle the sudden increase in visitors.

- **Infrastructure Failure Simulation:** For example, turning off a server or disconnecting a database to see how the system handles the loss of a critical component.

- **Peak Testing:** Generating excessive load for a very short period to observe how the system handles sudden spikes in activity.

-Tools for Stress Testing:

- **Chaos Monkey:** Created by Netflix, this tool is part of a set known as Chaos Engineering and allows simulating failures in infrastructure to test the system's resilience.

- **Stress-ng:** A tool that allows stress testing at the operating system level, simulating high demand conditions on CPU, memory, and other resources.
- **k6:** A modern open-source tool for load testing that can also be used for stress testing, particularly in APIs and microservices environments.

9.7.3. Importance of Load Testing and Stress Testing

These tests are critical for any application that will be in a production environment, as they ensure that the system can maintain good performance and stability even under adverse conditions:

- **Preventing Production Downtime:** An unexpected failure in a production environment can cause financial losses and damage a company's reputation. Load and stress testing help anticipate and resolve these issues before they happen.
- **Scalability Planning:** Thanks to these tests, development and operations teams can accurately determine when scaling the infrastructure is necessary, whether by adding more servers, optimizing the database, or adjusting system configuration.
- **Continuous System Improvement:** Performance tests provide valuable data that can be used to continuously optimize the application, improving user experience and reducing operational costs.

9.7.4. Considerations for Performing Load Testing and Stress Testing

- **Realistic Testing Environment:** It's essential that the tests are conducted in an environment that closely mirrors the production configuration, including network, servers, and other components, to obtain accurate results.
- **Constant Monitoring:** During the tests, it is crucial to use monitoring tools to track resource usage (CPU, memory, I/O) and detect potential bottlenecks.
- **Results Analysis:** After the tests, it's important to carefully analyze the results to identify areas for improvement and adjust the system accordingly.

9.7.5. Conclusion

Load testing and stress testing are crucial to ensure that software not only meets performance expectations under normal conditions but is also prepared to handle unexpected spikes in demand and critical situations. Investing in these tests contributes to the creation of more robust and reliable systems, improving user experience and ensuring service continuity in high-demand environments.

9.8. CHAPTER CONCLUSIONS

Software testing is a fundamental pillar to ensure the quality and stability of an application before deployment. Each type of test, from unit tests to load and security tests, serves a specific role in validating software. Test automation and proper test case management enable development teams to be more efficient and ensure that systems meet user requirements and industry standards. Implementing a comprehensive testing approach is essential for the success of any software project.

CHAPTER 10
BEST PRACTICES IN SOFTWARE DEVELOPMENT

The adoption of best practices in software development is essential for creating robust, maintainable, and high-quality applications. This chapter discusses methodologies, principles, and tools that enable developers to improve code quality, team efficiency, and customer satisfaction.

10.1. SOLID PRINCIPLES

The SOLID principles are a set of five key guidelines for object-oriented software design aimed at improving flexibility, scalability, and maintainability of code. Properly implementing these principles leads to more robust systems that are easier to modify and extend, reducing the likelihood of errors and simplifying development.

10.1.1. S: Single Responsibility Principle (SRP)

This principle states that each class or software module should have only one responsibility, meaning it should focus on doing one thing. This makes the code easier to understand and maintain because if a change occurs in one aspect of the system, only the relevant class needs to be modified.

- **Example**: Instead of having a class that handles both business logic and database access, you can separate them into two classes: one for business logic and another for database interactions.
- **Benefit**: It makes maintenance and testing easier because each class has a clear purpose, and changes in one part of the system do not have unintended side effects in other parts.

10.1.2. O: Open/Closed Principle (OCP)

The OCP principle suggests that classes **should be open for extension but closed for modification**. This means that new functionality should be added without changing existing code, reducing the risk of introducing errors when new requirements are implemented.

- **Example**: Instead of modifying an existing class to add new features, you can create a new subclass or use a design pattern like the Decorator to extend the behavior without modifying the original class.
- **Benefit**: It allows developers to add new functionality without compromising the stability of the existing code, minimizing the risk of regressions.

10.1.3. L: Liskov Substitution Principle (LSP)

The Liskov Substitution Principle states that objects of a subclass should be able to replace objects of their superclass without altering the correct functioning of the program. In other words, any derived class should be interchangeable with its base class without causing issues in the system.

- **Example**: If there is a Vehicle class with an accelerate method, all subclasses like Car or Bicycle must implement this method in a way that is consistent with the expectations of the base class.

- **Benefit**: It ensures that derived classes preserve the expected behavior of base classes, avoiding unexpected results or incorrect behavior when using inheritance.

10.1.4. I: Interface Segregation Principle (ISP)

The ISP states that no client should be forced to depend on interfaces it does not use. Rather than having a large and generic interface that encompasses many functionalities, it is better to have smaller, more specific interfaces that cover only what each class really needs.

- **Example**: Instead of having a Vehicle interface with methods for flying, sailing, and driving, more specialized interfaces can be created, such as Flyable for airplanes, Navigable for boats, and Drivable for cars.

- **Benefit**: It prevents classes from implementing methods they do not need, simplifying the code and making it easier to maintain. It also reduces the need to update all classes when a change is made to a very general interface.

10.1.5. D: Dependency Inversion Principle (DIP)

This principle states that high-level modules should not depend on low-level modules, but rather on abstractions. Details should depend on abstractions, not the other way around. This makes it easier for high-level modules to remain decoupled from specific implementation details, improving flexibility and code reusability.

- **Example**: Instead of having a PaymentService class depend directly on a concrete PaymentProcessor implementation, it can depend on an abstract interface IPayment. This way, the implementation of IPayment can be changed without modifying PaymentService.

- **Benefit**: It facilitates dependency injection and the changing of implementations, making the system more flexible and modular. Additionally, it makes unit testing easier through mocks or simulated implementations.

10.1.6. Applying SOLID Principles in Software Development

Proper implementation of SOLID principles offers multiple benefits throughout the software development life cycle:

- **Modular Code**: It facilitates the creation of code modules that can be developed, tested, and updated independently. This is particularly valuable in large teams where different developers work on different parts of the system.

- **Maintainability and Scalability**: Well-structured software according to SOLID principles can scale more efficiently, as new features are added by extending the system without modifying existing code.

- **More Efficient Testing**: Following SOLID promotes the use of interfaces and decoupled classes, which makes it easier to create unit and integration tests, making the system more testable.

- **Refactoring Ease**: Code that follows SOLID principles is easier to refactor when changes are needed, as responsibilities are clearly defined and dependencies are minimized.

- **Adaptability to Requirement Changes**: A design based on SOLID allows changes in requirements to be implemented with minimal impact, as the code is organized in a way that makes it easy to extend without modifying what already exists.

10.1.7. Conclusion

SOLID principles are essential for object-oriented design, providing a solid foundation for developing high-quality software. These principles help developers write flexible, maintainable, testable, and scalable code. By adhering to SOLID, development teams can build systems that support frequent changes and new requirements without compromising the stability or quality of existing code.

10.2. TEST-DRIVEN DEVELOPMENT (TDD)

Test-Driven Development (TDD) is a methodology that reshapes how software is built by promoting a process where tests guide development. Instead of writing code first and testing later, TDD advocates defining test cases before implementing any functionality. This ensures that each new feature is fully covered by tests from the outset.

10.2.1. TDD Cycle

The TDD process follows a constant iterative cycle with three main steps:

1. **Write a failing test**: Start by writing a test case for the new functionality. Since the code does not yet exist, this test will fail, confirming that the test is correctly written and that the functionality is not implemented.

2. **Write the minimal code to pass the test**: Implement the minimum code necessary to make the test pass. The goal is not to create the most complete or elegant solution but to ensure the test succeeds.

3. **Refactor**: Once the test passes, refactor the code to improve its structure, efficiency, or readability while ensuring all tests continue to pass.

This cycle is repeated for each new functionality, ensuring continuous test coverage and preventing future changes from breaking existing features.

10.2.2. Benefits of TDD

Adopting TDD brings several advantages that enhance both software quality and team productivity:

- **Improved code quality:** Since every line of code is written to make a test pass, developers focus on writing functional, correctly implemented code, reducing hidden bugs and ensuring that requirements are met.

- **Early error detection:** By writing tests before development, TDD helps identify errors early in the development cycle, reducing the cost and time required to fix issues later.

- **Continuous refactoring:** The iterative nature of TDD promotes constant refactoring, allowing for progressive design and structure improvements without fear of breaking existing functionality due to comprehensive test coverage.

- **Confidence in changes:** A strong test suite gives developers confidence when making changes or adding new features, knowing that existing tests will immediately alert them to any issues.

- **Behavior documentation:** The tests written during TDD serve as living documentation of the system's expected behavior, illustrating how the software should respond to various inputs or events.

- **More modular code:** TDD often results in more modular and decoupled code since developers break down software into smaller, easily testable components, fostering a flexible and scalable architecture.

10.2.3. TDD in the Agile Cycle

TDD fits seamlessly into Agile methodologies due to its iterative and continuous approach, aligning with the short development cycles characteristic of Agile. By implementing TDD, teams can incrementally develop small features and validate them continuously, contributing to frequent deliveries and overall product quality enhancement.

TDD also complements other Agile practices, such as Feature-Driven Development (FDD) or Behavior-Driven Development (BDD), aligning tests with user requirements and expectations to ensure the software meets both technical and functional needs.

10.2.4. Challenges of Implementing TDD

Despite its numerous benefits, TDD poses certain challenges:

- **Learning curve:** For developers unfamiliar with writing tests first, TDD represents a significant shift in their workflow. Learning to write effective tests and develop under this approach requires time and practice.

- **Initial time cost:** TDD may initially slow down development since writing tests before implementing code takes extra time. However, this investment often pays off later when the test suite enables quick detection and correction of issues.

- **Limited test coverage:** If tests are not written effectively or focus only on trivial cases, TDD can create a false sense of security. It's crucial to ensure tests cover all critical aspects of the software, not just the obvious ones.

10.2.5. Conclusion

Test-Driven Development (TDD) is a powerful methodology that can transform how software systems are built and maintained. By writing tests before code, developers ensure that each new feature is covered from the start and that future changes won't introduce unexpected errors. Despite initial challenges, the long-term benefits of TDD—such as improved code quality, reduced errors, and confidence in changes—make it a valuable practice for software development teams aiming to deliver high-quality products in an Agile and efficient manner.

10.3. CODE REVIEWS AND PAIR PROGRAMMING

Reviewing and collaborating between developers are key practices for ensuring quality and efficiency in software development. Code Reviews and Pair Programming not only improve code quality but also foster professional growth and teamwork. Both techniques are essential in an agile environment, where continuous delivery and constant code improvement are vital.

10.3.1. Code Reviews

Code Reviews involve having one or more teammates review code written by a developer before it is merged into the main repository. This process identifies errors, ensures adherence to coding standards, and facilitates knowledge sharing across the team. The main benefits of Code Reviews include:

- **Improved Code Quality:** By reviewing code before integration, errors such as logic issues, implementation mistakes, or style violations can be detected and corrected.

- **Long-Term Problem Prevention:** Code Reviews help spot issues that could lead to critical failures later, like architectural errors or poorly managed dependencies.

- **Code Consistency:** They ensure all team members follow the same coding guidelines, making code easier to maintain and read, especially in large teams.

- **Knowledge Sharing:** Developers gain a broader understanding of the system and learn best practices and design patterns.

- **Quality Culture:** Regular reviews foster continuous improvement and collaboration, focusing on enhancing software quality rather than criticizing the author.

Effective Code Reviews require regular sessions with clear, specific feedback, focusing on functionality, style, and best practices to ensure optimal code.

10.3.2. Pair Programming

Pair Programming involves two developers working on the same task using one computer. One acts as the "driver," writing the code, while the other, the "navigator," observes, suggests improvements, and reviews the code in real-time. Key benefits include:

- **Better Code Quality:** Having two sets of eyes on the code increases the likelihood of detecting errors and possible enhancements.

- **Continuous Learning:** It allows developers to exchange knowledge and skills, with experienced developers mentoring newer ones and vice versa.

- **Faster Problem Solving:** Real-time collaboration leads to quicker solutions and fewer bottlenecks.

- **Enhanced Team Collaboration:** It strengthens communication and fosters a collaborative work culture.

- **Increased Productivity:** Although it may seem that two developers working on one task is inefficient, the reduction in errors and need for later revisions can make it more productive in the long run.

10.3.3. Best Practices for Code Reviews and Pair Programming

To maximize the benefits of these practices:

- **Efficient Code Reviews:** Avoid overly extensive or superficial reviews. Reviewing smaller chunks of code (up to 400 lines) ensures focus and accuracy. Using tools like GitHub or GitLab can streamline collaboration and feedback management.

- **Constructive Feedback:** Maintain a respectful tone and provide clear, specific feedback aimed at improving code design and functionality.

- **Rotate Pair Programming Partners:** Rotating partners helps evenly distribute knowledge across the team and prevents specialization in specific code areas.

- **Document the Process:** Keeping records of key feedback and changes, particularly in Code Reviews, helps reference design or implementation decisions in the future.

10.3.4. Conclusion

Code Reviews and Pair Programming are essential practices that enhance code quality, promote teamwork, and ensure robust, maintainable, and error-free software delivery. By adopting these techniques, teams can foster a culture of continuous learning, collaboration, and shared responsibility in software development.

10.4. EFFECTIVE DOCUMENTATION

Documentation is a crucial component in the software development lifecycle as it enables developers, users, and future collaborators to understand how the system works, how to use it, and how to maintain it. Without proper documentation, even the best-written code can be difficult to understand and modify, negatively impacting long-term productivity and quality.

10.4.1. Types of Documentation

Each type of documentation serves a distinct purpose, contributing to different stages and stakeholders within the development process:

- **Code Documentation:** Code documentation consists of comments embedded within the source code to explain the logic, algorithms, design decisions, and the usage of specific classes and functions. Effective code documentation:

    I. Enhances readability by summarizing complex logic.

    II. Clarifies the purpose and functionality without requiring developers to analyze every line.

    III. Reduces onboarding time for new developers joining the project.

- **User Guides:** These guides are aimed at end-users, offering step-by-step instructions on how to use the system or application. Key elements include:

    I. Visuals: Screenshots, diagrams, and flowcharts.

    II. Use Cases: Real-world scenarios showcasing typical workflows.

III. Error Handling: Instructions for troubleshooting common issues.

- **Technical Manuals:** Intended for system administrators and developers, technical manuals delve into the system's architecture, configuration, and maintenance. They typically include:

    I. Infrastructure Setup: Details on servers, databases, and networking.

    II. Installation Procedures: Step-by-step instructions for deploying the software.

    III. Runtime Environments: Configuration settings for different environments (development, testing, production).

- **API Documentation:** API documentation explains how external developers can interact with the system through programmatic interfaces. Effective API documentation:

    I. Lists endpoints, methods, parameters, and expected responses.

    II. Provides code examples for quick integration.

    III. Is often auto-generated using tools like Swagger or Postman to ensure consistency and accuracy.

- **Requirements Specifications:** These documents define the functional and non-functional requirements, acting as a blueprint for development and testing. Components include:

    I. Functional Requirements: Specific features and functionalities.

    II. Non-functional Requirements: Performance, security, and scalability standards.

    III. Constraints: Legal, technical, or organizational limitations.

10.4.2. Best Practices for Documentation

Documentation is only effective if it adheres to key principles:

- **Clarity and Conciseness:** It should be easy to read and understand. Using simple, direct language is crucial, avoiding unnecessary technical jargon. Practical examples and concise descriptions help readers quickly grasp functionality.

- **Keep Documentation Updated:** As the software evolves, outdated documentation can cause confusion and errors. Keeping documentation in sync with the code and new features is crucial. Integrating documentation updates into the workflow (e.g., as part of each commit or pull request) helps maintain accuracy.

- **Automate Documentation:** Tools like Javadoc, Doxygen, or Sphinx can automatically generate documentation from code comments, ensuring alignment with the source code. Tools like Markdown or LaTeX are also used to create well-formatted, extensive documents.

- **Consistent Formatting:** Following a standard format throughout the documentation ensures consistency and ease of navigation. The structure should include clear headings, well-defined sections, and an index to help users quickly find the information they need.

- **Include Examples and Use Cases:** Practical examples are one of the most effective ways to explain complex concepts. Demonstrating how to interact with a system or use an API in a real-world scenario facilitates understanding and reduces the learning curve.

- **Versioning the Documentation:** For projects with multiple versions, maintaining separate documentation for each version ensures users can access the correct information corresponding to their software version.

10.4.3. Benefits of Effective Documentation

Well-crafted documentation offers numerous benefits for the development team and users:

- **Facilitates Software Maintenance:** Comprehensive, accurate documentation helps developers quickly understand the system's structure, making it easier to identify and fix errors and implement new features without negatively impacting existing functionalities.

- **Reduces Learning Curve:** For new team members, clear documentation reduces the time needed to understand the codebase and project practices, allowing them to contribute more quickly.

- **Increases Productivity:** By reducing the need for explanations and code searches, proper documentation frees up valuable time for developers to focus on writing new code rather than deciphering existing code.

- **Enhances User Experience:** User guides and technical manuals ensure that users can fully utilize the software's features, improving user satisfaction and reducing support inquiries.

- **Serves as a Source of Truth:** In collaborative projects, documentation acts as a source of truth where everyone involved can gain a shared understanding of the system's goals, requirements, and functionalities.

10.4.4. Challenges in Documentation and How to Overcome Them

Although effective documentation is essential, implementing it is not always easy. Common challenges include:

- **Time Constraints:** Documentation is often seen as a lower priority than developing new features, leading to future issues. A strategy to overcome this is integrating documentation creation into the development cycle from the start, making it a natural part of the process.

- **Outdated Documentation:** When documentation is not regularly updated, it becomes useless or even harmful. Automatic documentation tools and clear policies requiring updates as part of the development process can prevent this.

- **Too Much or Too Little Documentation:** Finding the right balance is essential. Too much documentation can be overwhelming and difficult to maintain, while too little may not provide enough understanding of the system. Clearly defining which aspects require thorough documentation and which can be summarized helps manage this balance.

10.4.5. Conclusion: Documentation as a Strategic Pillar in Software Development

Documentation is not just a complement; it is a strategic asset that drives the long-term success of any software project. Its importance is often underestimated compared to the creation of new features or code optimization, but its impact extends to all phases of the development lifecycle. Investing in high-quality documentation is not just a recommended practice—it is a necessity for ensuring the sustainability, scalability, and effectiveness of software over time.

-Promotes Collaboration and Transparency

In multidisciplinary teams where developers, designers, testers, project managers, and stakeholders interact, documentation acts as a bridge that connects various perspectives. It provides a common language and establishes a shared understanding, reducing misunderstandings and fostering efficient collaboration. Additionally, it ensures transparency by granting all involved parties access to the same information, allowing decisions to be based on clear facts and data.

-Enhances Project Scalability

As projects grow in size and complexity, solid documentation facilitates the onboarding of new developers and the integration of new technologies. A well-documented system can scale without creating bottlenecks, as each component is clearly described, allowing modifications or expansions without negatively affecting other parts of the system. This is crucial for constantly evolving projects, where adaptability can be a key factor for success.

-Improves Maintainability and Reduces Risk

Software is a living entity, subject to constant changes from updates, bug fixes, or new features. Without documentation, any alteration can become an arduous and risky process. Detailed documentation mitigates this risk by providing a clear map of the architecture, data flows, and component interactions, making it easier to identify potential failure points before they become critical issues.

-Optimizes Learning and Knowledge Transfer

Employee turnover is a common challenge in the tech industry. When a key team member leaves, knowledge loss can stall development. However, comprehensive documentation serves as a knowledge repository that remains even as personnel change, allowing for smoother transitions and minimizing the negative impact on the project.

-Increases End-User Satisfaction

From the user's perspective, a well-crafted, easy-to-understand guide significantly improves the overall software experience. Users are more likely to adopt and recommend an application if they can fully understand how to use it and solve basic problems independently. This not only reduces the support team's workload but also enhances the product's perceived value and professionalism.

-Supports Strategic Decision-Making

In agile development environments or projects where priorities frequently shift, having up-to-date documentation enables leaders to make informed decisions based on the current state of the project rather than assumptions. This is especially important during critical moments, such as mergers, acquisitions, or expansions, where clear documentation can make the difference between a smooth transition and a problematic one.

-Long-Term Commitment

In summary, effective documentation is not just about writing but about establishing a long-term commitment to quality, collaboration, and the continuous evolution of software. Implementing good documentation practices from the project's start and maintaining them throughout its lifecycle is an investment that, while potentially costly in terms of initial time and resources, translates into exponential benefits.

Projects that value and prioritize documentation are better positioned to face future challenges, maintaining their relevance, competitiveness, and adaptability in an ever-changing market.

10.5. SIX SIGMA AND SOFTWARE QUALITY

Six Sigma is a methodology focused on continuous improvement and reducing defects and variability in processes. Although traditionally used in manufacturing and other sectors, its principles have been successfully adapted to software development, aiming to improve process quality and efficiency while reducing product errors and failures.

10.5.1. Application in Software Development

In software development, Six Sigma focuses on process quality, aiming to eliminate errors and reduce variability at various development stages. Its goal is to deliver software with minimal defects, meeting or exceeding customer expectations while enhancing development team efficiency.

- **Product Quality Improvement:** Six Sigma analyzes the software lifecycle phases (planning, design, coding, testing, deployment, maintenance) to detect areas prone to defects. By applying its tools and principles, these processes can be improved, minimizing product failures.

- **Defect Prevention:** A key objective of Six Sigma is to prevent issues before they occur through strict controls and quality standards in every development phase. This reduces the risk of defects and minimizes costly later-stage corrections.

- **Process Optimization:** Six Sigma identifies inefficiencies, such as delays in code reviews, redundant testing, or communication failures between teams. Addressing these inefficiencies enhances development speed and overall productivity.

10.5.2. DMAIC in Software Development

The DMAIC cycle, a structured Six Sigma approach, helps solve problems and improve processes. Its application in software development includes:

- **Define:** Clearly define problems or improvement areas in the development process, such as frequent defects, missed delivery timelines, or quality issues. Set objectives and determine customer or stakeholder requirements.

- **Measure:** Collect relevant data about the current process, such as bug counts during testing, average development time per feature, or production failure rates. Measuring quantifies the problem and establishes a baseline for improvements.

- **Analyze:** Examine collected data to identify root causes of problems. For example, high error rates during testing could stem from poor requirement communication or deployment delays from inadequate test automation. Deep analysis highlights critical areas for intervention.

- **Improve:** Apply solutions to improve the process, such as implementing best development practices, automating tests, adopting continuous integration, or optimizing code reviews. The aim is to enhance efficiency, reduce defects, and shorten development cycles.

- **Control:** Establish monitoring and control mechanisms to ensure sustained improvements. Create key performance indicators (KPIs) to track software quality and development process efficiency, ensuring problems do not recur and fostering continuous improvement.

10.5.3. Benefits of Implementing Six Sigma in Software Development

Implementing Six Sigma principles in software development offers several key benefits:

- **Defect Reduction:** Six Sigma's rigorous approach helps teams detect and fix defects early, reducing the number of errors reaching production, thus increasing software stability and reliability.

- **Better Understanding of Client Requirements:** Six Sigma emphasizes customer satisfaction, aligning developed software closely with client needs, minimizing rework or post-launch corrections.

- **Process Efficiency Gains:** The methodology optimizes the development cycle by eliminating bottlenecks and inefficiencies, resulting in faster processes, predictable delivery times, and reduced last-minute fixes.

- **Continuous Improvement:** Through DMAIC, development processes are continually refined, ensuring long-term software quality improvement.
- **Cost Minimization:** Early defect detection and process efficiency improvements reduce costs associated with rework, production fixes, and system interruptions, lowering overall development expenses.

10.5.4. Six Sigma Tools in Software Development

- **Flowcharts:** Visualize workflow within the development cycle to identify problem areas.
- **Ishikawa (Cause-Effect) Diagrams:** Identify and analyze root causes of software quality issues.
- **Statistical Process Control (SPC):** Monitor process variability during development and testing, ensuring processes remain within acceptable limits.
- **Process Maps:** Detail each development stage, helping identify redundancies or inefficient steps.

10.5.5. Conclusion

Implementing Six Sigma in software development can transform team operations, enhancing both product quality and development efficiency. By applying the DMAIC cycle and using specific tools, teams can systematically identify, analyze, and resolve issues, ensuring customer satisfaction while reducing costs. Adopting this methodology fosters continuous improvement, essential in an agile, competitive development environment.

10.6. SOFTWARE QUALITY MODELS AND STANDARDS

Software quality models and standards are essential to ensure that developed software meets expected quality requirements from both a technical and user perspective. These frameworks provide structured guidelines for managing and improving software development processes, minimizing defects, and maximizing the final product's value. Below are some of the most relevant models and standards in the software industry.

10.6.1. ISO/IEC 25010: Software Quality Evaluation

The ISO/IEC 25010 standard is part of the ISO/IEC 25000 family, also known as SQuaRE (System and Software Quality Requirements and Evaluation). It defines a comprehensive framework for evaluating software product quality. This standard classifies software quality into two key dimensions: product quality and quality in use. These dimensions are broken down into a series of characteristics and sub-characteristics to thoroughly evaluate a system's quality attributes.

1. Product Quality:

•   **Functionality:** Ability of the software to meet functional requirements.

•   **Maintainability:** Ease with which the software can be modified to fix errors, improve performance, or adapt to new requirements.

•   **Usability:** Ease of use from the end-user's perspective.

•   **Reliability:** Ability of the software to operate without failure under specified conditions.

- **Performance Efficiency:** Effective use of system resources, such as response time and memory utilization.

- **Security:** Protection against unauthorized access and safeguarding of the data handled by the software.

- **Portability:** Ease of transferring the software from one environment to another.

2. Quality in Use:

- **Effectiveness:** Software's ability to help users achieve their objectives.

- **Productivity:** Efficiency in user interaction with the software.

- **Safety:** Ability to prevent adverse consequences, such as human errors or system failures.

- **User Satisfaction:** Degree of end-user satisfaction with the software.

Adopting ISO/IEC 25010 allows organizations to systematically measure and improve their software's quality, ensuring it meets both technical requirements and user expectations.

10.6.2. CMMI (Capability Maturity Model Integration)

CMMI is a model designed to guide organizations in improving their software development processes, aiming to ensure product quality and delivery efficiency. CMMI consists of five maturity levels that assess an organization's capability to develop software consistently and in a controlled manner:

1. **Initial:** Processes are unpredictable and reactive. Success relies on individuals rather than organized processes.

2. **Managed:** Projects follow planned processes, though practices are often reactive.

3. **Defined:** Processes are well-documented and standardized across the organization.

4. **Quantitatively Managed:** The organization uses metrics to manage processes, enabling quality and performance prediction.

5. **Optimizing:** Focus is on continuous process improvement through feedback and innovation.

CMMI is particularly useful for large organizations seeking to scale their development practices and improve quality through organizational maturity. By following the maturity levels, companies can ensure their software development processes are more predictable and that final products meet high-quality standards.

10.6.3. IEEE 730: Software Quality Assurance Standard

The IEEE 730 standard, developed by the Institute of Electrical and Electronics Engineers (IEEE), provides guidelines for creating Software Quality Assurance (SQA) plans. This standard outlines processes and practices to ensure that software meets quality requirements throughout its lifecycle.

- **SQA Plan Requirements:** IEEE 730 mandates that the SQA plan includes a detailed description of quality assurance activities, team responsibilities, required resources, schedules, and evaluation procedures. Acceptance criteria and metrics for evaluating software quality must also be defined.

- **Verification and Validation (V&V):** Verification ensures that the software meets specified requirements, while validation ensures that it fulfills the end-user's needs.

- **Quality Audits:** Regular audits are recommended to independently review and evaluate whether development activities and intermediate products meet defined quality standards.

Implementing IEEE 730 helps organizations formalize their quality assurance processes, ensuring adherence to best practices and maintaining quality throughout all software lifecycle phases.

10.6.4. Other Relevant Models and Standards

- **ISO/IEC 12207:** This standard defines processes, activities, and tasks across the software lifecycle, including development, operation, and maintenance. It is widely used as a reference framework for software lifecycle management.

- **ISO/IEC 27001:** While focused on information security, this standard also applies to software quality by ensuring that development processes meet high security standards.

- **ISO/IEC 9001:** A general quality management standard applicable to software development, focusing on customer satisfaction, continuous improvement, and efficient process management.

10.6.5. Benefits of Adopting Quality Models and Standards

Adopting software quality models and standards offers several key benefits:

- **Consistency and Stability:** Standards provide a common framework for development activities, ensuring team members follow consistent practices, reducing variability, and improving software stability.

- **Continuous Improvement:** Models like CMMI and Six Sigma focus on continuous process improvement, enabling organizations to optimize workflows and enhance product quality over time.

- **Regulatory Compliance:** In sectors like finance or healthcare, adhering to quality standards is a legal requirement. Standards such as ISO/IEC 25010 or IEEE 730 ensure compliance with current regulations.

- **Enhanced Communication and Collaboration:** Structured documentation and guidelines facilitate communication between development, testing, and operations teams, promoting more effective collaboration.

- **Customer Satisfaction:** Following recognized models and standards results in higher-quality software, enhancing customer satisfaction and building trust in delivered products.

10.6.6. Conclusion

The adoption of software quality models and standards is essential to ensure developed software meets the highest quality standards. These frameworks help organizations improve their development processes, ensure software stability, and meet both user and client expectations.

10.7. KNOWLEDGE MANAGEMENT IN DEVELOPMENT TEAMS

Knowledge management in software development teams is a crucial pillar for maintaining productivity, efficiency, and ensuring project continuity. In this context, knowledge encompasses not only technical skills but also accumulated experiences, best practices, and processes within the team over time. Effective knowledge management ensures that these assets are accessible, shared, and reused by the entire team, preventing the loss of critical information and enabling smooth task transitions among team members.

10.7.1. Knowledge Documentation

Knowledge documentation involves capturing and organizing relevant information in an accessible and understandable format for all team members. This includes:

- **Technical Guides:** Documents detailing the operation of critical system components, design patterns used, or specific implementation strategies.

- **Procedure Manuals:** Clear instructions on how to perform recurring tasks such as release management, automated testing, continuous integration, and deployment processes.

- **Knowledge Base:** A centralized repository compiling articles, tutorials, technical documentation, and FAQs about the project. Tools like Confluence, Notion, or GitHub Wikis are commonly used for this purpose.

- **Code Documentation:** Clear, concise comments in the code are essential. Automatically generated documentation through tools like Javadoc, Sphinx, or Doxygen allows developers to quickly understand the logic behind a function or module.

Good documentation should focus not only on how something works but also on the why behind important decisions, helping future developers understand the historical context of the project.

10.7.1. Knowledge Transfer

Knowledge transfer is a key aspect of knowledge management within a development team. Without a continuous flow of information among team members, projects risk becoming overly dependent on a few key individuals with critical knowledge. Best practices include:

- **Internal Workshops:** Sessions where developers share their expertise on specific topics, such as new technologies, design approaches, or solutions to complex project issues, fostering continuous collective learning.

- **Lunch & Learn:** Informal sessions where a developer or expert presents a brief topic during lunch, encouraging a relaxed environment for continuous learning.

- **Mentorship:** Assigning a mentor to new team members facilitates faster onboarding and ensures effective transmission of best practices and knowledge. Mentors can also guide tool usage, agile methodology, or system architecture.

- **Pair Programming:** This practice enables real-time knowledge transfer as two developers work on a single task, with one coding and the other reviewing, enhancing design decisions and code quality.

- **Task Rotation:** Encouraging rotation across different project components ensures all team members understand multiple system areas, preventing "knowledge silos" and facilitating collaboration when a team member is unavailable.

10.7.3. Knowledge Management Tools

Various tools support knowledge capture and transfer in development teams. Commonly used ones include:

- **Wikis:** Platforms like GitHub Wiki, Confluence, or

MediaWiki allow teams to store and organize documentation in an accessible, collaborative format.

• **Project Management Systems:** Tools like Jira, Trello, or Asana help document project management decisions, task assignments, and overall team progress.

• **Version Control Systems:** Repositories like Git or Subversion (SVN) maintain a detailed history of code changes, making it easier to review software evolution.

• **Communication Platforms:** Tools like Slack or Microsoft Teams enable quick communication among team members and the creation of specific channels for technical discussions or FAQs.

10.7.4. Benefits of Effective Knowledge Management

Proper knowledge management offers multiple benefits to a development team:

• **Reduced Critical Dependencies:** An accessible knowledge base reduces reliance on specific individuals, minimizing downtime if someone is absent or leaves the team.

• **Increased Productivity:** Organized, accessible information allows developers to quickly find answers, speeding up development and reducing downtime due to a lack of knowledge.

• **Facilitates Scalability:** As teams grow, knowledge management ensures new members quickly integrate, understanding workflows and technologies used in the project.

• **Fosters Innovation:** Sharing knowledge and experiences within the team promotes new ideas and approaches, improving efficiency and software quality.

• **Enhances Project Continuity:** As projects evolve, documentation and knowledge transfer ensure that personnel or requirement changes do not disrupt continuity and development quality.

10.7.5. Conclusion

Knowledge management in development teams is essential for maintaining productivity, project continuity, and ensuring efficient collaboration among all team members. Through clear documentation, continuous knowledge transfer, and appropriate tool usage, teams can capture and share knowledge effectively, improving the quality and speed of software development.

10.8. DEVSECOPS IMPLEMENTATION

DevSecOps is an evolution of the DevOps approach that integrates security throughout all stages of the software development lifecycle, from initial planning to deployment and operation. By embedding security into existing workflows, DevSecOps ensures that applications and systems are secure without sacrificing development speed and agility. This approach promotes automation, cross-team collaboration, and a "security-first" mindset.

10.8.1. Security Automation

Automation is a core pillar of DevSecOps. The goal is to integrate security into CI/CD (Continuous Integration/Continuous Deployment) pipelines, automating repetitive tasks like code review, security testing, and real-time monitoring. Key practices and tools include:

- **Static Application Security Testing (SAST):** Tools like SonarQube, Checkmarx, and Veracode analyze source code to detect potential vulnerabilities early in development, preventing critical issues from reaching production.

- **Dynamic Application Security Testing (DAST):** Tools such as OWASP ZAP and Burp Suite evaluate running applications for common vulnerabilities like SQL injection, Cross-Site Scripting (XSS), and other live-environment threats.

- **Automated Penetration Testing:** Tools like Metasploit and Nessus simulate attacks to identify potential weaknesses before real attackers can exploit them.

- **Security Monitoring and Incident Response:** Systems like ELK Stack, Splunk, and AWS GuardDuty monitor the production environment in real time, detecting anomalous patterns that could indicate intrusion attempts or emerging vulnerabilities.

- **Dependency Scanning:** Tools like OWASP Dependency-Check and Snyk scan project dependencies for known vulnerabilities in third-party libraries

Automating these activities ensures continuous security testing and validation without disrupting the development flow, enabling early detection and resolution of security issues.

10.8.2. Security as a Culture

Beyond tools and automation, DevSecOps success hinges on fostering a security culture across development, operations, and security teams. Everyone involved in the software lifecycle, from developers to DevOps engineers, should adopt a "security-first" mindset. Key strategies include:

- **Training and Awareness:** Developers need training not only in tools but also in secure coding practices (e.g., preventing SQL injection, handling authentication and authorization). Internal workshops, "capture the flag" sessions, and security updates help keep teams informed and aware of emerging threats.

- **Early Security Integration:** Using practices like Shift Left, security discussions begin in the early design and planning phases. Teams consider security requirements from the project's inception, identifying and mitigating potential risks early.

- **Secure Code Review:** Security should be integral to code reviews, ensuring both code quality and protection against common threats.

- **Access Management Policies:** Implement strict access controls based on the principle of least privilege, ensuring users only have access to the resources they need, minimizing breach risks if an account is compromised.

- **Secure Infrastructure as Code (IaC):** Given that infrastructure is managed and deployed as code, security configurations must be integrated from the start. Tools like Terraform and Ansible enforce security policies during resource provisioning, avoiding insecure default setups.

- **Team Collaboration:** DevSecOps requires close collaboration between security, development, and operations teams. Collaborative platforms and continuous feedback loops ensure that security issues are detected and addressed swiftly. Tools like Slack, Microsoft Teams, and Jira facilitate inter-team communication.

10.8.3. Benefits of Adopting DevSecOp

Adopting DevSecOps offers significant security and development efficiency benefits:

- **Reduced Vulnerabilities:** Continuous security integration helps identify and resolve vulnerabilities early, reducing the number of security defects in production.

- **Faster Delivery:** By automating security testing and related processes, teams maintain DevOps agility without compromising security.

- **Improved Incident Response:** Continuous monitoring and real-time alerts enable teams to detect and respond quickly to threats or incidents.

- **Regulatory Compliance:** DevSecOps simplifies implementing security controls and generating reports to ensure compliance with regulations like GDPR, HIPAA, or PCI DSS, reducing legal risks.

- **Shared Responsibility Culture:** Security becomes a shared responsibility across the team, enhancing cohesion and fostering a proactive security approach.

10.8.4. Conclusion

Adopting **DevSecOps** ensures security is not an afterthought but a core component of the software development lifecycle. By automating security tasks and fostering a shared security culture, organizations can develop applications efficiently and securely, protecting against threats.

10.9. CHAPTER CONCLUSIONS

Best practices in software development are essential for creating robust, maintainable, and high-quality applications. Applying principles like SOLID, adopting methodologies such as TDD, and emphasizing collaboration through effective code reviews and documentation improve project quality and efficiency. Furthermore, using quality standards and methodologies like Six Sigma, combined with implementing DevSecOps, ensures a comprehensive approach to delivering secure and reliable software. These practices form the foundation for successful software development and delivering high-quality solutions to end users.

CHAPTER 11
SOFTWARE PROJECT MANAGEMENT

Managing development teams is a critical component of successfully delivering software projects. It involves coordinating and leading professionals with diverse skills, ensuring the team aligns with project objectives and maintains a productive, collaborative work environment. Below are key aspects of development team management:

11.1. TALENT DEVELOPMENT AND TRAINING

Continuous skill and competency development is essential to remain competitive and maintain software quality. Effective strategies for talent development include:

- **Training Programs:** Implement regular training programs covering both technical skills (e.g., new programming languages, frameworks, and tools) and soft skills (e.g., time management, teamwork, and leadership). These can include workshops, online courses, and conferences.

- **Mentorship and Coaching:** Foster an environment where experienced developers guide new team members. Mentorship not only transfers knowledge but also creates a sense of belonging and support.

- **Performance Evaluations:** Conduct periodic performance reviews to identify areas for improvement and set clear goals. These evaluations can include self-assessments, peer reviews, and manager feedback.

- **Innovation Encouragement:** Motivate developers to explore new technologies and techniques through hackathons, innovation projects, or personal project time. This fosters creativity and can lead to significant product improvements.

- **Continuous Learning Culture:** Promote a mindset of ongoing learning, encouraging team members to acquire new knowledge and skills. This can include resource libraries, sharing relevant articles, and participating in developer communities.

11.1.1. Remote and Distributed Work Dynamics

With the rise of remote work and distributed teams, it is crucial to implement best practices for effective management:

- **Collaboration Tools:** Use platforms like Slack, Microsoft Teams, and Trello to keep team members connected. These tools facilitate real-time communication, task management, and project organization.

- **Flexible Work Hours:** Allow flexible schedules to accommodate different time zones and lifestyles, improving job satisfaction and productivity.

- **Effective Virtual Meetings:** Hold regular, well-structured meetings to keep everyone informed and aligned. Clear agendas and time limits ensure productive meetings and prevent fatigue.

- **Virtual Team-Building Activities:** Foster team cohesion through virtual team-building activities such as online games, contests, or informal gatherings to strengthen interpersonal relationships.

- **Clear Roles and Responsibilities:** Ensure that every team member understands their role and responsibilities as well as project objectives. This prevents confusion and ensures effective contributions.

11.1.2. Effective Communication in Multidisciplinary Teams

Effective communication is essential in multidisciplinary teams, where developers, designers, and stakeholders interact. Strategies for fostering effective communication include:

- **Sync Meetings:** Organize regular sync meetings where team members share updates and discuss challenges. These meetings keep everyone informed and aligned with project goals.

- **Shared Documentation:** Use accessible, up-to-date documentation as a reference for all team members. This can include wikis, cloud documents, and Kanban boards summarizing project progress.

- **Open Discussion Spaces:** Encourage open discussion and brainstorming spaces. This promotes idea generation and collaborative problem-solving, enhancing creativity and innovation.

- **Constructive Feedback:** Establish a culture of constructive feedback where team members feel comfortable giving and receiving input. This improves work quality and promotes personal and professional growth.

- **Celebrating Successes:** Recognize and celebrate both major and minor team achievements. This strengthens team spirit and motivates members to contribute enthusiastically.

11.1.3. Conclusion

Effective development team management involves a blend of continuous training, efficient remote work practices, and collaborative communication. By focusing on talent development, work dynamics, and communication, project leaders can create an environment where development teams thrive and deliver high-quality software.

11.2. PROJECT MANAGEMENT TOOLS: JIRA, TRELLO, ETC

Project management tools are essential for planning, organizing, and monitoring the progress of software development teams. These tools enhance transparency, improve collaboration, and ensure all team members are aligned with project objectives. Below are some of the most commonly used tools and their key features:

11.2.1. Workflow Customization in Jira

Jira is a powerful project management tool, particularly in Agile environments. Customizing workflows is crucial to adapt to different project types and teams. Key considerations include:

- **State Definition:** Configure states representing development stages, such as "To Do," "In Progress," "In Review," and "Done." These states should reflect the team's actual workflow.

- **Transitions:** Establish clear transitions between states to facilitate task movement. Transitions can include conditions and validations to ensure tasks meet specific criteria before advancing.

- **Custom Fields:** Add custom fields to capture project-specific information, such as "Priority," "Complexity," or "Assigned To."

- **Roles and Permissions:** Define user roles and permissions to control who can make workflow changes, assign tasks, or modify states. This maintains project integrity by restricting critical functions to authorized users.

- **Project Templates:** Use predefined project templates to streamline new project setups. Jira offers templates for methodologies like Scrum and Kanban, adaptable to team needs.

• **Reports and Dashboards:** Create customized dashboards to visualize project status and team progress. These can include burndown charts, task boards, and other reports to support informed decision-making.

11.2.2. Task and Sprint Management with Trello

Trello is an intuitive, board-based tool that helps teams visually organize and prioritize tasks. Here are some tips for maximizing its use:

• **Boards and Lists:** Create boards for specific projects and lists representing different work phases, such as "Backlog," "To Do," "In Progress," and "Done." This provides a clear workflow overview.

• **Task Cards:** Use cards for each task, including descriptions, assignments, due dates, and checklists, ensuring all relevant information is accessible in one place.

• **Labels and Priorities:** Implement a label system to categorize tasks, such as "Urgent," "Important," or "Low Priority," making it easier to identify critical tasks and prioritize work.

• **Sprints and Planning:** Manage sprints by creating dedicated lists and moving task cards as needed. This helps teams focus on specific tasks during short development cycles.

• **Integrations:** Leverage integrations with tools like Slack, Google Drive, and development platforms to enhance collaboration and keep everyone informed of important updates.

• **Automation:** Use Trello's Butler automation feature to create rules that handle repetitive tasks, such as moving cards or sending reminders, saving time and reducing administrative burden.

11.2.3. Project Management Tool Integration with CI/CD

Integrating project management tools with continuous integration (CI) and continuous delivery (CD) pipelines improves efficiency and collaboration between teams. Ways to achieve this include:

• **Repository Connections:** Connect project management tools with code repositories (e.g., GitHub or Bitbucket) to link tasks and commits, facilitating traceability between work and code.

- **Automated Updates:** Use webhooks and APIs to automate task status updates based on CI/CD progress. For example, automatically change a task's status to "In Progress" when a CI build starts.

- **Real-Time Notifications:** Set up notifications to alert the team of significant pipeline events, such as test completions or build failures, enabling swift responses to issues.

- **Project Dashboards:** Create dashboards integrating development metrics like completed tasks, average task completion time, and test failure rates, offering a comprehensive project view for decision-making.

- **Code Review Integration:** Integrate project management tools with code review systems to streamline pull request creation and tracking, ensuring the review process aligns with ongoing tasks.

- **Post-Implementation Reviews:** Conduct post-implementation reviews to analyze project performance, assessing how management tool integration with CI/CD impacted workflow efficiency and software quality.

11.2.4. Conclusion

Project management tools like Jira and Trello, combined with CI/CD pipeline integration, are vital for successful software development. Customizing workflows, managing tasks effectively, and connecting these tools to integration and delivery processes not only boost productivity but also foster collaboration and ensure the final product's quality.

11.3. PROJECT MEASUREMENT AND TRACKING: KPIS AND METRICS

Measuring and tracking projects are key elements for ensuring success in software development. Utilizing Key Performance Indicators (KPIs) and metrics allows teams to assess progress, identify areas for improvement, and make informed decisions. Below are various metrics and evaluation methods relevant to software development teams.

11.3.1. Productivity Metrics for Development Teams

The productivity of development teams can be measured through various metrics that help evaluate their speed, efficiency, and performance. Key metrics include:

- **Velocity:** Refers to the amount of work completed in a specific period, often measured in story points in an Agile environment. The average sprint velocity provides a clear idea of how much work the team can complete in the future, aiding in planning.

- **Delivery Rate:** Measures the number of tasks or features delivered in a specific period. This metric helps determine how quickly the team can move tasks from the backlog to "done," assessing workflow efficiency.

- **Cycle Time:** Refers to the time taken to complete a task from start to finish. A reduced cycle time indicates improvements in team efficiency and responsiveness to changes.

- **Lead Time:** Measures the total time from when a feature is requested to its delivery. Unlike cycle time, lead time includes the time a task spends in the backlog before starting. This metric is crucial for understanding overall process efficiency.

- **Failure Rate:** Evaluates how many tasks or features fail during testing or produce errors in production. A high failure rate may indicate issues in the development process or code quality.

- **Code Review Time:** Measuring the average time taken for code reviews provides insights into team collaboration and review quality. Excessive review times may signal communication issues or unclear requirements.

11.3.2. Software Quality Indicators

Software quality is essential to ensure that the final product meets standards and expectations. Useful metrics for evaluating quality include:

- **Test Coverage:** Indicates the percentage of code covered by automated tests. High test coverage suggests more comprehensive software evaluation, reducing the likelihood of production errors.

- **Number of Bugs:** Tracks the number of bugs detected during testing and in production. Monitoring bug numbers over time helps identify patterns and areas needing code quality improvement.

- **Bug Resolution Time:** Assesses how long it takes to resolve bugs from the time they are reported until they are fixed. A low resolution time indicates an agile, effective team in managing issues.

- **Code Complexity:** Using metrics like the cyclomatic complexity index helps identify code sections prone to errors or maintenance difficulties.

- **Software Stability:** Measures how long software can operate without failures. This metric is particularly important for critical applications where availability is essential.

- **Quality Reviews:** Regularly auditing code and conducting quality reviews provide valuable insights into adherence to best practices and coding standards.

11.3.3. Customer Satisfaction Metrics

Customer satisfaction is a crucial indicator of a software project's success. Evaluating the end-user experience can be achieved through various techniques:

- **Customer Satisfaction Surveys:** Conduct regular surveys with end-users to gather feedback on the product, including usability, functionality, and performance aspects.

- **Net Promoter Score (NPS):** Measures customer loyalty and their likelihood to recommend the product. A high NPS indicates strong customer satisfaction, while a low score highlights areas needing attention.

- **Feedback and Reviews Analysis:** Evaluating user feedback and reviews across various platforms provides valuable insights into the user experience, including positive feedback and constructive criticism.

- **Customer Retention Rate:** Measures the proportion of customers continuing to use the software over time. A high retention rate indicates user satisfaction and perceived value in the product.

- **Support Response Time:** Tracks how quickly the support team responds and resolves customer queries or issues. Fast response times are key to maintaining customer trust.

- **Usage Analysis:** Implementing analytics tools to track user interactions with the software can reveal which features are most used and where usability issues may exist.

11.3.4. Conclusion

Measuring and tracking projects through KPIs and metrics are fundamental to software development success. By focusing on productivity metrics, quality indicators, and customer satisfaction, teams can identify improvement areas and ensure that the delivered software meets expected standards. A strong measurement strategy not only optimizes team performance but also contributes to creating high-quality products that meet end-user needs.

11.4. RISK MANAGEMENT AND PLANNING

Risk management is a critical component of software project planning. It involves identifying, evaluating, and mitigating risks that could impact the project's success. Effective risk management not only helps prevent problems but also prepares the team to face unexpected challenges. Below are the key focus areas in risk management and planning.

11.4.1. Risk Identification and Analysis

Risk identification and analysis are the initial steps in risk management. They involve recognizing potential events that could threaten the project's success and assessing their likelihood and impact.

-Risk Identification Methods:

- **Brainstorming Sessions:** Bring together the development team, stakeholders, and other interested parties to discuss and document potential risks in a collaborative setting.

- **SWOT Analysis:** Evaluate the project's Strengths, Weaknesses, Opportunities, and Threats to identify potential risks.

- **Review of Past Projects:** Analyze lessons learned from previous projects to identify common risks that might recur in the new project.

- **Interviews and Questionnaires:** Conduct interviews with experts and team members to gather insights on potential risks based on their experiences.

-Risk Analysis:

- **Qualitative Assessment:** Classify risks based on their likelihood of occurrence and the impact they would have if materialized. This helps prioritize risks and focus mitigation efforts on the most critical ones.

• Quantitative Assessment: Use advanced techniques, such as Monte Carlo simulations, to model the financial or time impact of identified risks, providing a clearer understanding of possible project outcome variations.

11.4.2. Contingency Planning and Response Strategies

Once risks have been identified and analyzed, the next step is to develop contingency plans and appropriate response strategies.

-Developing Response Plans:

• **Risk Avoidance:** Modify the project plan to eliminate the risk or its impact. This may include changes in design, schedule, or scope.

• **Mitigation:** Implement actions to reduce the likelihood or impact of the risk. This could involve adopting best practices, training the team, or using appropriate technology.

• **Risk Transfer:** Shift responsibility for the risk to a third party, such as purchasing insurance or outsourcing certain activities to specialized vendors.

• **Acceptance:** Acknowledge that the risk may occur and establish contingency plans to manage its consequences if it materializes. This is suitable for low-impact risks that do not warrant significant mitigation efforts.

-Contingency Planning:

• **Define Clear Steps:** Outline specific actions to be taken if a risk materializes, including who will be responsible for implementing the response and how it will be communicated to the team.

• **Allocate Resources:** Ensure that resources and budgets are set aside for implementing contingency plans if necessary, providing a clear approach to handling unforeseen issues.

11.4.3. Risk Monitoring and Review

Risk management doesn't stop once a plan is established. Continuous monitoring and review throughout the project lifecycle are essential.

-Tools and Techniques for Risk Evaluation:

• **Periodic Reviews:** Hold regular meetings to review the status of identified risks, assess the effectiveness of response plans, and update the risk register as needed.

• **Risk Indicators:** Establish specific KPIs to measure risk exposure, such as the number of critical risks or the average time to resolve risks.

• **Project Management Software:** Use project management tools that integrate risk management, enabling more effective tracking and real-time risk updates.

-Updating the Risk Register:

• **Maintain a Living Document:** Keep a risk register that includes details on risk identification, analysis, response plans, and current status. This document should be continuously updated as the project progresses and new risks emerge.

11.4.4. Conclusion

Risk management and planning are essential for the success of any software project. By proactively identifying and analyzing risks, planning effective contingencies, and conducting ongoing reviews, teams can minimize the likelihood of problems and ensure smooth project progress. Well-implemented risk management not only protects the project but also fosters trust among team members and stakeholders, creating a more collaborative and resilient environment.

11.5. AGILE METHODOLOGIES IN PROJECT MANAGEMENT

Agile methodologies are iterative and incremental approaches to project management that promote flexibility, collaboration, and adaptability in software development. These methodologies allow teams to respond quickly to changes and focus on continuously delivering value to the customer. Below are the main Agile methodologies and their implementation in project management.

11.5.1. Scrum and Its Implementation in Software Teams

Scrum is one of the most popular Agile methodologies, designed to facilitate teamwork in complex and evolving environments. It focuses on incremental product delivery through short cycles called sprints.

- Roles in Scrum:

- **Product Owner:** Responsible for defining and prioritizing product requirements. Acts as a liaison between the development team and stakeholders, ensuring maximum value delivery in each sprint.

- **Scrum Master:** Facilitates the Scrum process by helping the team follow Agile practices and removing obstacles that may hinder progress. Also fosters collaboration and communication within the team.

- **Development Team:** A self-organizing group of professionals responsible for implementing product requirements. Each member brings diverse skills to achieve sprint goals.

- Scrum Events:

- **Sprint:** A fixed period (usually 2 to 4 weeks) in which a portion of the work is completed and a product increment is delivered.

- **Sprint Planning:** A meeting at the start of each sprint where objectives are defined, and user stories from the backlog are selected to be addressed during the sprint.

- **Daily Scrum:** A brief daily meeting where the team shares progress, obstacles, and plans for the day, fostering transparency and collaboration.

- **Sprint Review:** At the end of the sprint, the team presents completed work to stakeholders, gathering feedback for future sprints.

- **Sprint Retrospective:** A post-sprint meeting where the team reflects on what worked, what didn't, and how to improve in the next sprint.

- Scrum Artifacts:

- **Product Backlog:** A prioritized list of product requirements continuously updated, containing user stories and other development elements.

- **Sprint Backlog:** A set of Product Backlog items the team commits to completing during a sprint.

- **Increment:** The sum of all completed Product Backlog items during and across sprints, which must be ready for delivery.

11.5.2. Kanban for Visual Work Management

Kanban is an Agile methodology focusing on visualizing work and managing workflow. It uses a visual board to display task status and identify bottlenecks in the process.

- Kanban Principles:

- **Work Visualization:** Use a Kanban board to visually represent tasks in different workflow stages, helping teams see the current state and identify delays.

- **Work-In-Progress (WIP) Limitation:** Set limits on the number of tasks in progress at each stage to prevent team overload and enhance efficiency by completing tasks before starting new ones.

- **Flow Management:** Monitor and optimize workflow to maximize efficiency and reduce delivery time, using metrics like cycle time and lead time to assess team performance.

- Using a Kanban Board:

• Divide the board into columns representing different workflow stages (e.g., "To Do," "In Progress," "Done").

• Place task cards in the corresponding columns, moving them as they progress.

• Hold regular meetings to review the board, discuss progress, blockers, and priorities.

11.5.3. Comparison Between Scrum, Kanban, and Hybrid Methods

Choosing the right Agile methodology depends on project characteristics and team needs. Below are the pros and cons of Scrum, Kanban, and hybrid approaches:

- **Scrum**:

-Advantages:

• Clear structure and defined roles encourage responsibility and collaboration.

• Progress measured through sprints, enabling frequent product increments.

• Continuous feedback and improvement through reviews and retrospectives.

-Disadvantages:

• Requires significant commitment to planning and meetings, which may be challenging for smaller or resource-constrained teams.

• Sprint duration rigidity may not suit projects with highly dynamic requirements.

- **Kanban**:

-Advantages:

• Flexible workflow management, allowing quick adaptation to changes.

• Clear visualization of tasks, helping identify bottlenecks and optimize flow.

- No formal planning required, advantageous for teams with variable workloads.

-Disadvantages:

- Lack of formal structure can lead to role and responsibility ambiguity.

- Scaling in large projects can be challenging without clear work management and prioritization.

- **Hybrid Methods:**

-Advantages:

- Combine elements of Scrum and Kanban to suit specific team and project needs.

- Benefit from Scrum's structured planning and Kanban's flexibility.

-Disadvantages:

- Managing a hybrid approach can be complex and confusing if not communicated effectively.

- May require additional training for team members to understand integrated practices.

11.5.4. Conclusion

Agile methodologies like Scrum and Kanban offer valuable approaches to software project management, each with unique strengths and weaknesses. Choosing the right methodology should be based on team characteristics, project nature, and specific goals. By implementing Agile practices, teams can improve collaboration, increase adaptability, and optimize value delivery to clients, leading to more successful and efficient projects.

11.6. PROJECT SCOPE AND REQUIREMENTS MANAGEMENT

Managing scope and requirements is fundamental to the success of any software project. It ensures the team remains focused on the established objectives and delivers the expected functionalities within the allocated time and budget. This section explores techniques and practices for defining, controlling, and managing scope and requirements throughout the project lifecycle.

11.6.1. Scope Definition and Control

Clear scope definition is essential for setting project boundaries and avoiding uncontrolled scope expansion, known as "scope creep."

-Scope Definition:

- **Requirements Documentation:** Create a document detailing all functional and non-functional requirements of the project, including product features, constraints, and performance expectations.

- **Work Breakdown Structure (WBS):** Develop a WBS that breaks the project into smaller, manageable tasks. This helps identify all necessary activities and facilitates resource planning and allocation.

- **Scope Approval**: Obtain stakeholder validation of the scope, ensuring a shared understanding of the project's objectives.

-Scope Control:

- **Continuous Monitoring:** Conduct periodic project reviews to ensure it remains within the defined scope. This includes verifying that deliverables meet the established requirements.

- **Change Management:** Implement a formal process to handle scope change requests, evaluating their impact on budget, schedule, and resources before approval.

- **Change Log:** Maintain a log of all scope modifications, including justification and project impact, providing a clear reference to avoid misunderstandings.

11.6.2. Managing Requirement Changes

Requirement changes are inevitable in most software projects, and effectively handling them is crucial for project success.

-Change Request Evaluation:

- **Impact Analysis:** Assess how a proposed change will affect existing requirements, timelines, costs, and resources. Involve all stakeholders to get a comprehensive view.

- **Acceptance Criteria:** Define clear criteria for approving or rejecting a change, considering project alignment and product quality impact.

-Approval Process:

- **Change Committee:** Establish a committee responsible for reviewing and approving requirement changes, including key representatives from all relevant stakeholders.

- **Clear Communication:** Ensure all stakeholders are informed about approved changes and their implications, updating project documentation and adjusting timelines as needed.

-Managing Resistance to Change:

- **Foster Acceptance:** Involve stakeholders in decision-making to reduce resistance to change.

- **Training and Support:** Provide training and resources to help team members adapt to requirement changes and understand the reasons behind them.

11.6.3. Prioritizing Features

Feature prioritization ensures the development team focuses on tasks that provide the highest value to the project. Several techniques assist in this process.

-MoSCoW Method:

- **Definition:** This method classifies features into four categories:
- **Must Have:** Essential features that must be included in the release.
- **Should Have:** Important but not critical features for launch.
- **Could Have:** Desirable features to include if time and resources permit.
- **Won't Have:** Features excluded from this release but considered for future versions.
- **Benefits:** This approach helps manage stakeholder expectations and directs the team's efforts toward what truly matters.

-Priority Matrices:

- **Definition:** Use matrices to evaluate and prioritize features based on criteria such as customer value, implementation cost, and associated risk.
- **Evaluation:** Classify each feature based on these criteria, enabling informed decisions about which features to implement first.
- **Visualization:** Represent the priority matrix graphically to facilitate decision communication and align stakeholder expectations.

-Continuous Feedback:

- **Regular Reviews:** Conduct periodic review sessions with stakeholders to discuss feature prioritization and adjust priorities as needed.
- **Iteration:** Prioritization should be a continuous process, adapting to changes in project context and customer needs.

11.6.4. Conclusion

Scope and requirement management is critical to software project management. By clearly defining the scope, effectively managing changes, and appropriately prioritizing features, teams can ensure their projects align with stakeholder goals and expectations. These practices not only contribute to delivering high-quality products but also foster customer satisfaction and long-term project success.

11.7. TIME AND RESOURCE ESTIMATION

Time and resource estimation is a critical aspect of software project management. It enables teams to plan, allocate tasks, and ensure projects are completed on time and within budget. This section covers estimation techniques, resource planning, and schedule optimization.

11.7.1. Estimation Techniques: Story Points, T-Shirt Sizing

Accurate estimation of development effort is fundamental to project success. Several techniques facilitate this process.

-Story Points:

- **Definition:** This technique evaluates the effort required to complete a user story based on its complexity, risk, and size.

- **Point Scale:** A Fibonacci scale (1, 2, 3, 5, 8, 13, 21) is commonly used to assign points to user stories. This helps teams avoid underestimating more complex tasks by focusing on relative sizing.

- **Advantages:** Encourages team discussions about task complexity, enabling all members to contribute to the estimation process. Using points instead of hours reduces pressure for exact time predictions.

-T-Shirt Sizing:

- **Definition**: This technique uses T-shirt sizes (XS, S, M, L, XL) to categorize the complexity and effort of user stories or features.

- **Categories**: These quick classifications allow teams to estimate effort without delving into specifics. Clear criteria for each size standardize the estimation process.

- **Benefits**: Useful in early planning phases with limited requirement details. It provides a broad view of the effort required and enhances communication with stakeholders.

11.7.2. Human and Technical Resource Planning

Proper resource planning ensures that teams have the skills and tools necessary to meet project objectives.

-Human Resource Allocation:

- **Skill Assessment:** Evaluate team members 'skills and experience to assign tasks appropriately, considering both technical and interpersonal skills.

- **Workload Monitoring:** Track individual workloads to avoid burnout and ensure equitable task distribution. Tools like workload charts can aid in this.

- **Training and Development:** Identify training needs and offer development opportunities to enhance team skills, including new technologies and methodologies.

-Technical Resource Planning:

- **Tools and Technologies:** Select appropriate tools and technologies for project execution, from development environments to project management tools.

- **Infrastructure:** Ensure the availability and scalability of technical infrastructure, such as servers and networks. Cloud solutions or third-party services may be considered.

- **Testing and Development Environments:** Set up efficient testing and development environments to minimize production interference and streamline workflows.

11.7.3. Project Schedule Optimization

Optimizing the schedule is crucial for ensuring projects are completed on time and within budget. Key tools include Gantt charts and the PERT technique.

-Gantt Charts:

- **Definition**: A Gantt chart visually represents a project's schedule, showing tasks, their durations, and dependencies.

- **Usage**: Enables real-time project tracking, identifying delays, and allowing proactive adjustments. Gantt charts also facilitate stakeholder communication by providing a clear project overview.

- **Benefits**: Helps set realistic expectations and keeps team members informed about deadlines and progress.

-PERT (Program Evaluation Review Technique):

- **Definition**: PERT analyzes the tasks involved in project completion, identifying dependencies and calculating the time required for each task.

- **PERT Estimations:** Involves estimating three timeframes for each task: Optimistic (O), Pessimistic (P), and Most Likely (M). The Expected Time (TE) is calculated using these values.

- **Advantages:** Identifies the project's critical path—tasks determining overall project duration. This helps prioritize efforts and manage deadlines more effectively.

11.7.4. Conclusion

Time and resource estimation is an integral process requiring various techniques and tools. By applying estimation techniques like Story Points and T-Shirt Sizing, effectively planning human and technical resources, and optimizing schedules with Gantt charts and PERT, teams can improve estimation accuracy and enhance project success likelihood. Proper management of these aspects ensures high-quality software delivery within the established timeframes and budgets.

11.8. QUALITY MANAGEMENT IN SOFTWARE PROJECTS

Quality management in software projects is essential to ensure that the final product meets customer requirements and expectations. It involves setting standards, conducting audits, and fostering a culture of continuous improvement. This section covers the key components of quality management and how to effectively implement them in software development.

11.8.1. Quality Planning in Projects

Quality planning is the first step toward creating high-quality software. It involves defining the quality standards and metrics that will be used to evaluate project performance.

-Defining Quality Standards:

- **Internal and External Standards:** Establish clear criteria aligned with customer expectations and industry standards, such as ISO/IEC 25010 or CMMI. These standards may include functionality, performance, security, and maintainability requirements.

- **Requirements Documentation:** Create a requirements document specifying acceptance criteria and software features. This helps establish a shared understanding among all stakeholders.

-Defining Quality Metrics:

- **Quantitative Metrics:** Include metrics such as defect rate, test coverage, response time, and user satisfaction. These provide objective data to assess software quality.

- **Qualitative Metrics:** Collect user feedback on software usability and overall experience. Surveys and interviews can provide valuable insights beyond quantitative data.

-Integrating Quality into the Project Lifecycle:

- Integrate quality planning into all project phases, from requirements definition to final testing. This ensures that quality is considered at every stage, not just at the end of development.

11.8.2. Project Audits and Reviews

Audits and reviews are essential tools for ensuring compliance with the quality standards established during planning.

-Types of Audits:

- **Process Audits:** Evaluate the processes used in development to ensure adherence to best practices and established standards. This includes reviewing documentation, development procedures, and risk management.

- **Product Audits:** Review the final product to verify it meets specified requirements and is free from critical defects. These may include acceptance testing and code reviews.

-Project Reviews:

- **Code Reviews:** Implement practices where team members review each other's code to identify potential issues and promote learning and collaboration among developers.

- **Progress Reviews:** Conduct regular meetings to assess project progress against quality standards, allowing for early detection of deviations and necessary adjustments.

11.8.3. Continuous Improvement through Feedback

Continuous improvement is a crucial component of quality management, with feedback playing a central role in this process.

-Establishing Feedback Channels:

- **Surveys and Questionnaires:** Use periodic surveys to gather user feedback on the software experience, including functionality, usability, and performance.

- **Post-Mortem Review Sessions:** Conduct review sessions after project completion to discuss what worked well and what didn't. This provides an opportunity to learn from the experience and make improvements for future projects.

-Feedback Analysis:

- **Identifying Patterns:** Analyze feedback to identify patterns and trends indicating areas for improvement. This helps prioritize corrective actions and focus efforts on critical areas.

- **Implementing Changes:** Use feedback to adjust processes, tools, and development practices. This can include modifying procedures, enhancing training, or adopting new technologies.

-Fostering a Culture of Continuous Improvement:

- **Team Involvement:** Promote a culture where all team members feel responsible for quality. Empower developers to suggest improvements and actively participate in the feedback process.

- **Celebrating Successes and Learnings:** Recognize and celebrate achievements in quality improvement, motivating the team and reinforcing the importance of quality management in the organizational culture.

11.8.4. Conclusion

Quality management in software projects is a comprehensive process involving planning, audits, reviews, and continuous improvement through feedback. By establishing clear standards from the outset, conducting regular audits, and fostering a culture of continuous improvement, teams can ensure that software meets customer expectations and achieves high-quality levels. Effective implementation of these principles not only enhances the final product but also contributes to customer satisfaction and long-term organizational success.

11.9. PROJECT CLOSURE AND POST-MORTEM EVALUATION

Project closure is a critical phase that ensures all activities are completed, evaluated, and properly documented. This stage not only marks the conclusion of the work but also provides a valuable opportunity to reflect on the project and apply lessons learned to future endeavors. Below are the key components of project closure and post-mortem evaluation.

11.9.1. Documentation of Lessons Learned

Capturing lessons learned is essential for growth and continuous improvement within a team or organization. This documentation allows knowledge gained during the project to be shared and utilized in future projects.

-Identifying Lessons Learned:

• **Feedback Meetings:** Organize sessions with the project team to discuss what went well and what didn't. Creating a safe environment where everyone feels comfortable sharing their experiences and perspectives is crucial.

• **Documentation Review:** Analyze project documentation, including plans, schedules, and progress reports, to identify areas where planning or execution could have been improved.

-Recording and Storage:

• **Lessons Learned Templates:** Use standardized formats to document lessons learned, making them easier to understand and access. This may include context details, actions taken, outcomes, and future recommendations.

- **Lessons Learned Database:** Create a central repository where all lessons from past projects are stored. This can be a valuable resource for new teams and projects, offering quick reference to similar situations.

-Communication and Sharing:

- **Information Distribution:** Ensure lessons learned are accessible to all members of the organization, not just the project team. This may include presentations, webinars, or internal newsletters.

- **Integration into Organizational Culture:** Foster a culture that values learning and continuous improvement by encouraging teams to review and utilize the lessons learned database in planning new projects.

11.9.2. Project Performance Evaluation

Evaluating project performance is essential to measure success against initial objectives and established performance indicators.

-Defining Success Criteria:

- **Goal Review:** Compare project outcomes with the objectives set at the beginning, including scope, budget, timeline, and quality.

- **Establishing KPIs:** Use key performance indicators (KPIs) to assess project success. This can include metrics such as return on investment (ROI), customer satisfaction, and defect rates in the final product.

-Evaluation Methods:

- **Satisfaction Surveys:** Gather feedback from clients and stakeholders regarding their satisfaction with the product and process. Surveys can provide valuable insights into areas for improvement.

- **Benchmarking:** Compare project performance with similar projects within the organization or industry to identify trends and best practices.

-Documenting Results:

- **Closure Reports:** Prepare a closure report summarizing project outcomes, including objective achievement, lessons learned, and recommendations for future projects. This report should be shared with all stakeholders and archived for future reference.

11.9.3. Project Delivery and Transition Strategies

Project delivery is the final process in the project lifecycle, where the final product is handed over to the client or transferred to the support team.

-Preparation for Delivery:

- **Final Review:** Conduct a final product review to ensure it meets requirements and quality standards. This may include final testing, user documentation, and client validation.

- **User Training:** Provide training and support to end users on how to use the product, including training sessions, user manuals, and online resources.

-Delivery Process:

- **Formal Handover:** Conduct a formal handover meeting with the client and stakeholders, presenting the final product and discussing project outcomes. This establishes proper closure and alignment among all parties.

- **Transition Documentation:** Provide all necessary documentation, including user manuals, technical guides, and relevant information about product support and maintenance.

-Post-Delivery Support:

- **Support Plans:** Establish a post-delivery support plan, including resource allocation and a timeline for technical assistance, ensuring timely resolution of any issues.

- **Continuous Monitoring and Feedback:** Collect user feedback after delivery to identify potential issues and make improvements as needed, tracking usage and performance metrics.

11.9.4. Conclusion

Project closure and post-mortem evaluation are vital components of software project management. By documenting lessons learned, evaluating project performance, and establishing delivery strategies, teams can ensure each project contributes to organizational learning and the development of best practices. This approach not only improves the quality of future projects but also promotes a culture of continuous improvement and adaptability within the software development environment.

11.10. CHAPTER CONCLUSIONS

Software project management is a critical discipline encompassing various methodologies, tools, and approaches designed to ensure the successful delivery of software products. Throughout this chapter, we have explored essential aspects of project management, including planning, execution, monitoring, closure, and the implementation of continuous improvement practices.

This dynamic and ever-evolving field requires a proactive and adaptable approach. By adopting effective management practices, prioritizing communication, and fostering a collaborative environment, teams can enhance their ability to deliver high-quality products that meet client needs. Ultimately, success in software project management is not only measured by timely, budget-compliant delivery but also by customer satisfaction and the team's ability to learn and grow from each experience.

CHAPTER 12

ETHICAL AND LEGAL ASPECTS

In software development, ethical and legal considerations are fundamental to ensuring that the products created are not only functional and efficient but also responsible and fair. This chapter addresses the intersection of ethics and law within the context of software development, emphasizing the importance of social and professional responsibility for developers.

Key concepts such as intellectual property, including copyright, patents, and software licensing, will be explored. These are essential for protecting both developers 'innovations and users 'rights. Additionally, ethical dilemmas that may arise during the development process, such as data privacy, automation, and inherent biases in artificial intelligence, will be discussed.

As technology evolves and becomes integral to society, developers must be equipped with the knowledge and tools to navigate these ethical and legal aspects, ensuring a positive impact on the world around them.

12.1 INTRODUCTION TO ETHICS IN SOFTWARE DEVELOPMENT

Ethics in software development is an increasingly relevant field as technology integrates more deeply into everyday life. Software developers not only create tools and applications but also shape behaviors, influence culture, and significantly impact people's lives. This chapter addresses developers 'ethical responsibility, the dilemmas they face, and the importance of a clear code of conduct in their profession.

12.1.1 Social and Professional Responsibility of Developers

Software developers have both a social and professional responsibility that goes beyond merely creating functional code. This responsibility involves considering the societal impact of their work. For instance, when developing applications that process personal data, it is crucial to ensure the privacy and security of that data while being transparent about its use.

Developers should adhere to the principle of "do no harm," ensuring their applications do not contribute to harmful practices such as discrimination or misinformation. This is especially pertinent in an environment where technologies like artificial intelligence (AI) and machine learning can perpetuate existing biases if not properly managed. By adopting an ethical stance, developers can contribute to a fairer and more responsible technological environment.

12.1.2 Ethical Dilemmas in Software Development

Ethical dilemmas are common in software development and require careful analysis and informed decision-making. Examples include:

- **Data Privacy:** Developers must balance the need to collect data for service improvement with the obligation to protect user privacy. Excessive data collection or lack of transparency can lead to privacy violations.

- **Automation:** Automation and algorithms can increase efficiency but also raise concerns about job displacement and the dehumanization of processes. Developers should consider the human impact of their decisions and whether automation could perpetuate inequalities.

- **Bias in Artificial Intelligence:** AI systems can reflect biases present in the data they were trained on, leading to unfair decisions in critical areas such as hiring, credit, and criminal justice. Developers must be vigilant about these biases and actively work to mitigate them.

Analyzing these dilemmas through case studies helps developers recognize the complexity of their decisions and adopt a more thoughtful and ethical approach to their work.

12.1.3 Code of Conduct for Developers

A code of conduct provides an ethical framework for developers, establishing standards and principles that guide their professional behavior. It may include:

- **Integrity:** Encouraging honesty in development and project management, avoiding deceptive or unethical practices.

- **User Respect:** Prioritizing user experience and ensuring applications are accessible and non-discriminatory.

- **Collaboration and Transparency:** Promoting a collaborative work environment where open communication and feedback are valued.

- **Professional Responsibility:** Taking responsibility for the quality of their code and compliance with legal and ethical standards.

Adhering to a code of conduct reinforces developers 'commitment to ethics and helps build trust in their work and the software industry as a whole. This is crucial in a world where technology plays a significant role in daily life and societal shaping.

12.2. BASIC PRINCIPLES OF INTELLECTUAL PROPERTY

Intellectual property (IP) encompasses legal rights protecting creations of the mind, including literary, artistic works, and inventions. In software development, understanding these principles is essential for adequately protecting one's work and respecting others'. Below are key concepts related to intellectual property in software development.

12.2.1 Copyright and Software

Copyright protects original works of authorship, including software programs. Registering a software's source code under copyright grants the author exclusive rights to reproduce, distribute, and create derivative works. This means no one can use, modify, or distribute the software without the copyright holder's permission.

Understanding the importance of using licenses specifying how software can be used is crucial. Various licenses have different conditions regarding code redistribution and modification. By choosing an appropriate license, developers can protect their work and set usage rules, fostering a culture of respect and compliance within the software community.

12.2.2 Software Patents

Patents protect inventions, including certain software innovations. A patent grants the inventor exclusive rights to manufacture, use, and sell their invention for a set period, typically 20 years from the filing date.

Obtaining a software patent requires submitting a clear and detailed application to the relevant patent office. The invention must be new, useful, and non-obvious to someone skilled in the field. Software patents are suitable when innovative technology provides a competitive advantage and needs protection from competitors. However, the process can be costly and time-consuming, making careful evaluation essential.

12.2.3 Open-Source Software and Licensing

Open-source software allows developers to access and modify the source code, but understanding the associated licenses is critical, as they dictate usage, modification, and redistribution.

Common licenses include:

- **MIT License:** Allows users to do almost anything with the software, provided the license is included in any distribution.
- **GPL (General Public License):** Requires that any derived software also be distributed under the same license, promoting free distribution and modification.
- **Apache License:** Similar to the MIT license but includes patent clauses protecting users from patent claims by contributors.

Choosing the right license for a project is fundamental, affecting how software is shared and used and providing legal protection. Developers should consider their goals and context when selecting the most appropriate license.

12.2.4 Copyright and Fair Use Considerations

Copyright automatically protects original works, including software. Understanding the difference between fair use and copyright infringement in software is essential:

- **Fair Use:** A legal principle allowing limited use of protected works without permission, typically for criticism, teaching, and research. However, it is context-dependent and not clearly defined.
- **Copyright Infringement:** Occurs when software is used without the appropriate permission, including unauthorized copying, distribution, or modification.

Being aware of these distinctions helps developers avoid legal issues and promotes a culture of respect for intellectual property, protecting both their work and that of others in the software development community.

12.3. REGULATIONS AND COMPLIANCE IN SIMPLE TERMS

Regulations and compliance are critical aspects of software development, especially in a world where data privacy and security are increasingly relevant. This section focuses on the regulatory frameworks developers and organizations must consider to ensure their software is legal and ethical. Below are key topics in this area.

12.3.1. Data Privacy Regulations (GDPR, CCPA, etc.)

Data privacy regulations, such as the European Union's General Data Protection Regulation (GDPR) and the California Consumer Privacy Act (CCPA), establish specific requirements on how companies must handle personal information. Developers must understand the obligations imposed by these regulations, including:

•   **Consent:** Ensure explicit user consent is obtained before collecting and processing their data.

•   **Transparency:** Inform users about how their data will be used, who will have access to it, and how long it will be stored.

•   **User Rights:** Facilitate user access to their data, allowing them to correct or delete information as desired.

Complying with these regulations not only avoids legal penalties but also builds user trust.

12.3.2. Personal Data Protection Laws

Each country has its own personal data protection laws that developers must consider. For example, in Mexico, the Federal Law on Protection of Personal Data Held by Private Parties establishes principles for handling personal data. Ensuring applications comply with these laws involves:

- **Impact Assessments:** Conduct analyses to identify how data is managed and associated risks.

- **Security Measures Implementation:** Adopt protocols ensuring data security, such as encryption and access controls.

- **Staff Training:** Educate teams on the importance of data protection and how to handle sensitive information.

12.3.3. Accessibility Compliance Regulations

Accessibility is crucial in software development, ensuring that everyone, including people with disabilities, can use the application. Guidelines like the Web Content Accessibility Guidelines (WCAG) help developers create inclusive software. To comply with these guidelines, consider:

- **Inclusive Design:** Implement features such as alternative text for images and keyboard navigation.

- **Usability Testing:** Conduct tests with users with various disabilities to identify and fix accessibility barriers.

- **Continuous Training:** Stay updated on best practices and new accessibility regulations.

12.3.4. Information Security Standards Compliance (ISO/IEC 27001, NIST)

Information security is essential in software development. Standards such as ISO/IEC 27001 and guidelines from the National Institute of Standards and Technology (NIST) provide frameworks for managing information security. Key areas include:

- **Risk Management:** Evaluate and mitigate potential risks affecting data confidentiality, integrity, and availability.

- **Security Controls:** Implement appropriate measures, such as user authentication, encryption, and security monitoring.

- **Audits and Review:** Conduct periodic audits to ensure security policies are followed and updated as necessary.

Complying with these standards protects sensitive information, enhances organizational reputation, and builds user trust.

12.4. ETHICS IN ARTIFICIAL INTELLIGENCE AND MACHINE LEARNING

Ethics in artificial intelligence (AI) and machine learning (ML) has become a critical topic in developing technologies that profoundly impact daily life and society. With the growing use of algorithms and automated systems in various areas, addressing the ethical implications of their design, implementation, and use is essential.

12.4.1. Ethical Considerations in Data Use for AI

Data collection and use are fundamental to developing AI and ML systems but raise important ethical issues:

- **Transparency:** Users must understand how their data is used. Organizations should be transparent about data collection practices, including what data is collected, how it is used, and with whom it is shared. A lack of transparency can erode user trust and lead to technology rejection.

- **Consent:** Obtaining informed user consent is a key ethical principle. Users must be fully aware of the implications of their data usage and have the option to accept or decline. Data collection practices should be clear and accessible.

- **Privacy:** Protecting privacy is fundamental when using data for AI. Organizations must implement appropriate measures to ensure data is handled securely and comply with data protection regulations, such as GDPR. This includes using anonymization and encryption techniques.

12.4.2. Mitigating Bias in Machine Learning Models

Biases in machine learning models can lead to unfair and discriminatory outcomes, presenting significant ethical challenges:

- **Sources of Bias:** Biases can be introduced during the model training process due to unequal data, inadequate representations, or human errors in data collection. Identifying and addressing these bias sources is crucial to ensure models reflect an equitable representation of all populations.

- **Testing and Validation:** Organizations should implement rigorous testing and validation processes to evaluate model performance across different demographic groups. This involves using diverse and representative datasets during model training and evaluation.

- **Inclusive Development:** Promoting an inclusive approach to developing machine learning models involves engaging diverse, multidisciplinary teams in the design and evaluation process. This helps identify and mitigate biases that might otherwise be overlooked.

12.4.3. Responsibility in Automation and Algorithmic Decision-Making

As organizations adopt automated systems for decision-making, addressing the ethical implications of delegating responsibility is necessary:

- **Decision-Making Transparency:** AI systems should be transparent about how decisions are made. Users and stakeholders should access information on the criteria used in the decision-making process and underlying data. This fosters trust and enables people to challenge or appeal decisions they consider unfair.

- **Responsibility Implications:** Determining who is responsible when an automated system makes an error is a complex ethical and legal issue. Organizations should establish clear policies on responsibility for automated decisions, ensuring mechanisms are in place to address complaints and repercussions from erroneous decisions.

- **Social Impact:** Algorithmic decisions can profoundly impact people's lives, affecting areas such as hiring, credit, and criminal justice.

Organizations must assess the social implications of their AI systems and work to ensure that benefits are distributed equitably.

In summary, ethics in AI and machine learning is essential for developing and implementing responsible technologies. Addressing ethical considerations in data use, mitigating biases in models, and assuming responsibility for automated decisions are crucial steps in building AI systems that are fair, transparent, and respectful of user rights.

12.5. CYBERSECURITY PRACTICES AND LEGAL ASPECTS

Cybersecurity is a critical concern in software development, as the rise in digital threats requires developers not only to protect their applications but also to comply with current legal regulations. This section covers relevant regulations, legal protection against security breaches, and ethics in hacking, providing a comprehensive framework on how cybersecurity laws and practices are interconnected.

12.5.1. Cybersecurity Regulations in Application

As cyberattacks continue to rise, various laws and regulations have been implemented globally to protect applications and user data. Some of the most relevant regulations include:

•   **General Data Protection Regulation (GDPR):** This European Union regulation sets strict guidelines for handling personal data, requiring organizations to implement adequate security measures to protect user information. Non-compliance can result in significant fines.

•   Children's Online Privacy Protection Act (COPPA) and Personal Information Protection Acts: These U.S. laws provide guidelines on how organizations must protect personal information, particularly that of minors. This includes implementing robust security practices to prevent unauthorized access to sensitive data.

•   **ISO/IEC 27001 Standard:** This international standard provides a framework for information security management, helping organizations protect their data systematically and continuously. ISO/IEC 27001 certification demonstrates adherence to globally recognized cybersecurity standards.

Compliance with these regulations not only protects organizations from legal penalties but also builds user trust and enhances brand reputation.

12.5.2. Legal Protection Against Vulnerabilities and Security Breaches

Developers and organizations have legal rights and obligations regarding security vulnerabilities and data breaches. Understanding the legal framework surrounding these situations is essential:

- **Developer Responsibility:** Developers are responsible for implementing adequate security measures to protect applications from potential cyberattacks. This includes conducting regular security testing and fixing known vulnerabilities. Negligence in this regard can result in legal actions and fines.

- **Breach Notification:** Many laws require organizations to notify users and relevant authorities in the event of a data breach compromising personal data. Failure to notify or delayed notification can lead to severe penalties.

- **User Rights:** Users have the right to know how their data is handled and to be informed about the measures taken to protect their information. They can also sue organizations for damages if their data is compromised due to inadequate security measures.

Establishing clear policies for managing vulnerabilities and security breaches helps organizations protect their assets and maintain user trust.

12.5.3. Cybersecurity and Ethical Hacking

Ethics in hacking is a crucial topic in cybersecurity, especially in a context where hackers can be both threats and allies in combating cyberattacks:

- **Ethical Hacking:** Ethical hacking involves conducting penetration tests and security assessments of systems with the owner's permission. Ethical hackers use their skills to identify and fix vulnerabilities, helping organizations improve their security posture. This proactive approach is essential in cybersecurity.

- **Difference Between Ethical and Malicious Hacking:** The main difference lies in intent and permission. Ethical hacking is authorized and aims to improve security, while malicious hacking seeks to exploit vulnerabilities for personal gain or harm. Cybersecurity laws in many countries impose severe penalties for malicious hacking.

- **Professional Code of Ethics:** Cybersecurity professionals and ethical hackers must adhere to a code of ethics that promotes integrity, responsibility, and respect for user privacy. This code guides their behavior and ensures that their actions in cybersecurity benefit society.

Understanding the ethical implications of hacking and cybersecurity is essential for developers and IT professionals, as their decisions significantly impact data security and user trust.

12.6. LEGAL IMPLICATIONS OF SOFTWARE USE IN DIFFERENT SECTORS

Software use varies significantly across different sectors, each facing unique legal and regulatory implications. Understanding these regulations is crucial to ensure applications comply with legal requirements and protect both businesses and consumers.

12.6.1. Software in the Financial Sector and Regulatory Compliance (Fintech)

The financial sector, particularly in fintech, is subject to specific regulations aimed at ensuring security, transparency, and consumer protection:

• **Financial Services Regulation:** Fintech companies must comply with regulations such as the Bank Secrecy Act (BSA) and the USA PATRIOT Act, which mandate anti-money laundering (AML) measures and customer identification (KYC) diligence. This involves collecting personal and financial information and monitoring suspicious transactions.

• **Data Protection and Privacy:** Regulations like GDPR in Europe and CCPA in California set strict requirements on how companies handle and protect user data. Fintech companies must ensure that data collection, storage, and processing are legal and ethical, obtaining explicit user consent.

• **Cryptocurrency and Digital Asset Regulation:** As cryptocurrencies and other digital assets grow, regulatory frameworks are evolving. Fintech companies operating in this space must be aware of specific regulations regarding cryptocurrency classification, registration as virtual asset service providers, and initial coin offerings (ICO) regulations.

12.6.2. Healthcare Software Regulations

Developing healthcare software involves unique regulations designed to protect patient health and privacy:

- **Medical Device Regulation:** In many countries, software used as part of a medical device or significantly impacting patient treatment is classified as a medical device. It must comply with strict regulations from the FDA in the U.S. or CE in Europe, requiring rigorous testing and documentation before approval.

- **Health Information Protection:** The Health Insurance Portability and Accountability Act (HIPAA) in the U.S. establishes standards for the privacy and security of personal health information (PHI). Health applications must implement robust security measures to protect patient data and ensure confidentiality.

- **Telemedicine Regulations:** With the rise of telemedicine, regulations on remote healthcare delivery have become more relevant. This includes licensing requirements for healthcare providers and compliance with remote medical practice regulations.

12.6.3. E-commerce Software Regulations

E-commerce is subject to various regulations aimed at protecting both consumers and businesses:

- **Consumer Protection Legislation:** Online merchants must provide clear and accurate product information, including return policies, shipping, and associated costs. They must also ensure consumers have access to complaint and dispute resolution channels.

- **Payment Security and Privacy:** Standards like the Payment Card Industry Data Security Standard (PCI DSS) set requirements for securely managing credit card information. E-commerce companies must comply with these standards to protect customer payment data and prevent security breaches.

- **Advertising and Digital Marketing Regulation:** Online

advertising practices must comply with truthful and fair advertising regulations. Laws like the CAN-SPAM Act in the U.S. and GDPR in Europe regulate how companies can communicate with consumers through emails and targeted advertising.

12.7. CHAPTER CONCLUSIONS

Ethics in software development is not only a matter of professional responsibility but also a social imperative. Developers must be aware of the impact of their technical decisions on users 'lives and society. From data collection to automated decision-making, ethics should be a guiding principle to ensure software benefits the community and does not perpetuate inequalities or discrimination.

In conclusion, addressing ethical and legal aspects in software development is essential for building a fairer, safer, and more responsible technological ecosystem. Developers and organizations must commit to ethics, legality, and social responsibility, recognizing that their work impacts not only individual users but society as a whole. By doing so, they will foster an environment that prioritizes innovation while respecting and protecting everyone's rights.

CAPÍTULO 13
CURRENT AND FUTURE TRENDS IN SOFTWARE ENGINEERING

The world of software engineering is in constant evolution, driven by new technologies and approaches that transform the way we develop, deploy, and maintain applications. This chapter explores the most relevant trends and their impact on the industry, from artificial intelligence to the rise of augmented and virtual reality applications.

13.1. ARTIFICIAL INTELLIGENCE IN SOFTWARE DEVELOPMENT

Artificial intelligence (AI) has reshaped the landscape of software development, not only facilitating application creation but also enabling development teams to automate complex tasks and significantly optimize processes. As technology advances, AI becomes an essential tool that allows developers to tackle increasingly sophisticated challenges and deliver high-quality products in less time.

13.1.1. Programming Assistants

Programming assistant tools, such as GitHub Copilot and ChatGPT, have revolutionized how developers write code. These platforms use advanced language models and deep learning to suggest code snippets, autocomplete functions, and provide real-time solutions to common problems. By reducing the time developers spend writing code manually, these assistants not only increase efficiency but also help minimize errors, promoting better coding practices. Additionally, by providing contextualized examples and suggestions, these tools also serve as learning resources, helping developers—especially beginners—improve their skills.

13.1.2. Machine Learning and Deep Learning

Machine learning (ML) and deep learning (DL) have opened new possibilities in software development by enabling the creation of predictive models that analyze large volumes of data. These technologies are used in various applications, from recommendation systems to fraud detection and sentiment analysis. For example, in the context of software development, ML can be used to predict system failures before they occur by analyzing patterns in historical data. This not only improves software reliability but also enables development teams to anticipate and resolve issues before they impact end users, thereby optimizing the customer experience.

13.1.3. Process Optimization

AI also plays a crucial role in optimizing processes within the software development lifecycle. By automating software testing, AI-powered tools can identify and correct errors more quickly and efficiently than traditional methods. This reduces development time and enhances the quality of the final product. Additionally, AI can improve incident management by automatically classifying reported issues, prioritizing their resolution based on severity, and assigning tasks to the appropriate developers. This analytical and optimization capability allows teams to be more agile and respond quickly to changes in market needs or client requirements.

13.1.4. Impact on Collaboration and Innovation

In addition to improving efficiency and software quality, artificial intelligence fosters greater collaboration among teams. By automating routine tasks, developers can dedicate more time to creative and strategic activities, such as designing innovative solutions and planning software architectures. This focus on innovation is essential to staying competitive in a rapidly evolving tech market.

13.1.5. Ethical Considerations and Challenges

However, implementing AI in software development is not without challenges and ethical considerations. Excessive reliance on automated systems can lead to issues related to bias, security, and privacy. It is crucial for developers to understand the ethical implications of using AI and ensure their models are fair, transparent, and accountable. Continuous training in AI ethics and emerging technologies becomes essential for software professionals.

In summary, artificial intelligence is redefining software development by providing powerful tools that optimize processes, enhance quality, and foster innovation. As these technologies continue to evolve, their integration into the development workflow will become increasingly prevalent, making AI training and practical application essential for the future of software engineering.

13.2. DEVOPS AND CI/CD

The integration of DevOps and CI/CD (Continuous Integration and Continuous Deployment) automation has revolutionized software delivery, enabling shorter development cycles, better team collaboration, and a focus on continuous product quality. This holistic approach not only improves efficiency but also allows organizations to quickly adapt to market changes and user needs.

13.2.1. DevOps Culture

A strong DevOps culture is essential for successful continuous software delivery. It involves integrating development and operations teams into a collaborative workflow. This seamless collaboration fosters constant communication and mutual understanding, reducing the friction between traditionally siloed teams. Promoting a DevOps culture involves breaking down organizational silos, fostering shared responsibility, and adopting a mindset of continuous improvement.

DevOps principles also emphasize experimentation and constant feedback, allowing teams to learn from mistakes and optimize processes. This not only leads to faster software delivery but also enhances product quality by addressing issues before they reach production.

13.2.2. Deployment Automation

Automating integration and deployment processes is a cornerstone of DevOps. Tools like Jenkins, GitLab CI/CD, and GitHub Actions allow teams to automate repetitive tasks such as code builds, test executions, and production deployments. Automation speeds up delivery and reduces the risk of human error inherent in manual deployments.

Implementing CI/CD pipelines enables developers to make frequent code changes, automatically testing each change in a controlled environment before release. This ensures that issues are identified and resolved immediately, improving software stability and quality.

13.2.3. Infrastructure as Code (IaC)

Infrastructure as Code (IaC) is another critical component that complements DevOps practices. With tools like Terraform and Ansible, teams can manage IT infrastructure using code configurations, treating infrastructure as they would software. This provides consistency and reproducibility across development, testing, and production environments.

IaC allows teams to quickly provision and configure environments, especially useful in agile development environments where demands can change rapidly. Versioning infrastructure alongside code also means any configuration changes can be effectively tracked and rolled back, minimizing the risk of production environment errors.

13.2.4. Continuous Monitoring and Feedback

Continuous monitoring and feedback are essential aspects of DevOps and CI/CD. As software is deployed, real-time performance monitoring is crucial to identifying issues and areas for improvement. Tools like Prometheus, Grafana, and the ELK Stack help teams collect and analyze data on software performance, user experience, and other key metrics.

Continuous feedback enables teams to make quick, effective adjustments, enhancing software quality and ensuring user needs are met. Insights from monitoring also guide future product iterations, ensuring development remains aligned with customer expectations.

13.2.5. Conclusion

The integration of DevOps and CI/CD has optimized software development processes and transformed organizational culture by fostering collaboration and communication. By automating repetitive tasks, managing infrastructure as code, and adopting continuous monitoring, organizations can deliver high-quality software more quickly and efficiently. This approach allows teams to adapt to market changes and user needs, ensuring a competitive edge in a rapidly evolving technological landscape.

13.3. CLOUD COMPUTING AND CLOUD-NATIVE APPLICATION DEVELOPMENT

Cloud computing has radically transformed how applications are developed, deployed, and managed, providing a flexible and scalable environment that quickly adapts to changing business needs. This evolution has enabled companies to reduce operational and infrastructure costs while optimizing application performance and availability.

13.3.1. Cloud Services

Cloud service providers like Amazon Web Services (AWS), Google Cloud Platform (GCP), and Microsoft Azure offer a broad range of managed services, allowing organizations to focus on application development without worrying about the underlying infrastructure. These services include:

- **Storage:** Solutions like Amazon S3 and Google Cloud Storage enable users to store large volumes of data securely and scalably, with automated data recovery and backup options.

- **Compute:** Virtual machine instances like Amazon EC2 and Google Compute Engine provide on-demand compute resources, allowing companies to handle application load spikes without upfront hardware investment.

- **Data Management:** Services like Amazon RDS and

Google Cloud SQL offer managed databases, enabling developers to create, manage, and scale databases without extensive database administration knowledge.

13.3.2. Microservices and Containers

Adopting microservices architectures has changed how cloud applications are designed and deployed. This methodology promotes building applications from small, independent services that can be developed, deployed, and scaled individually. Key characteristics of this architecture include:

• **Modularity:** Microservices allow applications to be broken into smaller, manageable components, facilitating feature implementation and bug fixes without affecting the entire system.

• **Scalability:** Tools like Docker and Kubernetes enable developers to package microservices into containers that can be horizontally scaled. This means that if a part of the application needs more resources, multiple instances of that microservice can be deployed quickly and efficiently.

• **Continuous Deployment:** The microservices nature facilitates Continuous Integration and Continuous Deployment (CI/CD), allowing development teams to release new features and updates frequently and reliably.

13.3.3. Serverless Development

Serverless development is another emerging trend in cloud computing that allows developers to focus on writing code without managing server infrastructure. Platforms like AWS Lambda, Azure Functions, and Google Cloud Functions enable developers to execute code in response to specific events, such as HTTP requests or data uploads. Advantages of this approach include:

• **Cost-Effectiveness:** Instead of paying for always-on servers, the serverless model charges organizations only for the time code is executed, significantly reducing operational costs, especially for applications with variable workloads.

• **Automatic Scalability:** Serverless platforms automatically scale based on demand, meaning applications can handle high traffic volumes without manual intervention.

- **Agile Development:** By eliminating the burden of server management, development teams can iterate faster and focus on delivering customer value through new features and improvements.

13.3.4. Conclusion

Cloud computing has redefined application development, offering a broad range of tools and services that enhance flexibility, scalability, and operational efficiency. The adoption of microservices architectures and serverless development continues to shape the future of software development, allowing organizations to respond more effectively to market demands and user expectations. As technology advances, cloud computing will play a fundamental role in driving innovation and competitiveness in a constantly evolving digital world.

13.4. FUTURE OF SOFTWARE ENGINEERING: LOW-CODE AND NO-CODE

Low-code and no-code development platforms are revolutionizing how software is created, enabling non-technical users to participate in the development process and democratizing access to technology. These tools allow individuals and teams from various disciplines to build applications and solutions without deep programming knowledge, significantly shifting how software development is conceived and executed.

13.4.1. Development Acceleration

Platforms like OutSystems, Bubble, and Mendix are designed to enable users to develop applications quickly and efficiently. Key features that contribute to this acceleration include:

- **Visual Interface:** Drag-and-drop interfaces allow users to create applications using visual components instead of writing code. This simplifies the understanding of the design and functionality, enabling rapid iteration of ideas.

- **Simplified Integration:** Many low-code and no-code platforms offer pre-built integrations with various APIs and third-party services, making it easy for users to connect their applications to databases, external systems, and cloud services without complex configurations.

- **Reusable Templates and Components:** These tools often include libraries of templates and components that can be used to speed up the development of common applications, saving time and effort in building functionalities from scratch.

13.4.2. Rapid Prototyping

The ability to create prototypes quickly is a major benefit of low-code and no-code platforms, especially for startups and innovation teams needing efficient idea validation. Advantages of this feature include:

• **Agile Iteration:** Teams can develop prototypes in days, test concepts, and gather feedback from end-users. This allows for quick adjustments and product improvements before large-scale launches.

• **Risk Reduction:** By validating ideas through functional prototypes, organizations can identify issues and make necessary changes early in the process, reducing the risk of market failures.

• **Stakeholder Involvement:** Business users can actively participate in the development process with tools that allow them to express ideas and collaborate on solution design, resulting in products better aligned with user needs.

13.4.3. Limitations and Challenges

Despite numerous advantages, low-code and no-code platforms also present certain limitations and challenges:

• **Scalability:** Applications developed on low-code platforms may face challenges as user bases and functionalities grow. Some tools might not be designed to handle massive workloads, leading to performance issues.

• **Customization:** Although these platforms offer customization tools, they are often limited by the platform's capabilities. When applications require specific needs or complex logic, expert developers may need to integrate custom code or make deeper adjustments.

• **Vendor Lock-In:** Organizations that choose low-code and no-code platforms may become dependent on specific vendors, posing challenges if the vendor changes policies, pricing, or discontinues operations.

13.4.4. Conclusion

Low-code and no-code platforms are transforming the future of software engineering by opening software creation to a broader audience. While these tools promise to accelerate development and democratize technology access, organizations must be aware of their limitations and challenges. As the demand for quick and flexible solutions continues to grow, low-code and no-code platforms will likely become an integral part of the software development landscape, complementing the work of expert developers and enabling organizations to innovate more effectively.

13.5. EDGE COMPUTING AND ITS IMPACT ON DEVELOPMENT

Edge computing is emerging as a key solution to address the challenges associated with the growing volume of data generated by connected devices. By enabling data processing closer to the source, efficiency improves, and response times are optimized, which is especially relevant for applications requiring low latency and immediate processing. Below, the fundamental aspects of edge computing and its impact on software development are analyzed.

13.5.1. Local Processing

Local processing is a cornerstone of edge computing. By performing calculations and analysis on local devices such as IoT sensors, smartphones, and other mobile devices, several benefits can be obtained:

• **Latency Reduction:** By avoiding data transmission to cloud servers for processing, applications can deliver near-instant responses. This is crucial in scenarios where every millisecond counts, such as online gaming, industrial control systems, and augmented reality applications.

• **Bandwidth Savings:** Local data processing reduces the need to transmit large volumes of information to the cloud, lowering associated bandwidth costs and allowing more efficient use of network infrastructure.

• **Offline Operations:** Devices operating with edge computing can continue functioning even in environments with limited connectivity. This is vital for remote applications, such as crop monitoring or fleet management, where internet connectivity may be intermittent.

13.5.2. Critical Applications

Edge computing has become essential in developing critical applications requiring real-time processing. Key areas where its impact is particularly significant include:

- **Autonomous Vehicles:** These vehicles generate and process large amounts of real-time data for navigation and decision-making. Local processing allows them to react instantly to environmental changes, enhancing safety and driving efficiency.

- **Medical Devices:** In healthcare, edge computing enables devices like patient monitors to process data locally, vital for continuous monitoring and rapid intervention in critical situations such as arrhythmias or falls.

- **Surveillance Systems:** Intelligent security cameras can perform local video analysis to detect suspicious movements or recognize faces, reducing the need for constant cloud image transmission. This improves efficiency and helps maintain privacy by minimizing transmitted data.

13.5.3. Security Challenges

As edge computing becomes more widely adopted, significant challenges arise in terms of security and management:

- **Data Protection:** With the proliferation of connected devices, ensuring the security of locally processed data is crucial. Each edge device can become a potential vulnerability that attackers could exploit, requiring more robust cybersecurity approaches.

- **Distributed Infrastructure Management:** Edge computing infrastructure is inherently more complex than centralized systems. Managing and monitoring numerous dispersed devices require advanced administration and orchestration tools to ensure efficient and secure operations.

- **Regulatory Compliance:** Organizations must comply with data protection regulations, which can be complicated by the distributed nature of edge computing. Implementing security policies aligned with current regulations may require continuous updates as laws and regulations evolve.

13.5.4. Conclusion

Edge computing is transforming software development by offering solutions for fast and efficient data processing, enabling the creation of critical applications in sectors like automotive, healthcare, and security. However, this approach also poses new security and management challenges that organizations must address. As edge computing continues to evolve, its integration into the software development landscape will become essential for creating innovative and effective applications in an increasingly connected world.

13.6. APPLICATIONS IN AUGMENTED AND VIRTUAL REALITY

Augmented reality (AR) and virtual reality (VR) are revolutionizing how we interact with software, transforming various sectors from education and healthcare to entertainment and commerce. These technologies enable more immersive and enriched experiences, expanding the possibilities for software development. Below is an in-depth look at AR and VR applications and their impact on different fields.

13.6.1. AR on Mobile Devices

Augmented reality has gained significant traction on mobile devices, thanks to tools like Apple's ARKit and Google's ARCore. These platforms make it easier for developers to create AR applications that integrate digital elements into the real world.

- **Enhanced Interaction:** AR apps on mobile devices allow users to interact with digital objects overlaid onto their real environment. This results in more engaging interactive experiences, such as visualizing furniture in their home before purchase or playing games that blend physical reality with virtual elements.

- **Augmented Education:** AR is revolutionizing learning in education. For instance, apps can project 3D models of anatomical structures in biology classes, allowing students to explore complex details interactively and visually.

- **Marketing and Advertising:** Companies use AR to create innovative advertising campaigns. By scanning a QR code or an image, consumers can view additional content, such as interactive promotions or 3D product representations, increasing engagement and customer interest.

13.6.2. Simulations and Training

Virtual reality has become a powerful tool for creating training simulations across various industries, particularly in healthcare and technical training.

- **Medical Training:** VR allows healthcare professionals to practice medical procedures in a safe, controlled environment. For example, surgeons can simulate complex operations, refining their skills before performing real procedures. This enhances professional competence and increases patient safety.

- **Industrial Simulations:** VR is used in industrial settings to train employees on machinery operations, safety processes, and emergency handling. These simulations help workers familiarize themselves with equipment and working conditions without the risk of injury.

- **Interpersonal Skill Development:** VR is also used to train interpersonal skills, such as customer service or negotiation. Employees can practice in virtual scenarios, receive feedback, and improve their performance.

13.6.3. Immersive Experiences

Virtual reality offers immersive experiences beyond traditional screens, creating three-dimensional environments where users can interact meaningfully.

- **Gaming and Entertainment:** VR has transformed how we play games and experience media. VR games fully immerse players in virtual worlds, interacting with their surroundings in previously impossible ways, enhancing excitement and user engagement.

- **Virtual Tourism:** VR applications are changing how we explore the world. Virtual tourism platforms let users "visit" destinations from home, offering immersive experiences of iconic places, museums, and natural wonders.

- **Art and Culture**: VR is also being used for interactive artistic and cultural experiences. Virtual art galleries allow visitors to explore exhibitions in new ways, and immersive storytelling experiences transport users into unique narratives and environments.

13.6.4. Challenges and Future

Despite the opportunities AR and VR offer, there are challenges to address:

- **Accessibility:** As these technologies evolve, ensuring they are accessible to everyone, including people with disabilities, is essential. Developing inclusive experiences should be a priority for developers.

- **Implementation Costs:** AR and VR solutions can be expensive, limiting their adoption in some industries. As technology advances, costs are expected to decrease, increasing availability.

- **User Experience:** Effective AR and VR experiences require careful attention to usability and comfort. Poorly designed experiences can cause discomfort or disorientation, limiting user acceptance.

13.6.5. Conclusion

Augmented and virtual reality applications are transforming how we interact with software and the world around us. As these technologies continue to evolve, their integration across various sectors promises to enhance education, professional training, entertainment, and more. Addressing associated challenges, the future of AR and VR looks bright, offering exciting opportunities to innovate and enrich our digital experiences.

13.7. CHAPTER CONCLUSIONS

Current and future trends in software engineering offer vast potential to transform how software is developed and consumed. The integration of artificial intelligence, the rise of DevOps and CI/CD, and advancements in technologies like edge computing and augmented reality are redefining developers 'and users 'expectations. Embracing these innovations requires a balanced approach to seize opportunities without compromising software quality and security. Companies and developers adapting to these trends will be better positioned to face future challenges and harness the potential of an increasingly digital world.

CAPÍTULO 14
CONCLUSIONS AND NEXT STEPS

This final chapter wraps up the journey through the fundamentals, practices, and trends in software engineering, offering a summarized overview of the concepts learned, the skills necessary to advance in the field, and suggestions for further exploration. It also includes acknowledgments to everyone who supported this project.

14.1. RECAP OF KEY CONCEPTS

Throughout this book, we have explored a wide range of essential topics that are fundamental to developing quality software and managing technological projects. These concepts not only serve as the pillars of software development but also provide a framework for making informed decisions in an ever-evolving technological environment.

14.1.1. Software Engineering Fundamentals

We began our journey by reviewing the basic principles guiding software design and development. We discussed the importance of understanding user requirements, software architecture, and design patterns, as well as the need to apply solid principles that ensure efficient and sustainable development. Software engineering is not just about coding but also about understanding the context in which applications are developed and how they impact the end-user experience.

14.1.2. Architecture and Coding

In this section, we delved into how to structure applications efficiently. Software architecture is crucial in determining how different components and modules interact, affecting both performance and system scalability. We also discussed clean coding principles, emphasizing code readability, maintainability, and reusability. Implementing robust coding practices helps reduce errors and facilitates collaboration within development teams.

14.1.3. Software Testing

Software validation is a fundamental process to ensure quality and reliability. We analyzed different types of testing, including unit, integration, functional, and performance tests. Each type plays a unique role in the software development lifecycle, and implementing a strong testing approach improves the final product's quality while reducing development costs and time by detecting issues early.

14.1.4. Project Management and DevOps

Effective project management is vital for success in software development. We learned about coordinating teams, managing risks, using appropriate management tools, and applying DevOps principles. This culture of collaboration between development and operations teams enables continuous delivery of quality software, allowing agile responses to market and user needs. Implementing agile methodologies and automation tools also enhances efficiency in the software lifecycle.

14.1.5. Current Trends

Finally, we reviewed emerging technologies and current trends shaping the future of software development. Artificial intelligence, cloud computing, native cloud application development, augmented and virtual reality, and the proliferation of low-code and no-code development platforms are transforming how developers create and deploy applications. Understanding and adapting to these trends is crucial to remain competitive in a constantly changing technological landscape.

14.1.5. Current Trends

Finally, we reviewed emerging technologies and current trends shaping the future of software development. Artificial intelligence, cloud computing, native cloud application development, augmented and virtual reality, and the proliferation of low-code and no-code development platforms are transforming how developers create and deploy applications. Understanding and adapting to these trends is crucial to remain competitive in a constantly changing technological landscape.

14.2. KEY SKILLS FOR SOFTWARE DEVELOPERS

For those aiming to excel in the software industry, there are fundamental skills that must be continuously developed. These skills are not only crucial for creating quality software but also essential for a successful career in this constantly evolving field.

14.2.1. Problem-Solving

The ability to analyze and find solutions to complex problems is critical in software development. Developers often face unexpected challenges that require both critical and creative thinking. Problem-solving involves not only identifying the issue but also investigating root causes and proposing effective solutions. This can range from debugging code to optimizing algorithms and improving system efficiency. Cultivating analytical and logical thinking skills helps developers approach these challenges systematically and efficiently.

14.2.2. Continuous Learning

Technology evolves rapidly, so staying up-to-date with new tools, languages, and methodologies is essential. Developers should adopt a mindset of continuous learning through formal courses, online tutorials, conferences, or reading technical literature. This not only keeps professionals relevant in a competitive job market but also enables them to adapt to the changing needs of their projects and clients. Curiosity and a willingness to explore new technologies are valuable traits in any developer.

14.2.3. Teamwork and Collaboration

Effective communication and collaboration with other developers, designers, and stakeholders are vital for project success. Developers don't work in isolation; they need to interact and collaborate with various stakeholders, from project managers to clients. This includes sharing ideas, giving and receiving feedback, and managing conflicts. Teamwork fosters a positive and productive work environment where all team members can contribute to the project's success. Project management and communication tools like Jira, Slack, and Trello are essential for facilitating collaboration.

14.2.4. Quality Orientation

Adopting best practices such as writing clean code, conducting rigorous testing, and maintaining proper documentation ensures that software is maintainable and reliable. Software quality is measured not just by its functionality but also by how easily it can be understood and modified in the future. Developers should be committed to quality at every stage of development, from planning to implementation and maintenance. This involves following coding standards, conducting code reviews, and participating in testing activities to detect and fix issues before deployment.

14.2.5. Agile Mindset

Understanding and applying Agile principles allows teams to adapt quickly to changes and continuously improve development processes. Agile methodology focuses on flexibility, iteration, and collaboration, enabling teams to respond effectively to client needs and project changes. Developers with an Agile mindset can work more effectively in cross-functional teams, prioritize tasks, and adapt to new directions. Familiarity with Agile frameworks such as Scrum or Kanban is a significant asset in today's development landscape.

14.2.6. Conclusion

In summary, the key skills outlined are fundamental for any software developer aiming to excel in the industry. By focusing on problem-solving, continuous learning, collaboration, quality orientation, and an Agile mindset, developers will not only increase their professional value but also contribute to creating more effective and higher-quality software. Developing these skills should be an ongoing effort throughout one's career, adapting to new technologies and challenges in the software development field.

14.3. RECOMMENDED RESOURCES FOR FURTHER LEARNING

To continue learning and deepen your understanding of the topics discussed, here are some useful resources, including books, online courses, communities, forums, blogs, and podcasts. These resources are designed to help developers expand their knowledge and stay updated in the field of software engineering.

14.3.1. Key Books

• **Clean Code by Robert C. Martin:** This essential book helps developers improve their ability to write clean, readable code. Through practical examples, Martin explains design principles and best practices that can be applied to real projects, helping developers create more maintainable and error-free code.

• **Design Patterns:** Elements of Reusable Object-Oriented Software by Erich Gamma, Richard Helm, Ralph Johnson, and John Vlissides: Known as the "Gang of Four" (GoF), this book is an essential reference on design patterns in object-oriented programming. Readers will learn to recognize and apply solutions to common software development problems, enabling them to build more robust and scalable systems.

• **Continuous Delivery by Jez Humble and David Farley:** This book provides a comprehensive guide to automating deployments and implementing CI/CD practices. Through case studies and practical examples, the authors demonstrate how organizations can accelerate their ability to deliver high-quality software while reducing risks.

14.3.2. Online Courses

• **Platforms like Udemy, Coursera, and Pluralsight:** These platforms offer a wide range of courses in areas such as artificial intelligence, DevOps, software architecture, and Agile methodologies. Courses are often designed by industry experts and are accessible to different skill levels, from beginners to advanced.

• **Software Engineering for Beginners by Santiago Guido (Udemy):** This course is designed for those seeking a solid introduction to software development, covering the fundamentals of software engineering, recommended practices, and essential tools.

14.3.3. Communities and Forums

• **Stack Overflow:** One of the largest and most active forums for developers. Users can ask technical questions, find solutions to specific problems, and learn from others' experiences. The community is highly collaborative and offers a rich knowledge base.

• **GitHub:** A fundamental platform for open-source software development. GitHub not only allows developers to store and manage their projects but also provides opportunities to collaborate, explore open repositories, and contribute to existing projects. Learning to navigate and use GitHub is an essential skill for any developer.

14.3.4. Blogs and Podcasts

• **Martin Fowler's Blog:** An invaluable resource for those interested in software architecture, refactoring, design, and Agile practices. Martin Fowler is a leading figure in the development community, and his articles offer deep and relevant insights into software evolution.

• **Podcasts like Software Engineering Daily and Coding Blocks:** These podcasts provide informative discussions on current topics in the software industry, expert interviews, and analysis of emerging trends. They are an excellent way to stay updated while commuting or exercising.

14.3.5. Conclusion

Continuous education and community interaction are essential for professional growth in software engineering. These resources offer a solid foundation for diving deeper into various topics, acquiring new skills, and staying ahead in an ever-changing technological environment. By leveraging these books, courses, communities, and podcasts, developers can continue expanding their knowledge and contributing to the industry's advancement.

14.4. FAREWELL AND ACKNOWLEDGMENTS

With this book, I have aimed to provide a comprehensive guide for those entering the world of software engineering or seeking to strengthen their knowledge. Each chapter is designed to be a valuable resource that equips you to face the challenges of modern software development.

I want to express my deepest gratitude to everyone who has accompanied and supported me throughout the creation of this book: to my family, who have inspired and motivated me; to my colleagues, who have shared their knowledge and experiences; and to the readers, for trusting this content as a tool for their professional growth.

I hope the concepts and practices shared here prove helpful on your journey as developers and that you continue exploring, learning, and contributing to the fascinating and ever-evolving discipline of software engineering. Until the next coding adventure!

CHAPTER 15
APPENDICES

This chapter provides additional resources that complement the content of the book, offering tools, definitions, and references that may be useful for readers in their learning process and software development application.

15.1. GLOSSARY OF TERMS

Terms Related to Software Engineering

- **Algorithm:** A set of defined steps or instructions to solve a specific problem or perform a task.
- API (Application Programming Interface): A set of rules and protocols that allow different applications to communicate with each other.

- **Clean Code:** A concept referring to writing code that is easy to read, maintain, and understand.

- **Framework:** A support structure that provides a set of tools and libraries for application development.

- **Microservice:** An architectural approach that divides an application into small, autonomous services that communicate with each other.

- **Unit Testing:** A testing method that verifies the functionality of the smallest units of code in isolation.

- **Continuous Integration (CI):** A software development practice where code changes are automatically integrated and tested in a shared environment.

- **Continuous Deployment (CD):** An extension of continuous integration that allows developers to automatically deploy changes to production after passing tests.

- **Refactoring:** The process of modifying existing code to improve its structure and readability without changing its functionality.

- **Version Control:** A system for managing changes in source code that allows tracking and handling different software versions.

Terms Related to Project Management

- **SCRUM:** An agile project management methodology focused on the rapid delivery of products through short iterations called sprints.

- **Stakeholders:** People or groups who have an interest in or are affected by the outcome of a project.

- **Project Life Cycle:** The phases a project goes through from its initiation to completion, including planning, execution, and closure.

- **Risk Management:** The process of identifying, assessing, and mitigating potential risks that could affect a project's success.

- **MVP (Minimum Viable Product):** The initial version of a product that includes only essential features to be functional and gather user feedback.

- **Backlog:** A prioritized list of tasks, features, and bugs that need to be addressed in a project.

- **Kanban:** An agile method that uses a visual board to manage workflow and improve efficiency.

- **Gantt Chart:** A planning tool that graphically represents a project's schedule and tasks.

Cybersecurity Terms

- **Cybersecurity**: A set of practices and technologies that protect systems, networks, and data from malicious attacks.

- **Vulnerability**: A weakness in a system that can be exploited by an attacker to gain unauthorized access or cause damage.

- **Authentication**: The process of verifying the identity of a user or system.

- **Encryption**: A method of encoding information so that it can only be read by those with the decryption key.

- **Malware**: Malicious software designed to harm, infiltrate, or gain unauthorized access to systems.

- **Phishing**: An online fraud technique that uses deception to obtain confidential information, such as passwords or credit card numbers.

- **Firewall**: A device or software that controls access to a network by filtering incoming and outgoing traffic according to security rules.

Artificial Intelligence and Machine Learning Terms

- **Artificial Intelligence (AI):** A branch of computer science focused on creating systems capable of performing tasks that require human intelligence, such as voice recognition and decision-making.

- **Machine Learning:** A subfield of AI that uses algorithms to enable computers to learn from data and make predictions or decisions without being explicitly programmed.

- **Deep Learning:** A machine learning technique that uses artificial neural networks to model and solve complex problems, such as image recognition.

- **Unstructured Data:** Information that does not follow a predefined format, such as emails, images, or videos, requiring additional processing for analysis.

- **Predictive Model:** An algorithm designed to forecast future outcomes based on historical data.

15.2. DOCUMENTATION TEMPLATES

A collection of templates that can be used at different stages of software development and project management. These templates may include:

15.2.1. Requirements Specification Template

Software Requirements Specification (SRS)

-1. Introduction

-1.1 Purpose

Describe the purpose and functionality of the system to be developed.

-1.2 Scope

Define the system's scope, including its main objectives and boundaries.

-1.3 Definitions, Acronyms, and Abbreviations

List technical terms, acronyms, or abbreviations used in this document.

-1.4 References

External documents, standards, or specifications related to the system.

-1.5 Document Overview

Brief summary of the sections contained in this document.

-2. General Description

-2.1 Product Perspective

Describe the product in its context, mentioning how it interacts with other systems or products.

-2.2 System Features

List the most important system functionalities.

-2.3 User Characteristics

Describe the different types of users who will interact with the system, including their needs and experience levels.

-2.4 Limitations

Known limitations that may impact the system's development or performance (technological, time, budget constraints, etc.).

-2.5 Assumptions and Dependencies

List assumptions made for project development and delivery, as well as dependencies on other systems or external factors.

-3. Specific Requirements

-3.1 Functional Requirements

Detailed list of the system functionalities. Each functionality should include:

- Requirement ID: A unique identifier.
- Requirement Name: Brief description of the functionality.
- Description: Detailed explanation of the functionality.
- Priority: Define its priority (High, Medium, Low).
- Dependencies: Other functionalities that may affect or be affected by this requirement.

Example:

- ID: RF001
- Name: User Registration
- Description: The system must allow users to register using an email and password.
- Priority: High

- Dependencies: None

-3.2 Non-Functional Requirements

Description of the quality attributes the system must meet, such as:

- Performance: Response time, load capacity.
- Security: Authentication, authorization, encryption.
- Availability: Uptime rate, fault handling.
- Usability: Ease of use, accessibility.
- Portability: Compatibility with different operating systems or devices.

Example:

- ID: RNF001
- Description: The system must handle 1,000 concurrent users without affecting performance.
- Priority: Medium

-4. System Requirements

-4.1 Hardware

Specify the hardware requirements needed for the system to function properly.

-4.2 Software

List the platforms, libraries, and frameworks the system needs to run.

-4.3 User Interfaces

Describe the graphical and user interfaces the system will present, if applicable.

-5. Appendices

Any additional relevant information, such as flowcharts, UML diagrams, or detailed technical specifications.

15.2.2. Test Plan Template

Software Test Plan

-1. Introduction

-1.1 Purpose

Describe the objectives and scope of the test plan and how it will ensure that the software meets the specified requirements.

-1.2 Scope

Define which modules, features, and system functionalities will be tested, as well as what areas are outside the testing scope.

-1.3 Test Objectives

Define the main testing objectives, such as ensuring the software works correctly in different environments, verifying usability, and ensuring compliance with non-functional requirements.

-1.4 References

Relevant documentation, such as requirement specifications, user manuals, design guides, etc.

-2. Test Strategy

-2.1 Types of Tests

Describe the types of tests to be conducted and their purposes:

- Unit Tests: Ensure each code unit functions correctly.
- Integration Tests: Verify that different modules or components work together smoothly.
- Functional Tests: Validate that the software meets all functional requirements.
- Regression Tests: Ensure that new updates or fixes do not introduce errors in previously implemented features.
- Performance Tests: Evaluate system behavior under specific workloads.
- Security Tests: Ensure the system is protected against threats or vulnerabilities.

- Usability Tests: Assess software ease of use from a user's perspective.

-2.2 Test Entry and Exit Criteria

Establish criteria for when to start (entry criteria) and when to finish testing (exit criteria):

- Entry Criteria: Complete development, test environment configured, approved requirements, etc.
- Exit Criteria: All planned tests executed, acceptable defect level, requirements met, etc.

-3. Deliverables

-3.1 Test Cases

Specific test cases to be executed, including input data, actions, and expected results.

Example Structure of a Test Case:

- Test Case ID: TC001
- Test Case Name: Login Verification
- Description: Test that the system allows users to log in with valid credentials.
- Steps:
  1. Navigate to the login screen.
  2. Enter valid username and password.
  3. Press the login button.
- Expected Result: The user should be redirected to their dashboard.
- Actual Result: (To be completed during test execution).
- Status: Passed/Failed

-3.2 Bug Report

Format for reporting defects found during testing, including key information such as:

- Bug ID: Unique identifier.
- Description: Detailed explanation of the issue.
- Severity: Low, Medium, High, Critical.
- Status: Open, In Review, Closed.
- Steps to Reproduce: Detailed description of how to replicate the issue.

-3.3 Test Summary Report

A summary report at the end of testing, detailing results, defects found, passed and failed tests, and other relevant observations.

4. Test Environment

-4.1 Hardware and Software Requirements

Specify the necessary equipment and tools for testing (servers, devices, operating systems, databases, etc.).

-4.2 Testing Tools

List the tools to be used for test execution, bug tracking, automation, etc.

Examples:
- Test Management Tool: JIRA, TestRail
- Automation Tool: Selenium, JUnit
- Performance Testing Tool: JMeter, LoadRunner

5. Risk Management

-5.1 Risk Identification

Describe risks that may affect the testing process or software development, such as:
- Limited availability of test resources.
- Development delays impacting testing.
- Incompatibility between components or platforms.

-5.2 Risk Mitigation Plan

Propose strategies to reduce or mitigate identified risks.

-6. Test Schedule

-6.1 Testing Phases

Include a schedule showing different test phases (planning, test case design, execution, result reporting) and their estimated duration.

-6.2 Responsibilities

Assign responsibilities to various roles involved in testing (test engineers, developers, project managers, etc.).

-7. Approvals

-7.1 Review and Approval

Record signatures and approvals from stakeholders.

- Test Team Lead: Name and signature
- Project Manager: Name and signature
- Lead Developer: Name and signature

15.2.3 Project Plan Template

-1. Introduction

-1.1 Purpose

Define the general purpose of the project, its objectives, and the expected impact.

-1.2 Project Scope

Detail the project scope, specifying what will be included and what is out of scope.

-1.3 Project Objectives

Identify the key objectives to be achieved through the project implementation.

-1.4 Assumptions and Constraints

Specify the assumptions made for the project execution and the limitations that may affect it.

-2. Project Description

-2.1 Overview

Provide an overview of the project, including its goals, purpose, and approach.

-2.2 Project Deliverables

List the final products or deliverables that will be produced upon completion of the project.

Examples:

- Deliverable 1: Product or functionality A.
- Deliverable 2: System documentation.

-2.3 Success Criteria

Define the specific criteria that will be used to evaluate the success of the project.

-3. Project Management Plan

-3.1 Project Organization

Describe the organizational structure of the team, including roles and responsibilities.

Example roles:

- Project Manager: Responsible for project planning, execution, and closure.
- Development Team: Responsible for design, coding, and software testing.
- Stakeholders: Interested parties who will receive progress reports.

-3.2 Communication Plan

Establish how communication will occur between team members and stakeholders.

- Follow-up meetings: Weekly with the team.
- Progress reports: Sent to stakeholders every month.
- Communication channels: Email, project management tools (Asana, Trello).

-3.3 Change Management Plan

Define how changes in requirements, scope, or the project schedule will be handled.

- Change Requests: Must be submitted through a change request form.
- Approval Process: The change committee will review and approve change requests.

-4. Schedule and Planning

-4.1 Project Phases

Define the key phases of the project with their estimated start and end dates.

- Phase 1: Project Planning (Dates: dd/mm/yyyy - dd/mm/yyyy)
- Phase 2: Design and Specification (Dates: dd/mm/yyyy - dd/mm/yyyy)
- Phase 3: Development (Dates: dd/mm/yyyy - dd/mm/yyyy)
- Phase 4: Testing and Integration (Dates: dd/mm/yyyy - dd/mm/yyyy)
- Phase 5: Implementation and Closure (Dates: dd/mm/yyyy - dd/mm/yyyy)

-4.2 Detailed Schedule

Create a more detailed schedule, such as a Gantt chart, showing all project activities, deadlines, and task dependencies.

-5. Resource Management

-5.1 Human Resources

Identify the roles and skills needed to complete the project. Example:

- Backend Developer: Python programming and SQL databases.
- Testing Specialist: Conduct integration and regression tests.

-5.2 Material Resources

Define the material and technological resources required for the project.

- Hardware: Servers, workstations.
- Software: Development tools, test management software, etc.

-5.3 Budget

Specify the estimated project budget, breaking down costs into categories such as personnel, materials, and tools.

-6. Risk Analysis

-6.1 Risk Identification

List potential risks that could affect the success of the project.

- Risk 1: Delay in the delivery of key components from external suppliers.
- Risk 2: Lack of availability of the development team due to other tasks.

6.2 Risk Mitigation Plan

Provide strategies to mitigate or reduce the impact of identified risks.

- Mitigation for Risk 1: Establish clear contractual agreements with suppliers to minimize delays.
- Mitigation for Risk 2: Allocate additional resources or prioritize the project within the team.

-7. Quality Plan

-7.1 Quality Control

Describe how quality will be ensured at each phase of the project.

- Code Reviews: Conducted by peers before integration.
- Automated Testing: Ensure coverage of critical code.

-7.2 Quality Assurance

Define the standards to ensure deliverables meet the set requirements.

-8. Implementation Plan

-8.1 Implementation Strategy

Describe how the product or service will be implemented at the end of the project, including deployment and the transition to end users.

- **Deployment**: Roll out in the production environment over a weekend to minimize service disruption.
- **Training**: Provide training for end users and system administrators.

8.2 Maintenance Plan

Describe how support and maintenance will be managed after project delivery.

-9. Project Closure

-9.1 Acceptance Criteria

Define criteria to consider the project successfully completed.

-9.2 Lessons Learned

Document lessons learned to improve future project management.

-10. Approvals

-10.1 Review and Approval

Include signatures from key stakeholders.

- Project Manager: Name and signature
- Main Stakeholder: Name and signature

15.3. USEFUL RESOURCES AND TOOLS

This section provides a list of additional resources and tools that can help developers and project managers improve their efficiency and effectiveness at work. The tools and resources are organized into key categories:

1. Project Management Tools

Project management tools facilitate the planning, tracking, and collaboration on tasks and projects. Some popular options include:

- **Trello**: A visual board-based tool that allows teams to organize tasks using cards. Ideal for managing Agile projects and visually tracking progress.
- **Asana:** A platform that enables teams to create tasks, assign responsibilities, and set deadlines. It offers project tracking and real-time collaboration features.
- **Jira:** Commonly used by software development teams, Jira supports Agile project management, bug tracking, and user story tracking.
- **Monday.com:** A flexible tool for managing projects, tasks, and workflows, customizable to meet team needs.
- **ClickUp:** Provides multiple features for task management, time tracking, and collaboration, allowing teams to manage their work in one place.

2. Integrated Development Environments (IDEs)

IDEs are essential for software development, offering tools for writing, debugging, and running code. Some highly recommended IDEs include:

- **Visual Studio:** A Microsoft IDE widely used for C#, C++, and .NET development, offering powerful debugging tools and Azure integration.
- **IntelliJ IDEA:** A popular IDE among Java developers, offering advanced features like code autocompletion and multi-language support.
- **Eclipse**: An open-source IDE primarily used for Java development, also supporting other languages through plugins.
- **PyCharm**: A Python-specialized IDE that offers features like code analysis, debugging, and integrated testing.
- **Visual Studio Code:** A lightweight, highly extensible code editor popular among web and multi-language developers due to its wide range of extensions.

3. Popular Frameworks and Libraries for Software Development

Frameworks and libraries provide structures and functionalities that simplify software development. Notable options include:

- **React**: A JavaScript library for building user interfaces, widely used in modern web application development.
- **Angular**: A web application development framework from Google, designed for creating single-page applications (SPAs) in a structured, efficient way.
- **Django**: A high-level Python web framework that promotes rapid development and clean design, ideal for building web applications and APIs.
- **Spring**: A framework for Java application development, offering a comprehensive approach to building robust enterprise applications.
- **Flask**: A lightweight Python microframework, easy to learn and use, perfect for smaller projects and prototypes.

4. Online Learning and Certification Platforms

For those looking to continue their education and acquire new skills, several online platforms offer courses and certifications:

- **Coursera:** Provides courses in partnership with leading universities and companies, covering topics in technology, software development, and project management.
- **Udemy:** A platform where instructors create courses on a wide variety of topics, including programming and software development.
- **edX**: Offers online courses from renowned universities, with certification options in areas like artificial intelligence, web development, and more.
- **Pluralsight:** An online learning platform offering technical courses and learning paths for developers, designers, and IT professionals.
- **LinkedIn Learning:** Offers a wide range of courses on technical and professional skills, including software development and project management.
- **Codecademy:** An interactive platform that teaches coding in various languages, ideal for beginners and those looking to improve their programming skills.

15.4. REFERENCES

- Beck, K. (2001). Extreme Programming Explained: Embrace Change (2nd ed.). Addison-Wesley.

- Boehm, B. W. (1988). *A Spiral Model of Software Development and Enhancement.* ACM SIGSOFT Software Engineering Notes, 11(4), 14-24. https://doi.org/10.1145/74334.74337

- Cohn, M. (2004). User Stories Applied for Agile Software Development. Addison-Wesley.

- Dingsøyr, T. D., & Moen, R. (2015). An empirical study of the effectiveness of agile methods. *Journal of Systems and Software, 108*, 1-16. https://doi.org/10.1016/j.jss.2015.04.022

- Fowler, M. (2018). Refactoring: Improving the Design of Existing Code (2nd ed.). Addison-Wesley.

- Gamma, E., Helm, R., Johnson, R., & Vlissides, J. (1994). Design Patterns: Elements of Reusable Object-Oriented Software. Addison-Wesley.

- Highsmith, J. (2004). Agile project management: Making it work. *IEEE Software, 21*(6), 12-14. https://doi.org/10.1109/MS.2004.148

- Humble, J., & Farley, D. (2010). Continuous Delivery: Reliable Software Releases through Build, Test, and Deployment Automation. Addison-Wesley.

- Hunt, A., & Thomas, D. (2000). The Pragmatic Programmer: Your Journey to Mastery. Addison-Wesley.

- Kim, G., Behr, K., & Spafford, G. (2018). The Phoenix Project: A Novel About IT, DevOps, and Helping Your Business Win. IT Revolution Press.

- Kitchenham, B., & Pfleeger, S. L. (2002). Principles of survey research: Part 1: Turning lemons into lemonade. *ACM SIGSOFT Software Engineering Notes, 27*(3), 20-24. https://

doi.org/10.1145/507078.507081

• Martin, R. C. (2008). Clean Code: A Handbook of Agile Software Craftsmanship. Prentice Hall.

• Mohan, R. K. P., Suresh, A. S., & Das, A. (2017). Exploring the relationship between agile practices and software quality. *Journal of Software: Evolution and Process, 29*(6), e1891. https://doi.org/10.1002/smr.1891

• Patton, J. (2014). User Story Mapping: Discover the Whole Story, Build the Right Product. O'Reilly Media.

• Poppendieck, M., & Poppendieck, T. (2003). *Lean Software Development: An Agile Toolkit.* Addison-Wesley.

• Pressman, R. S., & Maxim, B. R. (2014). Software Engineering: A Practitioner's Approach (9th ed.). McGraw-Hill.

• Ramesh, B., & Tiwana, A. (1999). The role of information systems in the support of agile software development. *Journal of Software Maintenance and Evolution: Research and Practice, 11*(3), 137-160. https://doi.org/10.1002/(SICI)1099-045X(199905/06)11:3<137::AID-SMR164>3.0.CO;2-3

• Sommerville, I. (2016). *Software Engineering* (10th ed.). Pearson.

• Sutherland, J., & Schwaber, K. (2017). The Scrum Guide: The Definitive Guide to Scrum: The Rules of the Game. Scrum.org.

• Teixeira, D. B. M., Barros, A. D., & Lemos, P. L. (2019). A survey of software engineering models. *Journal of Software Engineering and Applications, 12*(2), 49-67. https://doi.org/10.4236/jsea.2019.122004

ABOUT THE AUTHOR

Santiago Guido

Santiago Guido is a software developer specializing in mobile application development. With over 10 years of experience in the tech industry, he has contributed to innovative projects across a wide range of sectors. His primary focus is on creating efficient, scalable mobile solutions that enhance user experience and streamline business processes. Beyond his professional work, Santiago is passionate about sharing his expertise through courses and educational materials, helping aspiring developers improve their skills in software development.

www.ingramcontent.com/pod-product-compliance
Lightning Source LLC
Chambersburg PA
CBHW062317220526
45469CB00008B/2541